*BLONDEL AND CHRISTIANITY*

# *Blondel and Christianity*

HENRI BOUILLARD

Translated by James M. Somerville

*CORPUS BOOKS* *Washington / Cleveland*

**CORPUS PUBLICATIONS**

EDITORIAL OFFICES: 1330 Massachusetts Ave., N.W. Washington, D.C. 20005

SALES & DISTRIBUTION: 2231 West 110th Street, Cleveland, Ohio 44102

*Library of Congress Catalog Card Number: 70-81906*
FIRST PRINTING 1970
*Printed in the United States of America*

# CONTENTS

# TRANSLATOR'S PREFACE

Henri Bouillard's analytic study *Blondel et le Christianisme* is surely among the better and more mature works on the philosophy of Maurice Blondel. Bouillard is neither a special pleader for Blondel, nor even a Blondelian himself (he is best known for his exhaustive three-volume study of Karl Barth), but he brings to his work the distance and proper detachment of the accomplished scholar. While a portion of the text takes the form of a forthright polemic against Henry Duméry's reading of Blondel, the controversial aspect of these sections does not narrow the scope of the work or make it less valuable as a contribution to an understanding of what Blondel set out to do.

Maurice Blondel wanted to create a philosophy that would be innately and spontaneously Christian and, at the same time, truly autonomous in the best tradition of scientific thought. The task was a formidable one, and in seeking to achieve it the philosopher drew fire from two sides. On the one hand, the old-line rationalists of the French universities were distressed because Blondel's use of the method of immanence in order to transcend the self-imposed limits of doctrinal immanentism seemed to them to threaten the very foundations of naturalism. On the other hand, certain conservative Catholics thought they detected in Blondel's position a large measure of the very immanentism he sought to overcome. This was especially true after 1896, when the author sought in his *Letter on Apologetics* to vindicate the strictly philosophical intention of his masterwork, *L'Action* (1893).

Blondel remained a controversial figure throughout the Modernist period, but with the passing of the years the number of those who seriously questioned his orthodoxy or his intention dwindled to a mere handful. Meanwhile, an entire generation of French Catholic intellectuals, many of them theologians, was nourished on his thought. Early in the 1930s, when his influence and prestige seemed to be on the wane, the old question of the nature and possibility of an autonomous Christian philosophy was revived, and the author played a prominant role in the debate that engaged himself, Bréhier, Gilson, and several others. Between 1934 and 1937 he entered upon what has been described as his second career with the publication of a monumental five-volume Trilogy on Thought, Being, and Action, to be followed in the next decade by the main elements of a second Trilogy on Philosophy and the Christian Spirit.

Since *L'Action* was out of print and not available to the general public, public, mimeographed and handwritten copies of the book made the rounds in student circles between the two world wars, and an unauthorized Italian translation was published in 1921. The posthumous reprinting of the book in 1950 sparked a new interest in Blondel, and since then the publication of valuable inedita, personal diaries, several volumes of correspondence, and new editions of early works has provided busy commentators with a wealth of material. The Blondel Centennial Year (1961) not only was the occasion for a variety of congresses, commemorative volumes, and scholarly articles, but it was also marked by the appearance in French of the present work, which is an expansion and revision of Bouillard's classic study of Blondel's fundamental intention, originally published twenty years ago. The availability of new sources and more than two decades of reflection on Blondel's thought combine to make *Blondel and Christianity* the mature work of a distinguished scholar. Its appearance in English adds one more book to the growing literature on Blondel available to American readers, and it also gives substance to the contention that, after three-quarters of a century, the philosophy of action retains its vitality and relevance.

Bouillard sets out to examine the background and genesis of Blondel's conception of Christian philosophy. He indicates how the author gradually refined his own fundamental intention; he discusses the early controversies, explores the stages of the Blondelian dialectic, especially in connection with the three phases of the idea of the supernatural, and offers a well-documented interpretation of the relation between the religious option and the ontological affirmation of the Absolute. Bouillard's work is a useful introduction to the whole of Blondel's thought. In addition, it treats a much larger question, which, in its own right, cannot be passed over by the professional philosopher and theologian: Where must one locate the frontier between reason and revelation, and how are we to determine the point of insertion of the supernatural into the context of rational inquiry?

JAMES M. SOMERVILLE

# AUTHOR'S PREFACE

Perhaps we should not rely too heavily on childhood or adolescent memories, since it is just possible that we were never taught some of the strange notions that have slipped into our heads. Nevertheless, I, like so many of my generation, have long remembered an idea, picked up from the catechism or religious instruction classes, that used to disturb me with increasing insistence: The mysteries of Christianity are incomprehensible truths that God imposes on us to test our obedience. When, in addition, courses in apologetics apparently set out to justify this notion, they provided me with more motives for doubt than reasons for belief.

Perplexed, one day I began to read Maurice Blondel's *L'Action*. This was around 1930, at a time when young students would band together to mimeograph the contents of this unavailable book. Many things escaped me in this first reading; but I discovered at least that Christianity has a meaning, that it answers a desire of the spirit, and that the obedience of faith is not an arbitrary matter: in a word, that one can believe without betraying reason.

Neither Christian doctrine nor Christian life seemed on this account to be reduced to the level of a simple humanism. On the contrary, Blondel taught me to see that the Gospel would lose its meaning if it did not bear witness to a supernatural gift and that man cannot open himself to God without a new birth.

Since that time the writer has had occasion to reread *L'Action* while becoming acquainted with other works of Blondel. He has never made *L'Action* his bible; other approaches seemed better suited to meet certain philosophical requirements. And as far as understanding the Gospel is concerned, he could hardly be unacquainted with the resources offered by the whole Christian tradition. Yet he always has been profoundly grateful to the one who, at every reading, provided him with valuable suggestions. Many others in times gone by have had the same experience and shared

*ix*

the same feeling. But does this not all belong to a past that is rapidly disappearing? Can the work of Blondel claim the interest of the new generation? Are we not less directly affected by it than formerly?

Since the famous thesis appeared in 1893, the world has been convulsed by two wars; the advent of Communism, social change, technical progress, and the aspiration of colonial peoples for independence and prosperity have altered the face of the world and imposed new problems; and the social sciences, psychology, and sociology have developed. Today all this invites the attention of the philosopher and theologian. Is anyone likely to be interested in a work that (except in the last publications, and even then only in a marginal fashion) could not take these changes into account, and whose eloquent and moralizing style betrays its age?

A vigorous and profound thought that has come to grips with an essential and permanent problem never dies. Even in a transformed world and a new universe of the mind it can always bear re-examination. On the question of the meaning of life, especially regarding the relation between thought or action and the exigencies and promises of Christianity, Blondel's philosophy has touched so effectively on the crucial point that it can still enlighten us today.

In some respects it is easier to understand it today than in the past. The passage of time helps us distinguish the essential from the peripheral, which has too often been the center of focus. It neutralizes the fascination or revulsion, equally magical in their effect, that was once associated with certain phrases. Studies on Hegel, Husserl's phenomenology, the philosophy of existence, the renewal of biblical and patristic studies, and even a better knowledge of Thomism have all served to make us more familiar with one idea or another that used to cause dismay. Finally, with old quarrels laid to rest, it is now possible to recognize the value of Blondel's thought without being partisan and to express reservations about it without becoming an adversary. One can learn from Blondelianism without professing it.

On the occasion of the centenary of Blondel's birth, it seemed useful, then, to publish the results of a new study of his more significant works. After offering the reader an overview of his work, I shall be principally concerned with *L'Action* of 1893 and the *Letter* of 1896, without, however, failing to indicate the direction of later developments when the occasion calls for it. Three points have been selected for detailed study: the genesis of the idea of the supernatural, the role of the religious option in the ontological affirmation, and the special character of Blondel's philosophy. These are three different perspectives bearing on a single relation: philosophy's openness to Christianity. I must specify, however, that I am not concerned with the Christian themes developed by Blondel, but with the specifically philosophical aspect of the movement of thought by which he leads the mind to them.

Our interpretation is based, as it must be, on the analysis and comparison of texts. Where they have given rise to different interpretations, a closer scrutiny has at times produced new light. We would be remiss, however, were we to fail to acknowledge our indebtedness to the numerous interpreters who have already attempted to clarify a difficult thought. Without passing over the older commentators (the Abbé J. Wehrlé, Père Auguste Valensin, Paul Archambault, and others), let us single out Jacques Paliard, Pierre Lachièze-Rey, Jeanne Mercier, Henri de Lubac, Jean Trouillard, and, even more specifically, those whose more important contributions directly concern our subject: Père Yves de Montcheuil, Henry Duméry, Albert Cartier, and Pierre Henrici. We have not always followed them—it would have been impossible in view of their divergent points of view—and we shall have occasion from time to time to indicate why we have not been able to accept this or that interpretation. But the very notions we discard (with all due friendship for the authors) have stimulated us as much as anything else to make a closer analysis of Blondel's thought.

We owe a particular debt of gratitude to M. Charles Blondel, to Mme Charles Flory, and to M. André Blondel, who allowed us to read and make use of their father's unpublished notes and manuscripts, carefully preserved at his home in Aix-en-Provence. Guided by his secretary, Mlle N. Panis, to whom we are equally grateful, we have discovered in these writings priceless indications concerning the genesis and development of Blondel's thought. This has enabled us to clear up several points that had previously remained obscure. Reading the notes and letters in which the philosopher lays bare his soul, we have been better able to grasp the spirit which animated his effort. May some of this filter through to those who read our work.

HENRI BOUILLARD

# BLONDEL AND CHRISTIANITY

# CHAPTER ONE

# The Work of Maurice Blondel

"Each philosophical effort does little more than translate a primitive and abiding idea and intention that seem capable of being expressed in a word, yet are scarcely exhausted by a shelf of books."[1] This general observation by Maurice Blondel might serve as an accurate description of his own work. During the course of an exceptionally long career, starting with *L'Action*, the celebrated thesis of 1893, and culminating with the appearance of his monumental testament comprising *La Pensée, L'Etre et les êtres, L'Action* (second version), and *La philosophie et l'esprit chrétien* (published between 1934 and 1946), he was moved by a single fundamental intention: to work out a philosophy whose autonomous movement would open spontaneously to Christianity. During the years when he was reaching the age of reflection, French public life was dominated by the lay ideal, fashioned under the influence of Comte, Taine, and Renouvier. A few years later the separation of Church and State would give institutional and political expression to a rupture that had long been implicit in the realm of ideas and morality, namely, the dichotomy between human reality and Christian reality. It was usually taken for granted that no philosophy could vindicate its right to the name unless it was "separated" from Christianity, totally independent of it, and consciously bent on ignoring it. Many made much of a "spiritualist" philosophy, but to the majority the idea of a "Christian philosophy" would have seemed as strange as the notion of a Christian physics. Blondel's originality lay in the fact that he wished to re-establish lines of communication, not by devising an apologetic that would confront philosophers with Christianity's claims on their belief (any such attempt would have remained exterior to the problem), but by constructing a philosophy which, by the logic of its rational movement, would lead spontaneously to Christianity and, without imposing faith, would inevitably pose the Christian problem. His purpose was to reclaim for philosophy an entire realm that had been abandoned, to enlarge its unduly restricted field, and thus succeed in "imposing on all minds straining toward the limits of Reason the religious problem in its most precise formulation, that is, from the viewpoint and with all the exigencies of the Christian supernatural."[2] It was this primitive and abiding intention that animated his effort and gave it its distinctive stamp.

Neither an apologist nor a theologian in the usual sense, Blondel was to treat with rare depth the central problem that confronted Christian thought in its encounter with unbelief; it was a problem that theologians and apologists had yet to bring into sharp focus, yet one they could not avoid. In any case, his work did elicit a notable response among them. Even those whose sympathies have remained quite foreign to his point of view no longer speak of him today as though he had never existed. During the first half of the present century probably no other work so profoundly influenced the development of French theology, nor has any other been of such value in assisting Christian philosophers to reconcile for themselves the fruits of their reflection and their faith.

It seems best to begin by presenting an overview of Blondel's work. Since the aim of such a synopsis is principally to provide the reader with a context for situating the analyses that are to follow, it will dwell preferably, but by no means exclusively, on those aspects of Blondel's writings that are concerned with the encounter between philosophy and Christianity. To avoid excessive repetition we shall confine this treatment to a few summary observations on fine points to be taken up later in more detail.[3]

## *L'Action*

Maurice Blondel belongs to a generation that was one of the richest in the history of French culture. It is approximately the generation of Barrès, Gide, Proust, Péguy and Claudel, of Matisse and Rouault, of Ravel and Debussy, of Bergson and Brunschvicg. Philosophy, under the earlier impulse of Lachelier and Boutroux, escaped the simplifications both of positivists and of scientists. In a parallel manner, Christian thought and literature, by dissociating themselves from formalistic and excessively conservative positions, rediscovered their original sources. Blondel is located in this double renewal.

He was born on November 2, 1861, in Dijon, of a very old Burgundian family. His father was a notary and amassed a fortune that assured Blondel a life free from financial concern. The family tradition passed on to him a good education and solid Christian values. His secondary schooling was done in his home town. He then graduated from the Facultés with the degrees of Licence ès Lettres, Bachelier ès Sciences, and Bachelier en Droit. The influence of two professors, Alexis Bertrand at the Lycée and Henry Joly of the Faculté des Lettres, helped direct him toward the study of philosophy.

Blondel became a student in 1881 at the Ecole Normale (which Bergson had just left) and his colleagues included Frédéric Rauh, Pierre Duhem, and Victor Delbos (of whom he became a very close friend). His teachers, Léon Ollé-Laprune and Emile Boutroux, both exerted an influence on the formation of his thought (the former for content, the latter for philosophical form). By the beginning of his second year, he had chosen as his thesis project *l'action*, a subject that caused surprise and was not accepted without some difficulty. After having succeeded in 1881 (following two failures) in the *concours d'agrégation*, he was named professor at the Lycée Mignet in Aix-en-Provence. Here he matured his thought by endlessly jotting down ideas that came to mind during long walks in the countryside of Provence. When he began to edit these notes, he asked for a leave of absence, and in the solitude of a country house owned by his parents at Saint-Seine-sur-Vingeanne in Burgundy, he wrote the work to which he chiefly owes his fame.

The defense of his thesis at the Sorbonne took place on June 7, 1893. The jury was disconcerted both by the method and the conclusions of the work, but was obliged to recognize its vigor. The complementary thesis, in Latin, dealt with Leibniz' *Vinculum substantiale*. This curious theory was one of the points of departure for Blondel's thought. He sought precisely in action "this substantial bond which constitutes the concrete unity of each being by assuring its communion with all."[4]

Published in November, 1893, with the title *L'Action, essai d'une critique de la vie et d'une science de la pratique*, and out of print as early as 1895, the work was never reprinted in its original form by the author, who wanted, even at this date, to incorporate important changes. It would be an error to conclude from this that it can henceforth be disregarded and that one need only refer directly to later writings. In fact, this is the work that constituted a breakthrough and has exerted the greatest influence. The works that follow are marked by the controversies that *L'Action* gave rise to and they would be incomprehensible to anyone who did not enter through this door. Finally, we shall have the opportunity to show that this book, despite its imperfections, remains Blondel's masterpiece; it is the work in which his original contribution appears most vigorously.

It is difficult to speak about such a monumental work in a few lines; any résumé tends to reduce it to banality. In order to review it properly, it would be necessary to analyze it successively from several points of view; nor can any commentary replace the reading of the text. Only an attentive study can enable one to understand this complex, dense, and, at times, obscure work. We will limit ourselves for the time being to describing its development and its essential characteristics.[5]

Its object is action insofar as it is constructive of the destiny of man. The initial question controls all further development:

> Yes or no, has human life and meaning, has man a destiny? . . . The problem is inevitable and inevitably man solves it; and this solution, right or wrong, but voluntary even when it is necessary, is carried in each one's actions. This is the reason why action must be studied: The very meaning of the word and the wealth of its content will be unfolded little by little.[6]

The viewpoint from which the author attacks the problem of the meaning of life is not quite identical with the anxiety of man torn between diverse cares nor with the more contemporary feeling of absurdity or contingency. In keeping with the spirit of Blondel's generation, the problem centers around the conflict between autonomy and heteronomy in human existence. Action is not only a fact; it is a necessity. It is often presented to me as an obligation and it imposes unwilling sacrifices on me. I cannot advance with all the clarity I desire nor always accomplish what I set out to do. And, once performed, my actions weigh on my whole life; I am their prisoner. I can neither abstain, nor be self-sufficient, nor find satisfaction, nor be liberated. It is this weight of necessity and heteronomy that must be justified. It must be shown that this necessity is in conformity with man's deepest aspirations, that heteronomy is the condition for authentic autonomy. All this the science of action must establish.

If the proof is to be rigorous, nothing must be presupposed, nothing taken for granted: neither fact, nor principle, nor duty. In order to escape from the constraints that weigh on them, men have invented a host of doctrines and attitudes. We must sympathetically follow them to the limit in order to determine whether they carry within them their own justification or condemnation.

> We must learn whether, deeper than the most outrageous negations or wildest extravagances of the will, there is not an initial movement which always persists and is loved and desired, even when it is denied or abused. We must seek in each man the principle of the judgment that is to be used on each man. . . . Instead of setting out from a single

point representing the radiant center of a doctrine proposed by one mind, we must take our position at the extremities of the most divergent radii in order to grasp at the center the truth that is essential to every consciousness and the movement common to every will.[7]

In all the attitudes men assume to escape from necessary subjections, Blondel will uncover a lack of equilibrium or "inadequation" between what we believe we will and what we actually do will on a deeper level, between the willed object and the spontaneous movement of willing or, in Blondel's consecrated terminology, between the willed will (*"la volonté voulue"*) and the willing will (*"la volonté voulante"*). The latter term does not refer to a blind or arbitrary dictate but to the spiritual dynamism that animates the whole man, including his intelligence and reason. The amplitude of this dynamism will be measured by making an inventory of the whole series of human endeavors and uncovering in each case an ever-recurring inadequation as one seeks to establish the equation between the willed and the spontaneous movement.

Contrary to the efforts of dilettantism, Blondel establishes first of all the idea that the problem of destiny cannot be avoided; the act by which one supposedly suppresses it affirms it in its entirety. He next shows, against pessimism, that the problem cannot have a negative solution: The will for nothingness conceals a contradiction. There is something. This affirmation, simultaneously necessary and consented to, springs forth from the deepest source of our willing. It is now a question of measuring its scope. The unfolding of this initial dynamism will be followed in concentric circles through the different fields of our activity. The most elementary datum is sensation. It bears within it a lack of consistency that leads man to surpass it by creating science. Science, in its turn, supposes a synthetic activity, the constitutive action of the subject. The determinism of consciousness necessarily gives rise to freedom. To be maintained and developed, freedom expands and is incarnated in execution: Met by the resistance of the body and the world, it constructs individuality. The individual then seeks and obtains a complement outside itself, aiming not only to exert an influence and elicit cooperation but to contract a deep union with another self, to found a society. It is in this way that willing engenders family, nation, and humanity. Man's intention extends still farther: It successively gives rise to a utilitarian ethics, a metaphysics, and a disinterested ethics suspended from an as-yet-undetermined absolute. Finally, man seeks to achieve self-fulfillment and to be sufficient unto himself by attributing a religious value to his natural action, by situating the infinite and the absolute in one of the finite objects encountered so far. But this subterfuge, which constitutes superstition, involves a contradiction: One turns back to phenomena to make them infinitely more than they are. The rigorous chain of human action's total expansion leads us, then, to the following conclusion: "It is impossible not to recognize the insufficiency of every natural order and not to experience a further need; it is impossible to find within oneself the wherewithal to satisfy this religious need. *It is necessary,* and *it is impracticable.*"[8]

Observe that each of the steps followed so far enjoys its own consistency. Blondel does not treat science or family or ethics as mere means to establish man's failure to equal the amplitude of the will. Each object is willed for itself. But the very motive that prompts a person to cling firmly to each level is also the one that forces us to go beyond it (even while retaining it). Note also that this progressive expansion of willing is, at the same time, necessary and consented to: "the apparent necessity of each step results from an implicit will."[9] What engenders society is the profound will of the individual, and the individual accepts not only the advantages society affords but also the restrictions it imposes. The restraints against which the will may revolt in act are ratified by an implicit will. A dialectic, at the same time rigorous and voluntary, forces us to accept the necessity as in conformity with our aspirations, and heteronomy as the condition of autonomy.

This same movement persists even beyond the natural order. The human will has gone through the entire order of phenomena without exhausting its own *élan*. It must now will and ratify itself. But it cannot attain itself directly, even though it necessarily wills itself. Out of this conflict arises the idea of the *Unique Necessary,* the idea of God. This idea leads to the point where man must choose for or against freely welcoming the transcendent. Here lies the inevitable option at the heart of the philosophy of action. Life's principal concern

> . . . is wholly involved in this necessary conflict that arises at the heart of the human will and imposes on it the obligation of making a practical option between the terms of an inevitable alternative, an alternative such that man either tries to remain his own master, staying entirely within himself, or delivers himself over to the divine order, more or less obscurely revealed to his consciousness.[10]

The role of the determinism of action[11] is to give rise to this conflict, after which the ensuing dialectic does little more than unfold the implications of one option or the other.

If one proposes to do without God or at least put him under one's control, this spells the death of action; it is perdition. Man cannot live unless he consents to introduce God into his life. But God is he who absolutely escapes man's grasp. By our own powers, then, we cannot reach our necessary end. Our destiny—absolutely impossible and absolutely necessary—is supernatural. All we can do is wait for the unknown Messiah through generous action. This waiting, however, is already a gift. If a revelation and a redemption have already been given, they must include dogmas and require a literal practice. Philosophy thus leads to the idea of the Christian supernatural. But at the same time it recognizes that it cannot affirm its reality; this affirmation requires faith and religious practice.

Finally, the role of philosophy is not to put us in possession of being, but to make manifest the relations between phenomena. Its necessary development, when fully consented to, leads inevitably to the ontological affirmation; but in itself it only constitutes a phenomenology. A first affirmation of being is certainly given from the start, but the definitive and possessive affirmation depends on our religious option. It is only with the acceptance of our destiny that our knowledge becomes a real possession of being. The science of action establishes the fact that there is no substitute for action. The religious option is the true solution of the problem of being.

This, in summary fashion, is the argument of Blondel's first work. It is not an ethical treatise or a series of edifying exhortations. It is a *phenomenology of action*. But it must be correctly understood. It does not propose merely to describe the contingent variety of particular acts or the states of consciousness that accompany them, but "simply to determine what is inevitable and necessary in the total unfolding of human action."[12] By setting forth "the chain of necessities which make up the drama of life and leading it forcibly to the conclusion,"[13] Blondel's phenomenology discloses the *logic of action*. And it is a rigorous logic in the course of which we find necessarily linked together the successive advances of action in search of a term adequate to the dynamism from which it takes its origin. There is, no doubt, a natural temptation to stop at one of the steps which the will explores and to find sufficiency therein. This can be done provisionally. But at rock bottom we cannot escape the dialectic of a destiny which prescribes that man open himself to the divine gift.

The strength of Blondel's dialectic resides in the fact that it does not construct an ideal as the term of action, beyond the reality that is originally given; it simply expresses the inescapable content of action. It might seem that a secret postulate animates and sustains it. In order to follow it, is it not necessary to admit at the outset that the human will is not content with any finite object and that it is directed toward a good which it finds nowhere in the natural world? This is the objection Boutroux raised against Blondel when the latter was defending his thesis: "Is not willing the infinite the point of departure and, as it were, the question which is begged in all your inquiry?" Blondel replied that willing the infinite is not the point of departure but the point of arrival of philosophical inquiry. The question is to know whether it may not be the real principle of human activity. To avoid any unwarranted assumptions we should not begin by supposing it present nor by supposing it absent. And when it arises as a hypothesis, when it is proposed to consciousness through education or history, we must resist it. Blondel stated:

> And this is what I have attempted to do. . . . This is the origin of the negative side of the method that alone appears to me to enjoy scientific rigor. So I examine all the varieties of attempts that can be made to escape my secret postulate; I seek with all my strength to pretend that I know nothing about it, to suppress it. . . . But after all these attempts there only results a system of linked affirmations which, little by little, lead us to set before reflective thought and the will's option what was already present at the beginning of the very movement used to flee from it."[14]

Therefore, Blondel does not measure the various steps of action against the antecedently known amplitude of the will; on the contrary, it is the inexorable development of action which progressively reveals the amplitude of the spiritual dynamism by which it is secretly animated from the beginning.

Let us not imagine, as a summary analysis could lead us to believe, that this dialectic is developed in a uniform and mechanical fashion, repeating the same process at each step. No, it is as flexible as life. It is true that there is at each step an inadequation between the willed will and the willing will. But in each instance the disproportion is manifested in ways as different as the forms of human activity are different among themselves. It is this variety that enters into the concrete richness of *L'Action*.

To emphasize the originality of *L'Action*, the work perhaps can be presented in two ways: It is a philosophy of the *universal concrete*, and it is also a *Christian* philosophy. In the *Remarks* collected by Frédéric Lefèvre, Blondel tells how he was led to study action.[15] He wanted to break out of an intellectual universe where "the notional, the formal, even the unreal, seemed to triumph"; he wanted to "rehabilitate the concrete, the direct, the singular, the incarnate."[16] The science of the general only retains the abstract. Inversely, the individual, as closed system, as atomic phenomenon, cannot enter as such into the unity of science. "Strictly speaking, there is neither a real science of the general nor an authentic science of the individual. What we must aim at and achieve is a science of the concrete where the singular and the universal communicate."[17] "The singular is the echo, in an individual being, of the total order, just as the universal is present at each real point which contributes to the harmony of the whole. The two are reconciled and meet in the concrete."[18] Action appears to exercise the mediating function by which the singular and the universal communicate; it is "the substantial bond which constitutes the concrete unity of each being by assuring its communion with all."[19] Thus Blondel was led to study action through his quest for a concrete philosophy.

As we have seen, he develops this philosophy by making manifest the link which unites the different steps of human activity. Because the same dialectic binds these steps together while maintaining their particular character, the phenomenology of action associates the intelligible universal with the given singular. This is one of the points most insisted on by the author: Each of the successive objects of the will appears as "a synthesis that cannot be reduced to its elementary conditions"; it must be considered "in its originality, independent of the relations it entertains with all the rest"; it is "what is heterogeneous and specific." "But at the same time, every term, without ceasing to be heterogeneous with respect to all the others, is linked to them by a solidarity such that one cannot be known or affirmed without implying all of them."[20] The science of action studies phenomena by manifesting at the same time their heterogeneity and solidarity. It shows how they imply one another and constitute a universe where all the parts, original with respect to one another, remain in communion. It "seeks to describe the concrete universal by inserting into it at its proper place this very description and this very effort."[21] The logic of action constitutes the science of the concrete.

According to such a philosophy, truth can only reside in a thought that is unified and in a total science. And just as being corresponds to truth, its affirmation (not just the spontaneous affirmation but the reflective affirmation) will emerge only at the end of the phenomenological disclosure (but it will necessarily emerge). No isolated link can carry the weight of being; the entire chain is necessary. Being is not peculiar to an isolated phenomenon, even though every phenomenon participates in being. Nor does it hide behind phenomena like an ever-fleeing phantom. In an obscure way it resides in the directed totality of phenomena. The ontological affirmation arises at the end and not at the beginning of philosophical reflection, according to this way of thinking. But then it does appear as informing all the objects of the will; for what is disclosed at the end was already secretly present from the start. Thus, a realism which is both critical and total becomes inescapable. From this point of view, once again, the philosophy of action is a philosophy of the universal concrete.

The integral unfolding of action, as we have said, imposes an alternative on our freedom, an option for or against hospitality to the transcendent and to the supernatural. If it is true that we cannot posit any object in being without positing the total series, it follows that we cannot affirm the reality of objects without passing through the point where the alternative either of opening ourselves to God or of closing ourselves off from him is imposed. And as the meaning of action changes according to whether or not our option is positive or negative, it is inevitable that, depending on our choice, the character of our knowledge will be altered: in one case it is privative, and in the other, possessive. The ontological affirmation is linked to our option. This does not mean that objective reality depends on our will; but rather that by our will objects become for us what they are in themselves. "By willing, it is not a question of making reality subsist in itself because an arbitrary decree creates it within us; it is a question, by willing, of making reality be in us because it is and as it is in itself. This act of the will does not make reality depend on us. It makes us depend on it."[22] Thus, the religious option is the true solution to the ontological problem. This is why, even if we can do without philosophy, we cannot dispense with acting. "The problem of life is not solved without living; and to say or to prove does not dispense with doing and being. . . . The science of practice demonstrates that there can be no substitute for practice."[23] Generous action, sacrifice, constitutes a true metaphysical experimentation which supplies for science, whereas science cannot supply for it. By the inalienable role which it attributes to effective action, Blondel's philosophy is, once again, a concrete philosophy.

Is it necessary to show the extent to which such a view differs from the popularized rationalism of the eighteenth century, from those philosophies (more or less inspired by Wolff) where knowledge is equated with the real because the real is reflected in its entirety in the possible? On the contrary, it comes to grips with the essential preoccupations of modern philosophy: the problem of relating representation to the act which posits it, of understanding the fact without making it disappear, of disclosing existence without dissolving it, of enlarging reason so that it may also include the irrational.

Is not the project of describing the concrete universal, of wanting to find absolute truth only in totality, reminiscent of Hegel? It does not seem that Blondel studied the German philosopher, although he undoubtedly knew of him through his friend Victor Delbos or through Lucien Herr. Be that as it may, there is a striking resemblance between *L'Action* and Hegel's *Phenomenology of Mind.* In both works a unique and multiform dialectic leads the mind from sensation to revealed religion, passing through consciousness of self, the relation between the exterior and the interior, and the different forms of scientific, social, and moral activity. The parallel could be extended rather far. But, along with curious similarities, there would also appear profound differences. The idea of phenomenology is not exactly the same in the two authors. Hegel devotes much of his attention to the consideration of history and historical categories; but this plays a minor role in Blondel. The purpose of philosophy for Hegel, the ideal of the wise man, is absolute knowledge; for Blondel it is the religious option which philosophy shows to be necessary.

By the link that he establishes between human existence and the option in the face of transcendence, Blondel resembles, on the one hand, Kierkegaard, Karl Jaspers, and Gabriel Marcel, especially the latter, who, in his search for a concrete philosophy, speaks of "the hidden identity of the way which leads to holiness and the road which leads the metaphysician to the affirmation of being."[24] On the other hand, by his concern for rational exigency, for the "logic of action," and for the concatenation of different spheres, Blondel's philosophy differs profoundly from those existential philosophies that lay special stress on discontinuity and ruptures. It is still more opposed to "existentialism" proper. It is not concerned with the contingent or even with the simple concrete but with the universal.

We have also pointed out that in some respects Blondel seems to have anticipated Husserl. Indeed, there is a certain analogy between Husserl's phenomenological *épochè* and the methodological reserve with which the author of *L'Action* provisionally suspends the affirmation of being in order to focus only on the linking of phenomena presented to consciousness. But this resemblance should not be exaggerated; the points of view of the two authors are quite different.

It is unnecessary at this point to enter into detailed comparisons. It is enough simply to show how Blondel's philosophy can be related to certain problems and modes of contemporary thought. As early as 1893, and before the terms gained currency, he was already proposing a kind of phenomenology of existence. This is why, in spite of certain outmoded expressions, his thought remains up-to-date. It also explains why it discon-

certed many of his early readers who were not sufficiently well prepared
to understand it.

*L'Action* is both a philosophy of the concrete and a religious philosophy or, more precisely, a Christian philosophy. As Victor Delbos observed
in felicitous terms:

> It was . . . the original thought of Maurice Blondel, when he con-
> ceived his book *L'Action* . . . to seek to master the order of external
> and conventional relations employed up to that time to compare
> philosophy and religion in order to establish a philosophy that would
> be religious not by accident but by nature, without, however, being
> religious by prejudice.[25]

In order to reconcile Christian faith and philosophy, the following
method has often been used: An effort is first made to constitute, outside
all Christian thought, a self-sufficient philosophy; then a way is sought to
hook Christianity onto it. The union therefore remains extrinsic and artificial. Spontaneously, Blondel assumed an entirely different point of view:
"I said to myself: suppose for a moment that the problem had already been
solved in the direction indicated by Catholicism with its *Unique Necessary*
as the term of human destiny: What is to be the normal attitude of the
philosopher and how can the autonomy of his search be maintained?"[26] It
is not a question of introducing dogma into philosophy or of elaborating
a confused amalgam in a gnostic fashion. Nor is it a question of situating
dogma at the point of departure of reflection as a postulate. Christianity
must not be the postulate; it is simply the directing hypothesis of the
philosophic effort. The latter must proceed without prejudice and according to its own autonomous law, even taking a strong stand against the
deliverances of tradition. The real question, then, is to know whether
thought's free investigation does not lead to an encounter with Christian
exigencies.

In the atmosphere of the Ecole Normale, Blondel frequently encountered an attitude of deliberate refusal even to examine Christianity. It
seemed that philosophy would have disqualified itself were it to give any
consideration to a doctrine which, while depending on a contingent fact,
still claimed to impose on the mind and human conduct supernatural
requirements originating from the outside—and all this under pain of perdition. This heteronomy therefore had to be justified by showing that it
answers the most profound desire of the human will. This accounts for
those chapters of *L'Action* which maintain "that to fulfill human aspirations man and nature are not sufficient, that action fully consistent with its
secret desire for autonomy must be subordinated to an action prior to the

action man can prescribe for himself, to an order higher than thought can construct and fully justify for itself, to religious expectation, to supernatural truth, to literal practice."[27]

By attempting to justify philosophically the ideas of the supernatural and of revelation, of dogma and religious practice, Blondel drew up the indictment against a "separated philosophy." This effort attracted attention. But all too often it was only the Christian stamp of his philosophy as reflected in the fifth part of the book (entitled "The Fulfillment of Action") that won this attention. Actually, it is in evidence much earlier. To begin with, the fourth part traces out the necessary genesis of the idea of God. But the idea thus arrived at is not that of primitive religions or of the natural religion of deism. The author had already shown their superstitious character. What Blondel describes is the Christian idea of God. No doubt, this idea can and must arise, more or less confusedly, in every human mind, even when it is ignorant of positive revelation. But Blondel determines its characteristics in the light of Christianity. It is a question of the *Unique Necessary*, of the one before whom our destiny is decided and in communion with whom alone we can hope for salvation. Even in these early pages the Christian idea guides the inquiry from the outside, and this can be seen even more clearly throughout the rest of the chapter. The development on the death of action has for its purpose the philosophical justification of the dogma of hell. The pages dealing with substitutes and anticipations of perfect action justify the Christian conception of detachment and sacrifice. Showing, finally, that we cannot attain our necessary end by our own power alone, this section leads, although in an unspecified form, to the Christian notion of the supernatural and prescribes the expectation of such a gift.[28]

But one must go back even farther: At the very beginning of the book Christianity forms the directing hypothesis for reflection. The problem of destiny is set forth in the Introduction, not in general terms, but in the Christian context: "These actions, fleeting and transitory as a shadow, carry with them, I am told, the weight of an eternal responsibility."[29] Farther on, what is made a test is the attitude of the dilettante when confronted with dogma." Finally, when the issue is moral and social activity, it is precisely the Christian notion that is developed (including, for example, the indissolubility of marriage).

In short, from one end of the book to the other, the author justifies the Christian view of the world and of life. And while admitting that this vision is his own, he sets it in parentheses, retaining it only as a directing hypothesis. He then progressively establishes that it alone answers the demand of man's deeper will. Having before his eyes the Christian datum and admitting, as a *believer*, that *it is so*, he shows, as a *philosopher*, that *it must be so*. It is in this sense that his philosophy is a Christian philosophy by nature and not simply by accident or prejudice. In what follows we shall see, especially in the last chapter, how this Christian character does not prevent it from being rational and properly philosophical.

## The Controversies

Up to the present *L'Action* has been described as it appears to the open-minded reader of today who considers it in itself, independent of the controversies it provoked. An attempt has been made to preserve it intact. But the controversies have served to leave a considerable portion of it in the shadows. No doubt, they did fasten on its original and essential aspects, but more often they viewed them from a perspective other than that chosen by Blondel. To this extent they have partially shifted the focus of the original problematic, thus occasioning a greal deal of confusion. A brief review of these controversies will provide an opportunity to understand better Blondel's thought on several points and to weigh its influence.[31]

The first difficulties came from the university and its philosophers. Thanks to Boutroux's patronage, on the day of the dissertation defense the board of examiners had been unanimous in rendering an officially favorable decision. However, the malcontents had not given up the fight. When Blondel sought a position on one of the faculties, the administration of higher education rejected his petition on several occasions on the grounds that he denied to philosophy its proper value and rational autonomy in order to end up with an exclusive supernaturalism. For its part, the *Revue de Métaphysique et de Morale*, in its November, 1893, *Supplément*, noting that the author of *L'Action* concluded with a doctrine of transcendence and the literal practice of Catholicism, announced that he would find "among the defenders of the rights of Reason, courteous but staunch adversaries"; for "modern rationalism has been led by the analysis of thought to regard the notion of immanence as the basis and very condition of all philosophical doctrine."[32]

Moved by this verdict, which made him a virtual outcast in the field of free thought and rational argument, Blondel, in a letter to the *Revue*, insisted on the rational and properly philosophical character of his effort. He said that in taking up the religious problem he only wanted to reclaim for reason some portion of its domain that had been abandoned in France. His method is precisely one that defines the notion of immanence:

Simply by following the continuous evolution of our rational exigencies, I make emerge from consciousness, from within, what appeared at the start of this movement to be imposed on consciousness from without. . . . Turning to action, reason discovers there more than when it is applied to reason itself, but without ceasing to be rational. And if I speak of the supernatural, what I am giving expression to is a cry of nature, an appeal of moral conscience, a requirement of thought.[33]

These clarifications won Blondel the sympathy and esteem of Xavier Léon, editor for many years of the *Revue de Métaphysique et de Morale.* Thus he began to win acceptance among philosophers. A little later, the new Minister of Public Education, Raymond Poincaré, having been informed by his cousin, Emile Boutroux, of Blondel's plight, intervened in his behalf. On April 30, 1895, having waited for two years, he was appointed *maître de conférences* at the University of Lille. He became *chargé de cours* on December 28, 1896, on the Faculté des Lettres at the University of Aix-Marseille. The next year he was appointed professor, and spent the rest of his life at Aix.

We must keep in mind all the difficulties just reviewed if we are to understand the famous *Lettre sur l'apologétique,* destined to elicit so much emotion from Catholic theologians. So far, *L'Action* had not drawn from them any serious protest;[34] in fact, it had been favorably received. But several laudatory commentaries seemed to Blondel to betray the real significance of his effort. For example, in the September, 1895, issues of *Annales de Philosophie Chrétienne,* the Abbé Charles Denis declared that the dominant thought of *L'Action* was to "bring Christian apologetics back to the area of psychology." Denis's intention was to praise the work, but Blondel saw in this appreciation a double misunderstanding: He had intended to work as a philosopher, not as an apologist in the current meaning of the term, and to approach the religious problem not through psychological analysis but through philosophical reflection. As a reply to Denis, he published in *Annales de Philosophie Chrétienne* a series of six articles (January to July, 1896) with the title *Lettre sur les exigences de la pensée contemporaine en matière d'apologétique et sur la méthode de la philosophie dans l'étude du problème religieux.*[35] His immediate purpose was to vindicate the properly philosophical character of his work, something that had been misunderstood, though in different ways, both by rationalist philosophers and by Catholics such as Georges Fonsegrive or the Abbé Denis. Although Denis provided the occasion for writing the *Letter,* Blondel was writing primarily for the philosophers, still smarting under their original excommunication.

In the first part he reviews the various apologetic methods currently in use, especially those based on Christianity's intellectual and moral congruity or its agreement with the laws of life and, secondly, those based on the classical apologetics of the manuals. While recognizing their respective merits and without pretending to substitute for them a new apologetics of his own creation, he shows their philosophical shortcomings to the degree that they do not answer the questions raised by modern philosophy when confronted with the idea of the supernatural.

The second part is devoted to a precise delineation of this problem, indicating the proper method for tackling it. These pages are among the most remarkable Blondel ever wrote; they specify, even for our own generation, the fundamental condition that every apologetics must satisfy. As Blondel sees it, the problem is as follows:

> Modern thought with jealous sensitivity regards the notion of *immanence* as the very condition for philosophizing. . . . On the other hand, there is nothing Christian or Catholic that is not strictly *supernatural*; . . . that is, it is impossible for man to draw out of himself what is, nevertheless, imposed on his thought and will.[36]

The Christian supernatural constitutes a double scandal for reason: On the one hand, it is authentic only if it is given from above and received, not simply found in and drawn out from ourselves; on the other hand, this gift, gratuitous in its source, obliges the receiver in such a way that, while powerless to save ourselves, we do have the power to destroy ourselves forever. "If it is true that the exigencies of Revelation are well-founded, then it cannot be said that we are completely at home with ourselves; and of this insufficiency, powerlessness, need, there must be some trace in man, purely as man, and an echo of it even in the most autonomous philosophy."[37]

In this way Blondel leads up to the only method he thinks capable of resolving the conflict, the "method of immanence," conscientiously applied to the examination of human destiny. It will consist in "establishing an equilibrium or equation within consciousness itself between what we seem to think and will and do and what we really do, will, and think."[38] By studying the interconnected system of our thoughts, it will appear that "the very notion of immance is realized in our consciousness only by the effective presence of the notion of the transcendent";[39] that the problem of the supernatural is the very condition of philosophy; that it is "indispensable as well as inaccessible to man."[40] To resolve the conflict between reason and faith, Blondel borrows rationalism's own method, but he develops it to its limits, showing how the respective exigencies of philosophy and theology are satisfied.

In the third part of the *Letter* the author shows how the logical development of modern philosophy has greater resources than medieval Aristotelianism for resolving the conflict between reason and faith; and he outlines "the conditions which any future attempt will have to satisfy, whether it be philosophical or apologetical, if it is not to be condemned to sterility from the outset."[41]

The effect of the *Letter* was the opposite of that produced by *L'Action.* Although it was favorably received by those philosophers who were familiar with it, notably by Brunschvicg,[42] it displeased a fair number of theologians. The latter were irritated by its rather impassioned criticisms of textbook apologetics and of scholastic theology. (Blondel would later apologize for having been too sweeping in his criticism.) The most distressing factor was that, unfamiliar with the problematic, the method, and even the vocabulary of modern philosophy, many misunderstood Blondel's thought and attributed to him heterodox opinions which were completely foreign to his outlook. When the encyclical *Pascendi* appeared with its condemnation of Modernism, many made the unfounded claim that it was aimed at him.

It was in this troublesome atmosphere that the *Letter* and *L'Action* were discussed, the latter now winning more attention because of the former. From the beginning both works had won enlightened defenders so that, in spite of the opposition, they began to exercise an increasingly broad influence on theology. But adversaries as well as champions usually read *L'Action* in the light of the *Letter* or, at least, on the basis of what they could remember about them. This resulted in a distortion of the problematic originally chosen by Blondel. To be sure, *L'Action* did contain principles useful for apologetics, but it was proposed as a specifically philosophical work. The term "method of immanence" did not even appear in the book but was suggested to the author by the criticism that appeared in the *Revue de Métaphysique et de Morale*; and while the term was suitable for his purposes, it was not indispensable, isolated from the context, it could lead to confusion. Even the *Letter* was concerned with the problem of methodology without claiming to put itself forward as an apologetics. But, more attentive to the title of the work than to its explicit statements and attracted by the timeliness of the apologetic question, most regarded Blondel as less a philosopher than an apologist. It was commonly thought that his primary aim was to substitute for classical apologetics a new apologetics based on the method of immanence; the central question was to know whether there was a way of effecting this substitution and to determine what value the method of immanence might have.

We cannot review here all the weapons used in the attack. Let it suffice to refer briefly to the two earliest criticisms: an article by Père M.-B. Schwalm, "Les illusions de l'idéalisme et leurs dangers pour la foi," in the *Revue Thomiste* (September, 1896), and a series of two articles by Abbé H. Gayraud, "Une nouvelle apologétique chrétienne," in *Annales de Philosophie Chrétienne* (December, 1896, and January, 1897). These publications, like others that were to follow later, are marred by gross errors of interpretation, a fact which greatly reduces the value of their judgments. In addition, the article in the *Revue Thomiste* is surprisingly haughty in tone. For example, after having supposedly found opposition between Blondel's texts and the Decrees of the First Vatican Council, and having claimed that he could point out "more than fifty similar instances," the author concludes:

> I can be permitted, then, in full justice to the young philosopher's text
> —and in all charity for his intentions, which are more orthodox than
> his text—to certify that his study swarms with propositions that are
> heretical, erroneous, or temerarious. I do not find using such qualifica-
> tions easy, but, once again, all I have to judge by is the logical implica-
> tion of M. Blondel's affirmations. It is regrettable that one is obliged
> to censor so severely one of those enterprising and dedicated "young
> men," but the one who loves well chastises well. One must chastise
> this arrogance of the School and this presumption of youth which
> treats with so little restraint a tradition and a philosophy whose value
> it is ignorant of.[43]

The bill of complaints against Blondel was a lengthy one. The main objections concerned the value of knowledge and the gratuity of the supernatural. On the first point he was accused of being a Kantian, that is, an idealist, a subjectivist, a fideist. Thus, Schwalm wrote: "M. Blondel is a neo-Kantian. For him the philosophical method is the Kantian method, pushed to its ultimate phenomenist consequences: Speculative reason knows that we have ideas; it does not know whether these ideas correspond to anything outside us. It is from practice and action that it learns the objective truth of what it thinks."[44]

This same objection, often repeated and developed, revealed in its authors not only a rather summary notion of Kantianism but a misunderstanding regarding the nature of Blondel's phenomenology of action. Introduced into France by Renouvier and Lachelier at the end of the nineteenth and the beginning of the twentieth centuries, Kant's philosophy exercised a considerable influence. Even if a thinker did not accept its essential conclusions, if he were living with the times, he could not escape the atmosphere it created. He had to face the problem it raised and inevitably make use of some of its vocabulary. This is what Blondel did. Quite appropriately, he accepted some of the findings of Kantianism while rejecting its restrictive conclusions. In *L'Action* he expressly found fault with it for having stabilized in an irreconcilable dualism the merely provisional tensions between pure and practical reason, sensibility and understanding, the phenomenon and the thing-in-itself.[45] He showed that action, as "a synthesis of willing, knowing, and being," re-establishes the bond between metaphysics, science, and ethics.[46]

For Blondel, action does not exclude thought; it includes it. By action "we must understand not only the concrete act of living thought which represents ourselves to ourselves along with all the rest, . . . but also the initiative by which our instincts, desires, and intentions are expressed in all the rest. . . ."[47] "I study in action what precedes and prepares, what produces and nourishes, what follows and develops the very fact of distinct thought."[48] The spiritual dynamism analyzed by the science of action engenders and directs all human activity, including thought. To cut the latter off from its source is to make it an abstraction, that is, a part artificially isolated from the whole to which it belongs; this can only succeed in making it unintelligible. It was this error that Blondel often criticized in his first writings under the name of intellectualism, but his purpose was to defend intelligence and enlarge the realm of the intelligible. He wanted to avoid limiting thought to representation, but to integrate it with the very act of thinking and the totality of life. "What I am proposing is fundamentally a kind of panlogism. . . . If I have seemed to be anti-intellectualist, it is because I wanted to recover for rationality areas which the philosophy of the idea—not to be confused with intelligence or intelligibility—excludes because it has restricted itself to what is only a virtual source of light while abstracting from real conditions and vital sources."[49]

Consequently, when Blondel opposes "a proof which is only a logical argument" to one "which results from the total movement of life" and declares that only the latter leads to being,[50] this does not mean that "reason is imprisoned in pure phenomena" and that "the transcendent and ontological use of reasoning"[51] is forbidden. It simply means, as will be explained later on, that the logical argument draws its efficacy from the spiritual dynamism which engenders it. When he writes concerning the proof for God that from action and "from it alone arises the indisputable presence and the compelling proof of Being,"[52] he does not mean to substitute an arbitrary dictate for failing reason but, rather, to relate rational argument to the concrete activity from which it springs.

Thought has an objective value, and it possesses it spontaneously before the philosopher intervenes. "What we know is real, just as we know it."[53] But the role of the philosopher is to justify reflexively this spontaneous objectivity and to define what it implies. In order not to establish by postulate precisely what he wants to justify, Blondel considers first all the objects of our thought as they appear, that is, as phenomena, without as yet making any pronouncement about their objective reality. This is a perfectly legitimate methodological procedure. But the dialectic of the necessary solidarity of appearances finally forces us to affirm the objective reality of the whole. It leads us to recognize not an unknowable thing-in-itself behind the phenomenon, but the very being of the phenomena themselves. Thus the ontological value of knowledge is justified.

Another difficulty remains. In the preceding paragraph we said that to affirm the reality of objects it is necessary to pose implicitly the problem of our destiny and to subordinate all that we are and all that in any way is for us to an option: the free acceptance or refusal of the Unique Necessary. Acceptance puts us in possession of being; refusal deprives us of it. This thesis, set forth in the last chapter of *L'Action*, has led some to suspect Blondel of fideism: The value of our knowledge would seem to be founded on faith. In this case the critics may be excused because of the obscurity of a text in which several lines of thought are mixed together and where an insufficiently precise vocabulary contributes to the confusion. In a later chapter it will be shown how Blondel subordinates to the religious option (but not explicitly to the Christian faith), not so much the objective value of our representation, but the spiritual value of our knowledge within the context of our concrete destiny. By the negative option "we deprive ourselves of the possession of known reality," without, however, suppressing "knowledge of reality."[54] "Truth, for those who reject it and refuse to live by it, is undoubtedly not the same as for those who are nourished on it, but it is nonetheless; and while entirely different in the two instances, its reign is no more affected in one case than in the other."[55] Those who refuse to open themselves to God are not on that account ignorant of the truth; but instead of saving them it condemns them. This condemnation, affecting their entire destiny, must necessarily affect the quality of their knowledge; not that this knowledge ceases to have reference to being. But, plagued by an inner contradiction, to the extent that it denies the spiritual dynamism that sustains it, it is privative and nonpossessive. This distinction between the *knowledge of being* (which is a necessary datum) and *being in knowledge* (where possession is subordinated to the free acceptance of the *Unique Necessary*)[56] may seem to be excessively subtle. Actually it is one of *L'Action*'s most profound insights, for it translates into the sphere of philosophy the Gospel message: "From him who does not have, even what he has will be taken." But perhaps in order to understand this distinction, it may be necessary to understand the distinction that it anticipates in its own manner, the one proposed later by Gabriel Marcel between *having* and *being*, between *problem* and *mystery.* Knowledge which obeys the laws of thought has an objective value. But being, in the strongest sense of the word, in offering resistance and giving value to everything else, is unveiled, beyond the purely objective, as a mystery, and it is unveiled only to a freedom that is prepared to welcome it.

Alongside objections about subjectivism and fideism came the accusation of "naturalism." The method of immanence, applied to the total unfolding of human action, leads one to regard the supernatural "as indispensable even though it is simultaneously inaccessible to man."[57] This fundamental thesis of Blondel's thought was and remains the most controversial. Even in 1896, Père Gayraud criticized it: "A Scholastic would say: What is invincibly postulated by human reason, what is necessary and indispensable to his nature, cannot be really supernatural. And the conclusion would be that the method of immanence ends by denying the supernatural and falls finally into naturalism."[58] The same objection has been formulated in another way: When the attempt is made from a purely philosophical standpoint to establish the necessity of the divine gift, is this not equivalent to claiming that there is in nature an exigency for the supernatural and, with Baius, denying the gratuity of the gift of God?

It must be recognized that this is a delicate question, that Blondel's texts, with a rather shifting vocabulary, are not always crystal clear, and that they do not resolve all the problems they raise. But to declare that they disregard the gratuity of the supernatural or only affirm it as a logical *non sequitur* is surely a misconception. Far from denying this gratuity, the explicit aim of the philosophy of action is to justify it. Indeed, it shows that the ultimate term of the unfolding of action is not the supreme flowering of human nature, but a going beyond; and this *"dépassement"* is not the work of man but the gift of God. The idea of the supernatural can be meaningful for the philosopher only if it designates something *inaccessible* to man. The reality of this gift remains beyond the grasp of man and of philosophy. We can neither produce nor accurately define it but only recognize and receive it. Blondel never tires of repeating this in a thousand different forms, not as a concession but as an essential conclusion of his dialectic. Few systems of thought can be of such assistance in conveying an understanding of the transcendence of Christianity or, in Gospel terminology, in helping one grasp the sense in which the kingdom of God is not of this world.

But here is the difficulty. The same movement of thought that conceives the supernatural as inaccessible simultaneously conceives it as necessary to man. Does not the second affirmation destroy the first? Short of disregarding divine wisdom and the consistency of creation, can one say that the divine gift is gratuitous, if it is indispensable? Let us observe first of all that if the apparent contradiction is real and definitive, then Christianity itself would be incoherent. Indeed, revelation teaches unequivocally that the gift of God is gratuitous in its source and that it is indispensable for man since he cannot refuse it without destroying himself. We have no other end but the possession of God and this end is inaccessible. This is a paradox that we cannot eliminate, any more than we can reconcile divine predestination and human freedom, or the unity of person and the duality of natures in Jesus Christ, etc. The irreducible paradox of Blondel's thought simply translates on the philosophical level the Christian paradox.[59]

Very well, one might reply; but this translation is not valid. For the necessity of the supernatural is the result of a free divine decree; it is a de facto necessity manifested by contingent events that cannot be deduced from anything else. Thus, it cannot be arrived at by a simple analysis of human nature. It will be shown in the next chapter that the author of *L'Action* and the *Letter* had no intention of deducing from his analyses either the divine degrees, salvation history, or the content of Christian preaching. All he sought to do was to set in relief the *a priori* without which we could not recognize that the exigencies proclaimed by Christianity do concern us. We shall see how the gratuity of the divine gift is, at one and the same time, guaranteed by the distinction introduced between various steps in the genesis of action and by the phenomenological character of this deduction, which reserves for a free avowal in faith a role for which there is no substitute.

Blondel's correspondence and personal notebooks reveal to us today how much he suffered from the recriminations and denunciations leveled against him. They also show the contrast between the intentions some attributed to him and his deep piety, his humble docility to the authentic teaching of the Church, and his concern to defend and communicate the purest Christian spirit. We find him consulting competent people, regretting infelicitous turns of phrase, sharpening his thought, urging restraint on those who in their enthusiasm were inclined to make improper use of it, and protesting against unjust allegations.

For many years he elected to suffer in silence. Trying to enlighten his adversaries by private correspondence, he followed the advice of competent authorities and refused to enter personally into public controversy. Other writers first came to his defense.

The first reply to the criticism of Père Schwalm (and of Abbé Gayraud) was offered by Père Laberthonnière in two articles for *Annales de Philosophie Chrétienne*.[60] Assuming the truth of Christianity, and proceeding as a theologian by beginning with the supernatural in order to determine the conditions for a philosophical solution, he showed how one spontaneously arrives at the conclusions reached by Blondel through his free investigation that set out from the natural order. In nature there are exigencies for the supernatural. "These exigencies do not belong to nature as such, but they do belong to it to the extent that it is penetrated and already pervaded by grace."[61]

The correspondence exchanged between Laberthonnière and Blondel when these articles were in preparation marked the beginning of a personal friendship and close collaboration. In 1905, Blondel assigned to Laberthonnière the position of editorial secretary for *Annales de Philosophie Chrétienne*, whose title and good will he had just purchased. Together they made use of this forum for eight years, until 1913. Their correspondence makes it clear that they were not always in agreement on all points. As early as 1898 when Laberthonnière's book, *Le dogmatisme moral*, made its appearance, Blondel had expressed his reservations, and throughout the course of their collaboration he exercised a moderating influence on his friend. But in all that was essential they fought the same battle.

Between 1905 and 1907, the review published a series of articles on the work of Cardinal Dechamps.[62] Although signed by Abbé Mallet, they were edited by Blondel himself. What they show is that Dechamps, whose apologetics had been approved by the First Vatican Council, was already pressing for the method of immanence in his study of "the interior fact," and relying on what is *in* man without being *of* him in order to lead the unbeliever to Catholicism. Under the pen name of Bernard de Sailly, Blondel also published in the same review interpretations of the philosophy of action,[63] a treatise on the notion of miracles,[64] and, somewhat later, observations on the need for an integral apologetics.[65]

Laberthonnière was not the only one to support Blondel in defending or explaining his views in the field of apologetics. Henri Brémond and others showed that Newman was a precursor. Abbé J. Wherlé, in 1911, devoted an excellent brochure to *La méthode d'immanence*; in it he sought to sort out misunderstandings and show the usefulness of the method. The same year the article of the Fathers Auguste and Albert Valensin, *Imma-nence* (*Methode d'*), appeared in the *Dictionnaire apologétique de la foi catholique.* Clear and well thought out, it was favorably received in a wide variety of circles and helped in large measure to allay suspicions.

These theologians and others too numerous to mention here did not restrict themselves to explaining Blondel's thought but took inspiration from it and made it bear fruit in their own work. Through them it pene-trated the fields of apologetics and theology. But this influence quickly spread beyond the so-called Blondelian circles, extending to some whose thought was basically Thomistic. Père de Poulpiquet is a case in point, with his effort to situate the role of the inner apologetics within the context of a total apologetics.[66] Another is Père Rousselot, who, in his treatment of the will's immanence in conceptual knowledge and the role of love in the assent of faith, clearly took his inspiration from *L'Action.*[67]

When the War of 1914–1918 ushered in a shift of perspectives and concerns which helped to calm the heat of passion, Blondel's influence became even more widespread and merged with other influences. Between 1920 and 1930, *L'Action,* with or without the author's permission, was mimeographed several times and attracted many readers in a wide variety of circles. Among the works published or brought to maturity between the two wars, a great number, including some of the more classic statements, owed much of their inspiration to Blondel. Passing over the living, we may settle on two names: Monsignor Brunhes, who did a short but much es-teemed work, *La Foi et sa signification rationnelle,* and Père de Mont-cheuil, whose vigorous teaching, deep spiritual life, and heroic apostolic activity were fed on Blondel's religious thought. Mention might also be made of the chaplains and directors of Catholic Action who drew inspira-tion from the same source; for it is a fact that, as conceived between the two wars, it owed no small part of its unique character to the direct or indirect influence of Blondel.

But the action of Blondel's thought was not limited to theologians; it greatly helped philosophers feel more at ease in their Christian faith since it offered them a way of establishing a symbiosis between faith and reflec-tion. One of Blondel's friends, Victor Delbos, a Catholic with a ratio-nalist temperament, was indebted to him for the gradual orientation of his thought toward a more Pascalian outlook, more open in any case to a serious consideration of religious matters. Later on (to say nothing of direct disciples like Jacques Paliard), Pierre Lachièze-Rey, thoroughly Kantian in other respects, drew on the Blondelian legacy in his treatment of wisdom and human destiny—and one might list other names, known or less well known, of writers deceased or still alive.

In a somewhat different vein, it is appropriate here to make mention of Père J. Maréchal, whose thought has had its own influence among theologians and owes no small debt to Blondel for its stress on the dynamism of the intellect.[68] Finally, Père G. Fessard owes to Blondel the first *élan* of his thought, and in the next chapter we shall indicate how *L'Action* helped him uncover the dialectic of the *Spiritual Exercises* of St. Ignatius Loyola.

In mentioning only a few names, we limit ourselves to the better aspects of Blondel's influence. It must be admitted, however, that it occasionally gave rise to erroneous or simplistic affirmations among those who had only a superficial or token training in philosophy and an insufficient awareness of the Christian tradition. These affirmations disturbed and irritated Blondel's defenders as well as his adversaries. But one cannot hold an author accountable for all the nonsense uttered in his name. Vigorous ideas are often misinterpreted even by would-be followers. St. Augustine and St. Thomas Aquinas would have to bear a weighty responsibility were it necessary to impute to them all the errors and folly lodged under the umbrella of their names. Besides, not even the most reputable theologians have all succeeded in grasping what is most profound in Blondel's thought. Efforts at popularization have only succeeded in providing the public with a somewhat emaciated version of it. Finally, to calculate its theological import, one would have to analyze the uses it might be put to beyond those already made. In what follows we can only offer a few brief hints.

Throughout the early years the influence of *L'Action* and the *Letter* was especially significant in the fields of apologetical methods and the theology of the act of faith. Here it profoundly modified the theology of the twentieth century by helping it rediscover and deepen traditional themes.

The sharpness of the *Letter's* attacks on the "old doctrinal apologetics" could have given substance to the false impression that the author rejected it outright with a view to substituting another. Actually, his intention was quite different, a fact which a careful reader can ascertain for himself by an attentive reading of the work and by Blondel's subsequent clarifications. It was not a question of proposing new arguments but of preparing the unbeliever to grasp the deeper sense of the old ones.

> Let us not wear ourselves out trying to beat the drum for existing arguments, proposing an object, when it is the subject who is ill-disposed. The fault never lies on the side of divine truth but on the side of man's preparation. . . . This role of subjective preparation is of

primary importance; it is essential and permanent if it is true that man's action throughout its entire range cooperates with God's.[69]

It was soon understood that the "method of immanence" or the "internal apologetics" was not a substitute for the "external or objective apologetics," but was to be joined with it to constitute an "integral apologetics." Its task was to prepare the subject by obliging him to face the religious problem and by disposing of the initial objection inspired by the doctrines of pure immanence.

But the method of immanence was often construed as a "threshold apologetics," whose apparent role was to stop short before entering the area of apologetics properly so called. As it turned out, however, Blondel's thought carried with it the obligation of deepening the very notion of an apologetic "proof." While it is authentically rational, this proof is not coercive as a scientific demonstration is. In requiring that man give up his claim of self-sufficiency, it releases its compelling power only to the one who consents to this kind of conversion. It is a *sign* that requires interpretation, a sign with a double meaning which is only perceived when one adopts the required religious dispositions and freely commits himself. This is especially true of miracles, and such was the import of the few lines in *L'Action* and the *Letter* dealing with them. At first, some believed that Blondel was rejecting their reality or probative value. But later explanations left no room for doubt about his position,[70] and they assisted theologians in deepening the theory of miracles.[71]

By showing the necessary role of freedom in the very perception of signs, Blondel helped theologians understand better the traditional thesis which defined faith as a free adherence. Instead of imagining an action of the will exterior to that of the intelligence—and therefore arbitrary—the act of faith was conceived as a concrete totality emerging from the spiritual depths of the human person. It was understood better how faith, an intellectual adherence, of course, was also an act involving the entire person, a gift of self to God who also gives himself, an act of filial confidence. With this clearly understood, it was easier to interiorize the role of grace.

While these ideas have become more or less commonplace, few today suspect how it took Blondel's penetration to rediscover them and years of controversy to clarify and gain general acceptance for them.[72]

There are other problems that the philosophy of action helped to bring into focus. One of its immediate effects was to lead theologians to undertake a new analysis of the relation between nature and the supernatural; and what is less known, it helped not a few recover what the ancients used to call "understanding of the faith," on the basis of which one might establish not only a theology, in the strict sense of the word, but a Christian vision of the world.

But the most valuable insight Blondel gave theologians was not so much the recovery of the idea that an "internal" apologetics should precede the presentation of the signs of revelation, nor that subjective dispositions are necessary for the perception of the signs (all such expressions are partially inadequate). His real contribution was to highlight the sense in which Christianity has a meaning for man so that there is always room for moving toward a Christian view of the world. By clarifying the meaning of revelation, he suggested to theology a means for its own deepening and interiorization, and this in turn was a reminder of the true role of apologetics, which is to make this meaning manifest.

An approach to several special problems gave Blondel the opportunity to demonstrate the fruitfulness of his method. Thus, in a remarkable letter to Abbé Pêchegut[73] on religious certitude, he shows that an objective knowledge of revealed truth is not a necessary condition for one's possession of the object to be believed; but neither is the good faith of the one who is ignorant of it a sufficient condition for its possession. For what saves us is not our certitude but the action of the Incarnate Word. In going beyond individual subjectivity and the simple representation of objects, the study of action enables us to define the relationship between good faith and religious faith, together with their respective participation in the divine initiative. These pages, which add precision to some scattered remarks in *L'Action* and the *Letter*, provide a valuable contribution to the theological problems of implicit faith and the salvation of unbelievers.

More important still is the series of articles entitled *Histoire et dogme, les lacunes philosophiques de l'exégèse moderne.*[74] They were drawn up in view of the biblical question raised by Loisy's exegesis. There was an apparent gap between biblical facts (history) and Christian beliefs (dogma). Theological "extrinsicism" conceived dogma as a block given once and for all without internal relation to history. All it asked of biblical facts was a proof supporting the authority of the Church. "Historicism," on the contrary, tended to separate Christian beliefs from the facts established by the historian. But in either case one of the necessary elements was sacrificed while the other lost its significance. Thus, Christianity either consisted in a supernatural endowment extrinsic to man or was reduced to a kind of divine element diffused throughout the course of history. The problem, then, was to show a bond between history and dogma that would ensure their unity without destroying their relative independence. This bond, said

Blondel, is Tradition as understood by the Church. All that was needed was
to clarify this notion and vindicate its role. Tradition is not simply the
conservation of an inert deposit.

> I will say that this is a conquering as well as a conservative force, that
> it discovers and formulates truths that the past has lived without
> having been able to enunciate or define, that it enriches our intellec-
> tual patrimony by releasing the total deposit bit by bit and by making
> it bear fruit. . . . It is founded, no doubt, on texts, but it is also and
> primarily based on something other than texts, on an experience that
> is always in act and which permits it to remain in some respects master
> of the texts instead of strictly subservient to them.[75]

It is "the collective experience of Christ verified and realized in us."[76]
"It has no need to innovate because it possesses its God and its all; but it
must perpetually teach us anew because it makes something that is implicitly lived become explicitly known."[77] It is this that allows us to set forth
"a philosophy of action that studies the multiple, regular, and methodically
determinable ways by which clear and formulated knowledge succeeds in
expressing more and more fully the profound realities that nourish it."[78]
On this basis we come to understand the inner bond that unites dogma to
biblical facts, and one can no longer say, with historicism, that in proposing
the God-Man for our adoration the Church is guilty of a substitution of
person.

On a difficult question that disturbed even the best Christians in those
days, these articles provided many intellectuals with light.[79] They were
favorably received even by those theologians who had reservations about
Blondel's thought in general. Their clarifications on the idea of Tradition
provided an efficacious contribution for resolving the then hotly debated
question of the development of dogma. It can be said that the majority of
theologians today have adopted the essential points of Blondel's solution.

Maurice Blondel's unusually astute mind also shed light in another
controversial area where "social Catholics" were pitted against the more
or less open partisans of *L'Action Française*. In a series of articles on *La
Semaine Sociale de Bordeaux*, he outlined the philosophical and theological principles underlying the two positions, criticizing the latter and seeking to justify the former. He reacted especially against the attempt to
disengage politics and economics from the judgment of morality and Christianity. He showed that all spheres of human activity are simultaneously
heterogeneous and intimately connected and that, above all, the supernatural order should penetrate and assume the natural order without being
confused with it. Thus he defended the work undertaken by the Semaines

Sociales, aimed at making the Christian idea penetrate even the organization of society.[80] Moreover, throughout his life he lent the project his sympathy, advice, and collaboration.

Between the *Letter* of 1896 and the War of 1914 Blondel, while publishing numerous articles, did not conclude any major work, not even the book on the Christian Spirit which he had been working on since 1900. He was embarrassed by the many suspicions that had been cast on his thought. Besides, caught up in apologetical and theological problems, he did not have the time to devote to a more directly philosophical work. Still, exclusive of his constant collaboration on the *Vocabulaire* of the Société de Philosophie, several strictly philosophical articles did make their appearance during these years. Three of them are especially worth mentioning.

First, the article "L'illusion idealiste" was an implicit reply to the accusations of Père Schwalm.[81] Realism and idealism, wrote Blondel, to the extent that they are absolutely opposed to one another, are but two species of the same "intellectualist" error which consists in separating the *fact* of thought from the *act* of thinking so that the former is uprooted from its vital origins.

The same illusion is treated from a broader point of view in the study entitled "Le point de départ de la recherche philosophique."[82] Here the author distinguishes two kinds of thought: *prospection*, or knowledge that is direct and synthetic, "attentive to the concrete work to which we tend"; and *reflection*, or "knowledge turned toward results obtained or procedures used as they are analyzed retrospectively through abstraction."[83] Philosophy brings together these two ways of knowing in an inquiry whose point of departure is not a particular object but a total way of considering the problem of destiny and the question of being. The datum it studies is inquietude, which is the inner disproportion, lack of equality, that characterizes human activity and stimulates it to seek progressively its proper equation. The true object of philosophy is action, that is, "the positive aspiration which stimulates the development of distinct thought and the moral life in each man," "the internal principle which orients, calls to order, and judges fragmentary acts and thoughts."[84] These pages are among the most illuminating that Blondel devoted to the conception of the philosophy that animated *L'Action.* They also marked the beginning of his future research on the distinct but unified stages of thought.

A few years before, in 1900, the writer had presented to the International Congress of Philosophy an entry entitled "Principe élémentaire d'une logique de la vie morale."[85] Taking up a project that he had tackled at the end of his thesis, he laid down the foundations for a "general logic" that would extend beyond, while including, Aristotelian logic. The same program would reappear in the ontological normative of *L'Etre et les êtres,* but the application would be different since the author was to modify his outlook over the intervening years.

## *TRANSITION*

The year 1913 marks an important date in the history of Blondel's work. Newspapers, dated May 15 and May 16, announced thut the review, *Annales de Philosophie Chrétienne,* had been placed on the Index, beginning with the volumes of 1905, covering exactly the period during which Père Laberthonnière had been editor. This move was especially aimed at the latter, whose works had also been put on the Index. Although Blondel was personally untouched by the condemnation, he shared in the suffering and submission of his collaborator and friend.[86] He himself assisted in framing the note published by the review's editorial committee, which reads in part as follows: "Catholics without reserve, philosophers persuaded of the ever imperfect character of our reflections and of the insufficiency of an apologetic effort that is always reformable, we have born witness to the authority to which we respectfully submit. And now we are about to have recourse to thoughtful meditation in order to examine, before God, the defects of our work."[87]

A practical consequence of this episode was that it was to lead Blondel over the years that followed to develop his thought in a progressively more cautious manner. Observing his direction, Laberthonnière in his correspondence was to express increasing dissatisfaction with what he regarded as an abandonment of the cause and an excessive concern for expediency. Blondel would insist on his fidelity and sincerity while continuing to express his own reservations about his friend's thought. But the latter, hurt by a decree that obliged him to remain silent, was to become more and more exasperated by criticisms that he had previously tolerated. In following their correspondence as it grew more infrequent, one observes the gradual, painful, and tragic separation of two great and equally noble minds who, while not ceasing to esteem and love one another, never succeeded in coming together again. The impartial reader cannot fail to suffer with both parties, while refusing to condemn one at the expense of the other.

From the time that his thesis could no longer be found in the bookstores, Blondel had never ceased contemplating the preparation of a revised work on the same question.[88] But in the course of the controversies, which lasted for many years, he defended his original positions and approved those writers who expounded them correctly. His adversaries, meanwhile, reproached him for defending obstinately texts they judged to be equivocal or incomplete. So it was that he publicly announced in 1913 his intention of publishing a considerably modified work.[89] In 1919, protesting against the charge of pragmatism,[90] he now refuses to attribute a pejorative meaning to the word "intellectualism," as he had done before the appearance of P. Rousselot's thesis, *L'Intellectualisme de saint Thomas*. By the same token he also expresses dissatisfaction with the name "Philosophy of Action," which he formerly accepted[91] or even used himself in describing his thought.[92] In *La Nouvelle Journée* of March 1, 1921, without disavowing the work of his thirtieth year, he once again announces a "revised and corrected expression" of his ideas, adding: "Before publishing again a recast version of *L'Action*, I plan to publish as a preparation, complement, and counterbalance, a book on Thought [*La Pensée*], a book on Being [*L'Etre*], while awaiting a testamentary book on The Christian Spirit [*L'Esprit chrétien*]." This was the first time that he made public this precise project. He had already referred to it in confidence, as an optative, in a letter to Paul Archambault, dated March 4, 1915.[93] To be sure, he had never claimed that *L'Action* constituted an entire philosophy, but he was in the habit of saying quite willingly that the proper object of philosophy is action.[94] Henceforth, this object would be "a congenital Unity . . . that can be analyzed into a real trinity of thought, action, and being, before terminating in the final and explicit union."[95] In developing a work according to this plan, Blondel has in mind taking issue with the charge of "unilateralism" leveled at his first book. And as the main lines of his thought become more precisely defined in his mind, he occasionally offers a taste of the future work, as in the Remarks collected by Frédéric Lefèvre and published under the title, *L'Itinéraire philosophique de Maurice Blondel* (1928) and in the 1930 adaptation of the *Vinculum*, a reworking of his original Latin thesis.

Insofar as it is possible to judge by the writings, short and rare, published between the end of World War I and the year 1928, Blondel's essential preoccupation was to analyze and validate "real" knowledge, that concrete and unitive knowledge whose final, though gratuitous, term is mystical experience. In *Le procès de l'intelligence* (1921),[96] he established the distinction and solidarity between "notional" and "real" knowledge. The former, the work of discursive reason, builds a world of representations and "lives by mimicking or similitude." Real knowledge or knowledge by action presents us with being itself to the extent that it is singular and unique; it is intuitive and unitive.[97] It is for this type of knowing that the word "intelligence" must be reserved; one cannot exalt intelligence or understanding without bringing it to the fore. To describe its manner of operation, Blondel has recourse, not to St. Augustine, not to Newman, but paradoxically to a philosopher who is regarded as the typical intellectualist, St. Thomas. Père Rousselot's thesis, published in 1908, having revealed a knowledge by affinity or connaturality in Thomism, now stimulates Blondel to use these notions to analyze "real" knowledge. But, in reaction to Rousselot and especially against Bergson (whose complexity, by the way, Blondel did not entirely appreciate), he then moves to demonstrate the necessary contribution of notional knowledge to unitive and intuitive knowledge.

*Le problème de la mystique*[98] (1925) should be read as a prolongation of *Le procès de l'intelligence*. The author maintains that philosophy can and should contribute to the study of this question of mysticism. Having been severely criticized for his conception of unitive knowledge, he here defends it and shows that it allows us to situate philosophically mystical experience. While the latter is, of course, a gratuitous gift, it does find its point of attachment in the human spirit, which is concrete knowledge.

We must admit that, in spite of the incontestable merit of his analysis, the distinction between the two types of knowledge, as defined by Blondel at that time, is artificial. It was an attempt to take up again the distinction established in *L'Action* between knowledge of phenomena and knowledge of being. But in *L'Action* it was a distinction that was essentially methodological; it did not concern two forms of knowledge, but two aspects of a single knowledge. The dialectic that established it at the start suppressed it at the conclusion by reintegrating the totality it had originally made manifest through analysis. Here, on the contrary, the distinction hardens in spite of the author's desire to restore a final solidarity; it is no longer a matter of dialectic but of congealing into abstractions. Notional knowledge is described without nuances, without any regard for the variety of its forms and their various adaptations to the real. We are told that even the most realist type of metaphysics is "a skeleton of knowledge," a container without content, a mere frame.[99] The distinction as here presented merits the reproach Blondel would later address to Newman who had inspired him: "It emphasizes perhaps too unilaterally the antithesis abstractly considered without paying sufficient attention to the strange wedding of these two conjugated thoughts and to the fecundity of a union which at first appears to be without love."[100] *Le procès de l'intelligence*, published during this intermediate period when the author had not yet developed the details of his great work on *Thought* (*La Pensée*), is one of his least perfect efforts. He was to recognize very soon the defects of his own conception. In the work that appeared in 1928 under the name of F. Lefèvre, which reported several conversations held with Blondel, the author no longer distinguishes two forms of knowledge operating separately but two kinds of thought present in all our thoughts.[101] It is this thesis that is developed in the first two volumes of the Trilogy. The same year, 1928, he writes to P. Archambault: "Action is not all to one side; it participates in the two thoughts that communicate in it and which serve to pro-move it, just as action serves to fecundate them. I would no longer say, then, that metaphysics is nothing but a schema, a shell."[102] In a letter to *Archivio di Filosofia* (September, 1932), he blames himself even more emphatically for having gone too far in stressing the emptiness of our speculative knowledge. Unfortunately, these two retractions would seem to refer, beyond *Le procès de l'intelligence*, to certain passages in the *Letter* on apologetics which, in spite of certain ambiguous phrases, had a quite different meaning. Apparently Blondel reread them through the prism of his more recent thought or the interpretation of someone else.

The years 1928–1931, then, represent a second turnabout in his evolution, following that of 1913–1920. And this time what is modified is not only the analysis of knowledge but also the philosophy of the supernatural. In this matter, too, he yields before the criticism of certain theologians and partly retracts the presentations in *L'Action* and the *Letter*. Until 1931 none of Blondel's writings gives evidence that he was in the process of working out a substantially new doctrine on this point. No doubt, after the period of the controversies he does avoid certain controversial expressions. He no longer says that philosophy conceives the supernatural as a *necessary* hypothesis. He gives up trying to justify the phenomenological *epoché*, which was the occasion for so many misunderstandings and whose scope even his theologian friends seem to have failed to grasp. He recognizes the possibility of a pure nature. But for a long time he declined to draw the logical consequences from this concession. Indeed, after having briefly made it, he insists that he is considering man only in his concrete, transnatural state, and he thinks that philosophy should be able to find in man an echo of the divine call inscribed in his nature. In this respect there is no difference between *Le problème de la mystique*, on the one hand, and *History and Dogma* or *La Semaine Sociale de Bordeaux*, on the other. But in 1932 *Le problème de la philosophie catholique* gives notice of a major change.[103]

This disparate work comprises three parts: a commentary on extracts from the *Letter* on apologetics, a reworking of the studies signed by Abbé Mallet on the work of Cardinal Dechamps, and reflections on the problem of Christian philosophy raised by Bréhier and Gilson. Against Bréhier, Blondel defends the idea of Christian philosophy (though he prefers the term "Catholic philosophy"), and in completing Gilson he shows that a philosophy merits this name, not precisely because historically it has undergone the influence of Christianity but when it opens minds and hearts to faith.

The first and especially the third part of the book provide him the occasion for defining the place of the idea of the supernatural in philosophy. The exposition suggests and, in fact, insists that the author is groping. But one thing is clear: the positive role accorded from now on to the consideration of the state of pure nature.[104] Of course, he says, this state has not existed and does not exist by itself apart, as a historical or psychological fact. But it could have so existed, and, in a sense, it is not an unrealized possibility since the proper condition of the spiritual creature remains effectively subordinate to the order of grace.[105] Thus, it is "possible, legitimate, useful, to examine what spiritual being admits of and requires regardless of the circumstances." This study will reveal in a being endowed with reason a *desire* for supernatural beatitude that is at once *natural* and *inefficacious*. We recognize here the thesis expounded in 1924 by Père Guy de Broglie in a well-known article, "De la place du Surnaturel dans la philosophie de saint Thomas."[107] Blondel makes explicit reference to it.[108]

But, he adds, philosophy can and should go farther, if it considers that the speculative possibility is actualized in fact. Philosophy should not limit itself to possibles, to essences, but should be concerned with contingent realities and singular existences in their dramatic history. Alongside a "pure philosophy" there is room for a "mixed philosophy," which, cautiously, without confusing domains, will clarify the notions of sacrifice, asceticism, rite, prayer, cult, and sacrament, and study the repercussions in the natural man of the various states—transnatural, supernatural, rebellious—manifesting in this way the philosophical appropriateness of Christianity.[109] "If the essential philosophy, concerned with the essential and universal conditions of spirits, leads us to the threshold of the mystery of God and the desirable beatitude, there is a real philosophy which, *servatis servandis*, is concerned with states realized in us but not entirely without us."[110]

But before building up this real philosophy, it is indispensable to reach a clear understanding of the realm of essences, possibilities. "We need a metaphysics of the necessary to prepare the way for and define a philosophy of the contingent and a science of the concrete."[111] This metaphysics of the necessary or essential philosophy leads man to acknowledge his insufficiency and to the recognition of a supernatural possibility. This real and mixed philosophy, which studies the appropriateness of Christianity, constitutes in the proper sense of the word the philosophy of religion. The real philosophy will make its appearance in the Trilogy (*La Pensèe, L'Etre et les êtres, L'Action*), the mixed philosophy, in *La philosophie et l'esprit chrétien.*

## THE TRILOGY AND THE CHRISTIAN SPIRIT

Matured over a long period of time, released at last as a philosophical testament, the individual volumes of this vast ensemble appeared in rapid succession, the five volumes of the Trilogy between 1934 and 1937 and the two dealing with The Christian Spirit between 1944 and 1947. Taken together they offer a nonpolemical but constructive reply to the objections raised by *L'Action* and the *Letter*. As suggested by the foregoing indications, they are not limited to an explanation and development of controversial works. They range over a much broader field, but always reflect the same fundamental intention in a different manner. Instead of a phenomenology of existence we are immediately confronted with a metaphysics which includes a theory of thought, an ontology, and a study of acting. The direct treatment of Christianity is taken up only in a separate work.

Contrary to what one might have expected, *La Pensée* does not offer a critique of knowledge along the classical Kantian lines. It sets forth the organic development of thought beginning with its obscure genesis in the cosmos, tracing it up the line of its spontaneous ascent in the organism, in psychism, in consciousness, until one reaches the level of its flowering in the intellectual life. From its origin to its term, it assumes two aspects: *noetic*, that is, unitary and universalizing, rational and connective; *pneumatic*, that is, open to the singular, the unique, the ineffable. These two distinct and related functions vitalize thought with an insistent impulse, with a rational and vital rhythm that advances both nature and intelligence. Their constant inadequation or imbalance causes the idea of God to arise in man and determines it. It leads to the desire for a deeper communion with him in view of the hypothesis of a possible supernatural which would represent the consummation of thought. And while its realization is uncertain, it at least indicates the conditions for gaining access to the spiritual life.

A vigorous dialectic, analogous to that found in *L'Action*, thus discloses what is implicated in every thought; it leaps across the gulf that is inherent in thought and which divides it into two elements, only to find that this same gulf is awaiting once again on the next level. The distinction proposed several years before between notional and real knowledge has been broadened to the dimensions of the cosmos and has recovered its pro-moving or promotional value as an impulse. It is no longer proposed in a way that depreciates the concept and makes speculative knowledge empty; for the *noetic* and the *pneumatic* are not two adequately distinct types but "two thoughts in each of our thoughts,"[112] "two forms that are insufficient in isolation, that are not distinctly joined together, that can be defined neither in their separate being nor in their union, which takes place, as in the case of all generation in nature, in the night."[113]

The reciprocal advance of these two elements in quest of their unity is seen to be especially fruitful in the genesis and expansion of the idea of God. It enables Blondel to define in pages of admirable strength the inevitable distinction and necessary relation between "the God of philosophers" and "the God of religious tradition," a distinction that will engage the exercise of human freedom and lead man to the essential option.[114]

It is possible that the same dialectic of the two thoughts might throw some light on certain aspects of knowledge by faith. For this knowledge indissolubly binds together two irreducible elements. The first is connective and conceptual, namely, dogma and the effort of our spirit to grasp its signification or its advance toward religious truth. The second is unitive, intuitive, and ineffable, expressing communion with God in the personal and reciprocal gift. The former is noetic, the latter is pneumatic. Now the danger of many a theory is that they favor one of the two elements to the detriment of the other. This can be avoided once one establishes between them a dialectical relation analogous to the one that animates the theory of the two thoughts. Here is one of the points where the work we are analyzing could provide theology with an instrument not offered so directly by the earlier writings.

As regards the scope of human knowledge, the dialectic of *La Pensée* rejects as incomplete the empiricist, rationalist, and idealist theses. The author remains faithful to his decision not to seek plenary truth except in the whole, but without underestimating the relative truth of the elements. He sets for himself the task of justifying the value of intelligence or understanding, even in its abstract and discursive expressions. All this notwithstanding, he did not succeed in satisfying all of his inveterate critics. Against the work under discussion, some theologians returned to almost the same charges that were originally lodged against the early writings. To satisfy their demands and avoid every misunderstanding, Blondel subsequently declared most explicity that he subscribed to all the fundamental truths of traditional philosophy required by the dogmatic teaching of the Church: He recognized the ontological implications of first principles, the objective value of knowledge in all its stages, the objective truth of concepts, and the living immanence of realities in them.[115] Later he would substitute for the term "intellectual option" (which some felt smacked of pragmatism) the word "agnition."[116] It does not seem that these efforts won the definitive success desired. To the end of his life Blondel had to put up with certain irreconcilable adversaries. Surely there is no obligation to follow him: Different minds follow different paths and reality is exceedingly complex. But to maintain that he destroys the objective value of human knowledge is so evident a misinterpretation, after the Trilogy, that one can scarcely take such a charge seriously.

Thought, Blondel observes, leads us to something other than itself: If it is already being, it is not by itself alone the whole of being. There is room, then, to expand our inquiry to the mysterious domain of being, and the essential task will be to reconcile the idea of absolute Being with that of contingent beings. This is the object of the volume entitled *L'Etre et les êtres*. It unfolds a concrete and dynamic ontology, notably different from that of the Wolffian tradition. A spontaneous feeling, an implicit notion of being forcibly present in us, hierarchizes the variety of beings experience offers us (matter, organism, person, universe), and is not exhausted in any of them. It only matches its own fullness in the affirmation of the absolute Being. Being in itself is intimately present and acting throughout the whole created order. This insertion gives to contingent beings their consistence; it hierarchizes them and animates the universe with a directed dynamism. Expressive of the plan of creative activity upon them, principle of their progressive realization, it constitutes their norm. In dealing with the "ontological normative," which is the most original part of his book, Blondel unfolds this regulative dynamism from the level of matter up to that of persons and to the conditions of their realization, up to the essential option which concerns the destiny of the spirit when faced with a gratuitous liberality, a possible supernatural.

As in the case of thought, ontology introduces us through this option to the problem of action. The work that Blondel devotes to this subject is not a mere reworking of his thesis. Before unfolding the stages of human action and the conditions for its achievement, he devotes a volume to the exploration in metaphysical terms of the problem of secondary causes in their relation to the mystery of pure "Acting." It is only then that he feels justified in approaching the problem of human action in its relative autonomy and with its necessary connections. The dialectic of the latter work is noticeably similar to that of the thesis. But in order to avoid the appearance of proposing too rigid a linking of the steps, especially when there is question of the supreme truths of philosophy and religion, the term "determinism," so characteristic of the thesis, is usually replaced by the more flexible "implication." Some important bits of the original work reappear unchanged, while others are deliberately suppressed. The most significant omission is the total absence of the final part of the thesis devoted to dogmas, religious practice, and to the bond of knowledge and action in being. The direct consideration of the Christian supernatural, relegated to another book, is replaced by a development of the "rational possibility of an exotic and supreme wave."

A tight unity runs through the whole Trilogy. In thought, in our idea of being, in our action, "there is everywhere imposed on us a provisional duality that we become aware of only by reason of a natural and ineradicable tendency towards unity, . . . . everywhere we encounter at the heart of all contingent reality an inadequation which . . . . opens up a farther horizon and imposes an initiative under the pressure of an inner stimulus and through the attraction of a superior end." "An infinite is everywhere present," which our thought should recognize and our action should welcome.[117] This is the locus of the option that gives us access to the spiritual life and disposes us to receive the gratuitous communication of God, should it be offered. The Trilogy thus constitutes a "philosophy of insufficiency," a metaphysics of the creature. Its soul is the aspiration for the transcendent God with whom man dreams of enjoying the gift of communion.[118]

The fundamental intention of this work, then, is visibly the same as that of the first *Action*. The thought retains the same concrete and dynamic character; the method is always that of implication. Throughout, a care for rational connection is allied with a deep spirituality, an ardent charity. Here too philosophical reflection is open to the deliverances of Christianity. In some respects, the final work is only a development of the original one. Yet the overall design and the inner constitution offer differences significant enough, and the changes introduced into certain themes are notable enough to warrant one's speaking of a second philosophy (on condition that the reader does not conclude from this that the later thought is heterogeneous with respect to the earlier). The work of 1893 was a "philosophy of action," which, situating itself, as it were, at the heart of action itself, bore witness to a dialectic of real life and described its inner logic; it was a phenomenology of existence. The Trilogy is presented as a "speculative philosophy," as a metaphysics. The science of action through action is expounded only at the end, that is, in the last volume, which returns to *L'Action* of 1893 with significant modifications. One can most assuredly say that this ensemble only develops the original potentialities in an enlarged perspective, that the speculative philosophy of the Trilogy only makes explicit that "metaphysics of the second power" sketched out in the final chapter of *L'Action*. But this inversion of the earlier procedure modifies the procedure itself. In the first philosophy, the judicative principle was the spiritual dynamism that vitalized human action in its total unfolding.[119] In the second philosophy, the judicative principle is being.[120] No doubt, the difference is to some extent only apparent: The dynamism of action tended to being, whence it proceeded, and the being referred to in the Trilogy is a normative dynamism. But the first philosophy aimed at an ontological affirmation through the development of a phenomenology; the second is an ontological affirmation from the start.[121]

The Trilogy is a vigorous work whose richness cannot be exhausted by any analysis. Its appearance was greeted as a philosophical event and its author was recognized as a metaphysician of stature. And rightly so. Yet it appears to be, especially today, much less close than the first *Action*, whose method anticipated certain current forms of thought. Another consideration also relegates it to a position of inferiority. The thesis of 1893, admirably composed, with its regular and compelling advance, with its brilliant and crisp style, burst forth in a single *élan*, carrying the reader on in spite of himself. The Trilogy, on the contrary (with the exception of *L'Etre et les êtres*, whose composition as a whole reveals a certain artistry), is burdened with repetitions, words of caution, backtracking. The dialectic has lost its bite and the style its brillance and movement. These faults can be explained in part by the fear of objections and the concern for avoiding misunderstandings. They can also be partly explained by the adverse conditions under which the author labored during the period of composition. Deprived of the use of his eyes after 1927, not only did Blondel have to retire from teaching but he had to dictate his works. Clearly these conditions made editing more difficult. They explain also why the later work is less deeply involved than the earlier in the great movements of the period. It is true that to the end of his life Blondel sought conscientiously to keep abreast of developments and to have his say regarding new tendencies, whether in philosophy, religion, or politics. But, being unable to read, his knowledge of affairs was undoubtedly less precise and immediate. Again, his later writings have about them an air of timelessness, a fact which does not detract from their worth; one bows, rather, before the courage they bear witness to, and it would be regrettable were one to allow oneself to be turned away from their rich substance by mere external defects. But one can also understand why many readers prefer the first *Action* and regard it as the philosopher's masterpiece.

*La philosophie et l'esprit chrétien* follows the Trilogy, but actually constitutes a new series. What succeeds the philosophy of insufficiency and expectancy is the philosophy of the Christian religion. After having studied the necessary implications immanent in all spiritual beings, whether they are aware of them or not, one tackles Christianity in its historic and contingent reality, in its Catholic form, with its dogmas, cult, and discipline. But, in the mind of the author, this is still a study that is "specifically philosophical," though of an unprecedented kind. It is a question of analyzing what in Christianity is "thinkable, consistent with our human reality, relatively intelligible, naturally incapable of being discovered yet perfectly desirable and good, in spite of the demands it places on us and in spite of what surpasses, if not our vague aspirations, at least our natural possibilities and human demands."[122]

The first volume sets forth the correspondence between man's rational initiative and the provisions of the divine plan for salvation. From the initial supernatural vocation of humanity to the accomplishment of redemption, the providential plan is adapted to our nature and even to to the deviations of our freedom. The various Christian mysteries resolve philosophical enigmas at a higher level than is inaccessible from the point of view of nature. Thus, we find juxtaposed the mystery of the Trinity and the philosophical enigma of a solitary God; the mystery of our supernatural vocation and the enigma of a destiny that cannot be achieved; the mystery of the incarnate Mediator and the enigma of a constant mediating function; the mystery of redemption and the enigma of reparation for faults. The second volume describes the risks humanity runs and the assistance God provides to support the individual Christian along the road to eternal life: the Church, the sacraments, the message of evangelical perfection, eschatological perspectives.

This work with its profoundly religious inspiration offers an overview of the meaning of Christianity that may not be available anywhere else. Several points that are developed are especially suggestive, for example, where the author indicates the correspondence between Christian mysteries and philosophical enigmas. Unfortunately, defects in composition and style, which are even more apparent than in the Trilogy, make reading the book a trial. Secondly, it adds few new ideas not already found in the earlier works. Many points had already been treated in various articles and excursuses, and in a more vigorous fashion. The fundamental intention of this development was already in evidence at the end of the first *Action*. Indeed, since that distant era religious thought has been considerably enriched, and, stimulated largely by Blondel's own philosophy, French theology has set for itself the task of discovering the significance of the Christian mystery for man. Due to other influences, there has been a development of religious phenomenology, while biblical theology and patristics have scaled new heights. These various developments tend to make the reader more exacting. That is why, no doubt, *La philosophie et l'esprit chrétien* did not cause much of a stir.

Blondel died on June 4, 1949, without having been able to complete the third and last volume. But he did leave, ready for the press, two complementary studies: *Le sens chrétien* and *De l'assimilation*, which the publisher was to bind together under the general title: *Exigences philosophiques du Christianisme*. Dictated twenty years earlier, more swift in movement, more direct, more accessible to non-philosophers, these studies have more to recommend them. The first considers "the Christian spirit" from the philosophical point of view, showing the appropriateness and consistency of dogma and the Christian life. The second examines how the intussusception of the divine life in man is possible and realizable. Throughout, the author insists, as he had already done so often, on the distinction between the two gifts: that of nature and that of grace, and on the need for a new and mortifying birth if one is to welcome the second.

Whether one is dealing with the different studies on the Christian spirit or with the Trilogy itself, as in *L'Action* and the *Letter* on apologetics, the crucial question remains that of the place accorded the idea of the supernatural in philosophy. As already indicated, the Blondelian dialectic unfolds from now on according to the principles established in *Le probléme de la philosophie catholique*. Here are the principal steps.

The constant inadequation that divides and advances thought, being, and action manifests the presence of a perfect Thought, a Being in itself, and a pure Acting—creative principle and term of our aspiration. Our insufficiency, our incompleteness, imposes upon us the need to affirm the existence of God, his presence in us, and his necessary cooperation.

This affirmation gives rise in its turn to an alternative, to an option: After having recognized once and for all this necessary assistance, we have the choice either of turning our thought and activity toward the scientific conquest and organization of the world, making use of the divine assistance in order to preoccupy ourselves with our own action alone; or of recognizing that the witness offered to God by the universe and by our thought prevents us from limiting ourselves simply to the enjoyment of the world and ourselves, that we have a "religious" obligation "to attach" ourselves to him in place of simply using his assistance in order to take hold of the rest. Only the second attitude corresponds to the original and constant thrust of thought and action. Consciousness of the divine assistance, be it implicit or explicit (but always irresistible), gives rise to the need to tend toward a union with the one who is the principle and end of every being and of every activity. We carry within us the *natural desire* for a more interior communion with God: *Omnia intendunt assimilari Deo.*

But at the same time this aspiration seems to be chimerical. The dialectic that has led us to the affirmation of God has made us recognize him as perfect, pure, inaccessible, transcendent, as the one in comparison with whom we dare not measure ourselves. By our own power we cannot enter into communion with him. Thus, the same reason that gives rise to and grounds the natural desire for this communion shows with equal force that such a desire is *inefficacious.*

What is to be our attitude in view of this tragic conflict? Shall we limit our aspirations as in the case of Greek wisdom? "It is, no doubt, conceivable that the role of reason could be to restrain us against an excessive ambition; and it would be no small blessing were the rational being to contemplate from afar and through the veil of mystery the vaguely glimpsed splendor of an inaccessible happiness."[123] A state of pure nature is conceivable. But we do not have the right to stop with this single consideration.[124] For even in such a state we would be unable to achieve stability in accordance with our powers. Bound to the God it depends on, the spirit "does not cease to be attracted by the force which from on high gives rise to all the movement from below."[125] We cannot abolish the insuppressible aspirations of our being or beat back its ascent to a higher vocation. From this situation there arises, at least implicitly, the hypothesis "of a supernatural, that is, of a complement which alone is capable of attaining what is humanly and metaphysically unattainable; an increase that is not due to nature and need not exist at all but which, once given, cannot be legitimately or inculpably neglected, repressed, turned aside from its true meaning and end."[126]

No autonomous inquiry of reason, no natural experience can certify for us whether the desired union is really offered. Only a positive revelation, authenticated by signs and received in faith, could provide us with this information. Only this revelation could define the nature and modalities of the divine gift if it is really offered. Philosophy does not provide details about the content of any dogma. But it obtains "certitude concerning a need, a certain need for an indeterminable Something, which is a principle of inquietude and insatiability."[127] In this respect it is in accord with the aspirations and beliefs of primitive religions concerning supra-natural interventions and an alliance between man and God, aspirations which even at times show through learned forms of unbelief.

> The most autonomous metaphysics can and ought to hollow out within itself a necessary void which no doubt remains indeterminable as regards its deeper foundations but whose boundaries and outline nonetheless prefigure the virtualities of an eventual solution. . . . There is then, purely from the rational point of view, a place prepared for a hypothetical supernatural, even though reason has no power of its own to require, define, or discern it.[128]

In view of these conditions, do we not have the duty to inquire whether this intervention has been effectively granted? And even though we may be ignorant of its historical reality, must we not adopt an attitude of docile expectancy and, through detachment, sacrifice, and generosity, create in ourselves spiritual dispositions that permit us to recognize and welcome it and which, in case it has not been given, would still constitute a life most in conformity with our deep aspirations? Thus, it remains philosophy's role to define precisely the conditions for this purification.

Such is the procedure common to the three works, *La Pensée, L'Etre et les êtres,* and *L'Action,* and reflected in *La philosophie et l'esprit chrétien* and *Exigences philosophiques du Christianisme.* In the next chapter we shall show how this differs from the approach of the first *Action,* what are its advantages, what also are the difficulties to which it gives rise.

This concludes the summary presentation of Blondel's work. From now on this study will concentrate on certain definite points, on those most delicate questions raised by the confrontation between philosophy and Christianity. These points will be studied especially as they occur in *L'Action* of 1893 and the *Letter* of 1896, and further developments of Blondel's thought will be analyzed or indicated in a more cursory fashion.

The preference accorded the early writings does not imply any lack of esteem for the later ones. On the contrary, we have indicated clearly the peculiar worth of some of them, especially *La Pensée* and *L'Etre et les êtres*, and we have provided a more complete view of their overall design than many historians who loudly proclaim their superiority. But when it is not possible to analyze everything in detail, is it not better to choose what one judges to be best? We freely recognize that the Trilogy provides "welcome complements, developments that are more mature, numerous clarifications," that it represents on certain points "an undeniable deepening."[129] But we will not go so far as to say: *"L'Action* was the *élan*, the seed, the promise. The Trilogy is maturity."[130] *Action* appears to be more than a promise: It is the masterpiece. The author of the statement we have just cited recognizes this himself implicitly since the very article in which he makes the above statement toward the end and which seems to aim at presenting what is essential in Blondel's thought is limited to an analysis of *L'Action* and expresses the hope that it be prescribed in the program of university studies.[131]

When we stress differences between the Trilogy and *L'Action*, when we speak of the second or later philosophy, we do not mean that Blondel "renounced" his "first inspiration" or "betrayed his starting point." Objections which some have opposed to the idea of a second philosophy,[132] to the extent that they might concern what we had written previously on this subject, were included in our own exposé. In the past as well as today, we announced at the start, showed along the way, and repeated at the end that the evolution of Blondel's thought took place against the background of a single fundamental intention, an intention that remained in force up to the end even when the author, for extrinsic reasons, spoke in a slighting manner, and not without injustice, of his first writings and introduced into the later ones this or that element which seemed to be less in accord with this original intention.

# CHAPTER TWO

# Genesis of the Idea of the Supernatural

When it sets out to follow the integral unfolding of human action, philosophy ends by regarding the supernatural as indispensable and simultaneously inacessible to man. Such is the thesis, as one will recall, which Blondel developed in *L'Action* of 1893 and in the *Letter* of 1896.[1] Readers will also remember the opposition it stirred up both on the part of philosophers and theologians. It is now time to examine this thesis more carefully. We shall approach it as it was first presented by the author, without considering the explanations he gave shortly afterward or the modifications he later introduced. The latter we shall take up briefly after the original presentation.

Henry Duméry's critical essay on the *Letter* of 1896 was inspired by the same concern to grasp Blondel's thought in its first state. This short study with its vivid contours and clear distinction deliberately turns aside on certain points from previous interpretations. We should keep this especially in mind. So that the reader may situate our scattered remarks, it will be useful to begin by presenting in a few words the central idea of this new interpretation.

Philosophy for Blondel, says Duméry, is essentially a reflective and critical analysis. It consists in ordering and linking together in an intelligible series, in an ideal frame, the various conditions for acting, while reserving for freedom and the effective option the task of realizing them in fact. It is this reservation that permits him to insert the notion of the supernatural into this ideal framework of conditions for acting without infringing upon the transcendence and gratuity of the divine gift. Leaving to faith the task of pronouncing on the *reality* of the supernatural, philosophy looks only to the *intelligibility* of the idea.[2]

So when Blondel establishes in philosophy the *necessity* of the supernatural, he has no intention of demonstrating that it is "required in fact by a man called to the supernatural,"[3] but simply that philosophy is unable not to introduce the hypothesis and that, moreover, it is unable not to recognize the coherence of this hypothesis.[4] In other words, "for Blondel, philosophy, or critical reason, or purely human nature, does not require that the supernatural be given in fact. It requires that it become a problem and that this problem be resolved under certain conditions. It refuses to say more or go any farther. For it knows that man remains free in his options even after reflection has had its word, just as God remains free in his gifts even when his bounty has been poured out."[5] Practical verification belongs to the free conscience, to the concrete subject. If this verification is positive, "it will then be demonstrated—but then only—that action wanted the supernatural in fact because God's grace was urging it to want it."[6]

The interpretation we have just summarized contains, as may have been noticed, a polemical point. What is the target of this interpretation? Is it not all previous interpretations? Duméry insists, as a matter of fact, on the novelty of his discovery;[7] and he easily dismisses both Blondel's partisans as well as his adversaries, reproaching the first for praising him and the second for attacking him for holding a thesis he never upheld.[8] Nevertheless, as far as the necessity of the supernatural is concerned, only a single interpreter is criticized by name, Père de Montcheuil. "He manages," writes Duméry, "to confuse the necessary hypothesis of the supernatural inscribed on the ideal plane and the effective need for divinization experienced by a nature directed in fact to a supernatural vocation. . . . He failed to conceive clearly the type of relationships that the intelligible order has with respect to the order of realizations."[9] As is clear, it is precisely against this view that Duméry directs the polemical points of his interpretation.

In the following chapter we shall have occasion to explain in what sense the celebrated text of de Montcheuil calls for certain corrections and precise clarifications, but also the sense in which the various complaints addressed to him by Duméry are excessive. We limit ourselves here to two points.

To recognize in the real spirit of man an effective need for divinization, and to admit that human nature, even when called to the supernatural, requires that the supernatural be given in fact: These are two very different theses. Duméry seems to confuse them. Père de Montcheuil held that Blondel developed the first while excluding the second.[10]

Again, Duméry is led to see in Blondel himself the confusion which he blames de Montcheuil for, between the intelligible order and the order of realization, between the necessary hypothesis of the supernatural inscribed on the ideal plane and the effective need for divinization. Should it not be admitted that the exegesis that is criticized faithfully reproduces the original?

Duméry admits, in fact, that Blondel on several occasions uses formulas that do not favor his interpretation and which seem to him to be "very equivocal."[11] He quite honestly cites a certain number of these texts (one could add many others).[12] Blondel repeatedly says, holds Duméry, that man really wills the infinite, that he needs the supernatural, that "if our nature is not at home in the supernatural, the supernatural is at home in our nature,"[13] that "it is thus inevitable that the titles to naturalization which it leaves in us are never erased,"[14] etc.[15] "Does this not all mean," continues Duméry, "that we effectively will the supernatural without being able to give it to ourselves? Yes, without any doubt, this is the meaning of such formulas. But they are written only to designate the end to be attained, the resolution of the option. Without being too careful about it, Blondel confuses the stages and speaks sometimes from the point of view of philosophical premises, sometimes from the point of view of practical decision. . . . Carried away by his subject, he manages to express himself, sometimes like a philosopher, sometimes like a believer."[16] In this he does not remain faithful to the end regarding the radical distinction that grounds the method of immanence, the distinction between the formal level of reflection and the real level of action.[17] Thus, the interpreter must set things back in place according to their proper order and reinstate the progressive sense of the demonstration.

A remark that is quite extrinsic to all this suffices to make these statements somewhat disturbing. The texts from Blondel cited here, and still others one might adduce, hold so important a place and play such a role in the *Letter* and in *L'Action* that to call them equivocal and confused is to read equivocation and confusion into the very heart of Blondel's thought. It is to allow not only that Blondel did not remain faithful to the end to the method of immanence, but that he grew confused at the very moment when he was trying to define this method. For, among the formulas that Duméry regards as equivocal, is the definition of the method of immanence itself; others are preparatory to it or a commentary on it. That is surely enough to give comfort to all those who have reproached Blondel for his confusion.

We surely do not claim that Blondel's thought is always clear or exempt from ambiguity. But it does seem that here in any case he is not confused and that there is no ground for distorting the obvious sense of his statements. It suffices if one understands what he is saying. Blondel indicates his intention of showing that we will the supernatural effectively without being able to give it to ourselves. But the effective will that he wants to exhibit through the method of immanence is not the *explicit* act of willing that is exercised within the realm of faith; it is an *implicit* act of willing which the dialectic (not introspection) causes to be recognized at the source of the spontaneous activity in every man, even of unbelievers. Besides, the object of this willing is not the supernatural under the *positively determined* form accorded it by Christian revelation but the supernatural that is still *undetermined* and of which philosophers, even the pagan philosophers, have had a presentment. Once this double distinction has been grasped, one can easily see that Blondel's demonstration remains entirely prior to the act of faith and does not move out of the domain of philosophy, as he conceives it.

We propose to show by an analysis of the texts that the thesis of *L'Action* and the *Letter* is in fact the one we have just outlined. Perhaps in the course of this investigation we shall discover certain clear distinctions that neither Blondel nor his friends have made enough of. Perhaps we may also so justice by another route to Duméry's best insight, which would be to establish that Blondel did not confuse what he had a right to deduce or infer as a philosopher and what he could affirm only as a believer.

## THE ENCOUNTER OF PHILOSOPHY AND CHRISTIANITY

*The Problem.* To understand how Blondel was led as a philosopher to envision the necessity of the supernatural, one must recall how his attention was caught by the conflict between modern philosophy and the Catholic faith.

Deeply Christian, with the soul of an apostle, the youth from the Provinces who arrived at the Ecole Normale in 1881 had made up his mind to spread his convictions among his companions. Often he ran up against a stone wall. Even the idea of examining Christianity was met by a determination not to accept it, and all this in the name of philosophy. How could any philosopher take seriously a doctrine which presumed to require under pain of eternal damnation submission of the mind and will to a supernatural order coming entirely from the outside? Or again: "Why should I be obliged to investigate and take into account some kind of event that took place nineteen hundred years ago in an obscure corner of the Roman Empire when I have no qualms about my ignorance of so many other contingent events concerning which, were I to whet my curiosity about them, would lead to an impoverishment of my interior life?"[18] It was the shock Blondel experienced in encountering such an attitude that made him reflect. To bring such minds to focus on Christian exigencies, it would be first necessary to clear away the objection that arose from prejudice and show that the exigencies proclaimed by preaching do correspond to an inner call with the result that heteronomy is here a condition for true autonomy. Only philosophy could maintain such a dialogue with philosophers.

On the one hand, at the time when Blondel was writing the draft of *L'Action*, Spinozism held an attraction for many thinkers, and there was also interest in the post-Kantian systems that had undergone its influence. It is true that Hegel was known in France only by a small number of people, but Secrétan, Ravaisson, and Lachelier had drawn attention to Schelling among those in university circles. We have no reason to believe that Blondel had read any of Hegel's works before writing his thesis. But from his notes and correspondence we do know that he had read Schelling's *Transcendental Idealism*.[19] On the other hand, through his friend Victor Delbos, who was a student of Spinoza and his posterity, he maintained permanent contact with these doctrines.[20] To him they all seemed like an attempt "to find a substitute for Christianity," to offer "a naturalized and inverted supernatural."[21] There was a need to demonstrate philosophically the failure of this attempt and the necessity of remaining open to the supernatural as such.

It was in these terms that the conflict between modern thought and Christianity presented itself to Blondel and led him to examine, as a philosopher, the question of the supernatural. And it was precisely this problematic that was presented in the *Letter on Apologetics.*

> Modern thought with jealous sensitivity regards the notion of immanence as the very condition for philosophizing. This means that if among current ideas there is one achievement which it clings to as representing progress, it is the idea, which is fundamentally correct, that nothing can enter into man which does not come out of him and which does not correspond in some way to a need for expansion, and that no historical fact, traditional teaching, or obligation added from without can be accepted as true or admitted as a precept unless it is in some way autonomous and autochthonous. On the other hand, there is nothing Christian or Catholic that is not *supernatural. . . .* strictly supernatural; which means that it is impossible for man to draw out of himself what is, nevertheless, imposed on his thought and will.[22]

It should be noted that Blondel does not define here what he will later call the method of immanence.[23] He simply sets forth the problem that the method should enable one to resolve: the apparent mutual exclusion of philosophy and Christianity. While admitting at the outset that rationalist thought has legitimate exigencies, he presents it at this early date as it understands itself, that is, as in apparent contradicition with the very notion of the supernatural. The relationship he establishes between philosophy and Christianity is not yet the one he will definitively adopt. Prior to the synthesis he wishes to bring about by his dialectic, what he outlines here is an antithesis between two concrete expressions of the spirit.[24]

The philosophy he has in mind at this point is the kind that inspired the review of *L'Action* that appeared in the *Revue de Métaphysique et de Morale*, which portrayed him as attacking the very nature of philosophy. "Modern rationalism," wrote the anonymous editor (L. Brunschvicg), "has been led by the analysis of thought to make the notion of immanence the basis and very condition for every philosophical doctrine."[25] This declaration was analogous to some of the statements of Blondel's comrades at the École Normale. It reflected, even more exactly, what some acute minds had borrowed from Spinozism, in whose name they were in the process of rejecting faith and Catholic practice. On the contrary, Blondel thought that "the notion of immancence . . . far from excluding, actually required, if completely developed, the transcendent truths to which it seemed at first to be hostile."[26] But in the passage of the *Letter* we are commenting on, before introducing the distinction between the method of immanence, which Blondel accepts, and the doctrine of immanence, which he rejects, he sets out to expound for Catholic readers the antithesis between rationalism and Christianity. He notes, incidentally, for the sake of some of this latter group, that the feeling of antithesis is not merely to be written off as a disease of "sick" minds, but as expressing, rather, the discomfort of man when confronted with the divine.[27]

The Christian supernatural, he goes on to explain, offers a twofold scandal for the philosopher: On the one hand, it is authentic only to the extent that it is given from above and received; and, on the other hand, this gift, gratuitous in its source, is obligatory for the one for whom it is destined, so that while we are powerless to save ourselves, we have the power to destroy ourselves forever.[28]

What seems at first to constitute a formal incompatibility is at the same time the very thing that makes a meeting of the two possible. If Christianity were to be presented as optional, and if it were praiseworthy to refuse the divine gift it proclaims without fear of sanction, then to renounce a higher vocation would leave us on the level where man might spontaneously choose to lift himself up. But the moment revelation looks on a neutral or negative attitude as a positive defection, the moment our poverty can contract a debt of the kind that only eternity can repay, "then the encounter has taken place, the difficulty breaks forth, the problem is defined. For if it is true that the exigencies of revelation are well founded, it cannot be said that we are entirely at home with ourselves alone; and of this powerlessness, of this insufficiency, of this exigency, there must be some trace in man-purely-man, some echo, even in the most autonomous philosophy."[29]

It is of the utmost importance to understand these declarations well: They introduce us to the heart of the problematic that is defined in the *Letter*. We see that what preoccupies the author is the philosophical problem of the meeting of philosophy and Christianity, not the theological problem of the relationship between the human creature and his supernatural destiny. Thus, Blondel is not led to ask how this relationship takes diverse forms depending on whether one views man in the hypothetical state of pure nature, or in the state of integral nature, or in a state of nature that has fallen, or in a world that has been redeemed. Later on he will take these problems into consideration, but during the period we are discussing he leaves them outside his purview. When he speaks here of "man-purely-man," he is not thinking of a state of pure nature,[30] but of real man, such as he is and knows himself, independent of the Christian faith. It cannot be said, however, that he was at this time making any direct appeal to what he would later call a "transnatural" state; for "man-purely-man" is not exhibited as knowing about the existence of a first prevenient grace. Again, Blondel does not examine here the relation of man to God according to the various states theologians distinguish. The question he proposes concerns knowing what man bears necesssarily within him, *if* the exigencies of Christianity in his regard are founded, and if he ought, on that account, to have some means for recognizing that they do indeed concern him. *If it is true*, says the *Letter*, that the acceptance of the divine gift proclaimed by the Gospel is necessary under pain of damnation, *it must be* that there is some trace of it in man-purely-man, that is, even in the one who does not know about, or rejects, Christianity; *it must be* that there is, consequently, an echo of this in the most autonomous philosophy. "Since the refusal of the state to which he is destined is not a pure privation for man, but a positive defection, what must be found, even in a life closed to faith, is some element of what has been rejected."[31] There is no evading the fact that one can never erase "the titles for naturalization" that the supernatural leaves in us, if it is true that "turning away from one's destiny does not really withdraw us from it."[32]

Here Blondel points out to the believer, then, what the hypothesis of the truth of Christianity necessarily implies, and he tells him that it is on this basis that the philosopher will be able to find a meaning in Christianity. What the believer calls an echo should, in fact, appear to the philosopher under the form of an inner need.[33] Blondel addresses the latter as follows: "Confronted with this rationalism which makes of the notion of immanence the condition for every philosophy, the question today is to know whether, on the basis of the only order retained, an imperious need for the other does not reappear."[34]

What must now be clarified is the question of what this "need" consists in and how it is revealed to the philosopher. To begin with, a simple examination of the original problematic already provides a valuable indication of the scope of subsequent developments. If, as a philosopher, Blondel sets out to demonstrate the need or necessity of the supernatural, it is in order to lead minds to take seriously the exigencies proclaimed by Christianity. His demonstration aims, then, at establishing, not that *God ought* to give himself to man under penalty of leaving his creation unsatisfied, but that *man ought* to welcome God's free gift announced by Christian preaching.

This latter obligation or necessity is proclaimed, as we know, by the Gospel message itself. But it is still necessary that it be recognized as such by us. This cannot be, says Blondel, unless we see in its external proclamation a reply to an expectation, to an "imperious appetite,"[35] unless we recognize in it, in some sense, the object of our implicit willing. It is not enough to present dogma in its inner splendor; the subject must also be prepared to welcome it.[36] Nor is it enough to examine carefully the history of the great Christian fact. "Whence comes the urgency that I ought to take this fact into account, when I can legitimately show no interest in so many other facts that are equally real? To what extent will I be responsible for a voluntary abstention? So many questions that remain without answer because it is not enough to establish separately the possibility and the reality, but I must go on to show the necessity for us of adhering to this reality of the supernatural."[37] Note well the formula Blondel uses here. It indicates exactly what he expects from philosophy when confronted with Christianity: It must show the necessity incumbent on us to recognize the reality of the supernatural.

Thus, according to him, philosophy ought to exercise the role of a "subjective preparation"[38] for faith. Without "claiming to cause faith to arise in a soul," philosophy will show "that man cannot pass it up with impunity, but that he cannot by himself gain possession of this life which is necessary for him, but impracticable."[39] It thus defines "the spiritual dispositions that prepare one for an understanding of the facts and a practical discernment of truths proposed from another source."[40]

These various indications all lead us in the same direction: When philosophy, according to Blondel, makes manifest the need for the supernatural, it does not require that God reveal himself; it simply uncovers the *a priori*, thanks to which we can grasp and admit the exigencies of the revelation.

*The Method and Its Scope.* By what method is this *a priori* laid bare? By the very same method that made the conflict come to the surface and which identified the difficulty. The "method of immanence," which initially seemed to exclude the idea of the supernatural, is the only one capable, says Blondel, of situating it properly. To succeed in this, all that is needed is to apply it integrally to the examination of human destiny.[41]

It consists in "establishing an equation or balance in consciousness between what we seem to think and will and do, and what we do, will, and think in reality, so that amid deliberate negations or ends that are artificially willed, we recover once again the deep affirmations and incoercible needs they imply."[42]

This formula, which the author expressly proposes as the very definition of the "method of immanence," as he understands its use, Duméry ranks among those "very equivocal" formulas which are faulty in the method of immanence because they skip ahead too rapidly and confuse the plane of reflection with that of action.[43] It is our opinion that if the interpreter sees here and elsewhere a confusion, this is because he does not share with Blondel the latter's understanding of the relationship he establishes between reflection and action. We shall demonstrate this later on when, having followed the movement of *L'Action* on several essential points and having grasped the method in its very exercise and application, we shall be more equal to the task of explicitating his concept. For the moment, let us accept Blondel's statements according to their obvious sense. We shall see that he expects from philosophical reflection and the method of immanence more than Duméry says he does.

The author of the *Letter* in the phrase already cited presents under a name he did not invent the method he had already defined and applied throughout *L'Action*. It consists in manifesting at each step a new imbalance between the willed-will (*la volonté voulue*) and the willing-will (*la volonté voulante*), until the final condition for their equation makes its appearance. This unfolding of the steps is not effected by means of introspection but by reflection. Popularizers have all too often given a psychological interpretation to Blondel's thought, an interpretation sometimes favored by his language, but one which is eliminated by supplementary explanation. Duméry is certainly justified in protesting against such a misrepresentation,[44] as are de Montcheuil,[45] Cartier,[46] and several others. Blondel's *"volonté voulante"* (will-willing) is not a conscious or subconscious will which careful introspection enables us to discover and which we might compare to the *"volonté voulue"* (willed-will) as one might compare two projects in order to see if they are compatible. As the second edition of *L'Action* indicates, the *"volonté voulante"* is to the *"volonté voulue"* what the scholastic *voluntas ut natura* was to the elicited will.[47] What this means is that, at the very heart of every free decision, it is the originative will that the elicited will necessarily implies. It does not exist alongside the *"volonté voulue,"* but operates within it as its principle and as the rule which permits one to judge. At the very core of "what is willed and done," it is "what wills and acts."[48] As such, it escapes all introspection. It only appears in a regressive analysis as the condition for the possibility of the *"volonté voulue,"* which, alone, is an object of direct knowledge. When one discovers a lack of harmony between the two wills, what must be understood by this is a logical flaw, a contradiction interior to the *"volonté voulue"* itself.

Therefore, when Blondel, searching by the method of immanence for the conditions that will enable the human will to equal itself, believes that he finds in this will a need, an appetite for the supernatural, do not imagine that he thinks he is reading in our consciousness, as though he had made a discovery, a demand for the supernatural. We are perfectly right in rejecting such a manner of understanding.[49] No, Blondel does not mean to discover, even in man in the concrete, "a telltale trace of the supernatural on the empirical level."[50] On the contrary, addressing himself to the unbeliever, he supposes that the supernatural is absent from consciousness and that no need for it is experienced. Besides, even were this need to be more or less clearly felt, it would hold no interest whatsoever for philosophy as long as it did not appear to be clothed with a quality of necessity; and it is not by any kind of empirical verification that one establishes a bond of necessity. Blondel knows this, and he calls attention to it most emphatically in the first part of the *Letter.*

We do not believe, however, that when he speaks of the "felt need for an increase," he is betraying his own thought by the inopportune use of the vocabulary of introspective psychology.[51] When he shows "that the progress of our will compels us to acknowledge our insufficiency, leads us to the felt need for an increase,"[52] he is not claiming to make the unbeliever *verify* a need discovered in consciousness, but he hopes to *elicit* this consciousness by his dialectic, which is something very different and does not imply in oneself any "psychologism."

Shall we say that the word "need," even used without the qualifier "felt," is unfortunate because it "returns to the psychological level"?[53] Does it necessarily return us there? Are there not unconscious needs? One can surely impose a bad interpretation on the need or will for the supernatural of which Blondel speaks so often. (For other reasons, terms like "exigency" or "to postulate" can also lend themselves to equivocation.) The word "opening"[54] is more precise. But does it suffice to communicate all Blondel wants to say? In wanting to purify his language excessively, do we not run the risk of weakening his thought? The moment one reaches a certain degree of depth of interrogation, all language becomes inadequate. The essential thing is that discourse correct words by playing one off against the others and that the reader be able to follow the line of argument.

Blondel, we said, does not invite the unbeliever to verify a need for the supernatural by a psychological inventory of consciousness. Yet he believes that he can lead him through rational reflection to conclude that the supernatural "is postulated by thought and action,"[55] even for one who is ignorant of or refuses Christianity, even for one who puts aside the idea of such a demand.

"Simply by following the continuous evolution of our rational exigencies, I succeed," he says, "in making emerge from consciousness, from within, what appear to be imposed on consciousness from without at the start of the movement. . . . And if I speak of the supernatural, it is still a cry of nature, an appeal of moral consciousness and a demand of thought that I make understood."[56] "It is in our very action," he points out, "that the need for the supernatural is discovered."[57]

He adds, of course, that the discovery and recognition of this need in no way prejudices the reality of the supernatural proclaimed by Christianity. In taking hold of "the natural bond of necessity that joins the most exact beliefs and practices to the total determinism of ideas and sentiments,"[58] one does not affirm their intrinsic truth. It is only to the eyes of faith that the truth of dogma and the reality of the Christian supernatural become apparent. It is impossible to insist too much on the reserve Blondel constantly imposes on philosophical reflection.

But neither should we restrict the role he attributes to this reflection, which goes so far as to discover in human action itself the need for the supernatural. The method of immanence applied to action will, he thinks, lead the unbeliever to recognize that in spite of himself he wants the supernatural, even in the act by which he refuses it. This is a real will in the very bosom of the effort that denies it, a will that remains implicit by reason of the fact that it is not known or is denied, a will which is nothing less than contradiction interior to its own negation. According to Blondel, manifesting this will is the only means of making the unbeliever recognize that the exigencies of Christianity do concern him and that submission to these exigencies is the only way by which he will realize the fulfillment of his action.

This role of philosophy is clearly stated in a passage of *L'Action*, which also provides us with a new clarification:

> Let no one misunderstand the strictly philosophical plan that inspires this inquiry; it always revolves around this same thought: "How equal the term willed to the very principle of the voluntary aspiration?" For one cannot lead men to submission save by making them understand that it is the secret of their true independence. So, it is necessary to aim at true independence in order to understand the secret of the necessary submission. Moreover, as long as it is a question of the supernatural, we have to do with a preoccupation that is profoundly human and rather like a cry of nature that makes itself heard. It is a question of seeing how this notion of the supernatural is necessarily engendered and how the supernatural seems necessary for the human will so that the equation of action may be established in consciousness. It is not a question of determing the actual content of divine revelation. . . . The role of the philosopher is to make sure that, fully consistent with our secret desire, we move even to the plane of literal practice; its task is to express the inevitable exigencies of thought and a kind of natural prayer of the human will. Nothing more, but nothing less.[59]

According to Henry Duméry, Blondel borrows the idea of the supernatural from Christian teaching and, as a philosopher, establishes the fact that it "can be integrated and ought to be integrated into the internal logic of action."[60] That is correct. But we see from the above text that this is not enough. Blondel wants to show how this notion is "necessarily engendered." This does not represent a lapse in the consistency of his thinking. At the beginning of the preceding chapter, he explains why it is necessary to determine the "genesis" of the idea of revelation.[61] "Were it necessary to consider that revelation itself comes entirely from without, as a datum that is entirely empirical, the very notion of dogma or of a revealed precept would be totally unintelligible."[62] "It is not even from revelation (in the hypothesis that it exists), nor from natural phenomena (in the hypothesis that it does not exist) that man can come to the idea of revealed precepts of dogmas. This notion rises up from an inner initiative."[63] Indeed, each time that Blondel speaks of the supernatural as a philosopher, what he wants to make heard is a "cry of nature." He shows that what appears at first to be imposed from without wells up also from within; that the Christian idea corresponds to a demand of thought. When, as a philosopher, he affirms the necessity of the supernatural, he does not merely mean that this notion must be viewed as a hypothesis and that one will thus be led to recognize its logical coherence. He declares in a more precise and demanding fashion that the "supernatural seems necessary for the human will so that action may be put in equation in consciousness," that is, so as to "equal the term willed to the very principle of the voluntary aspiration." The philosopher, he thinks, should go so far as to establish this very thing, if he wishes to resolve the conflict in which the autonomy of reason runs directly up against the apparent heteronomy of the Christian supernatural.

To soften the obvious sense of these express declarations is to weaken Blondel's thought. But if one is to adhere to this obvious sense, do we not expose him once more to the very legitimate criticism of theologians? Do we not forget that the Christian supernatural is a gratuitous gift of God when one claims to establish, as a philosopher, that its notion is necessarily engendered and that it appears to be necessary for the achievement of human action? We have said that this demonstration has as its goal the preparation of minds for the recognition of the reality of the supernatural, but that it does not seek to conclude of itself to its reality or impose a necessity on God. The objection can, nevertheless, take another turn, for it is a question of learning whether the demonstration does not exceed the limits the author wanted to impose on it.

There is no other way to find this out than to follow the demonstration from beginning to end. For this purpose, the *Letter* of 1896 cannot suffice. Its summary indications take the form of references that can scarcely be understood if one does not keep clearly in mind the progressive movement of *L'Action.* Moreover, addressed to believers in order to explain the exigencies of philosophy when confronted with the religious problem, the *Letter* constantly interweaves the perspectives of the believer and of the philosopher, and if this is not the result of confusion in the mind of the author, the reader has to pay close attention if he is to avoid confusion. His best guide will be the linear development of *L'Action,* which expounds for philosophers a linked succession of philosophical analyses.

## STAGES IN THE GENESIS OF THE IDEA
## OF THE SUPERNATURAL

It is not rash to suppose that, in a philosophical work that matured over a long period of time and was composed with care, the division into sections was not accidental but represents advances in the thought. This legitimate presumption, too often overlooked, will lead the reader of *L'Action* to the following observation: The genesis of the idea of the supernatural takes place in three steps, which, respectively, correspond to the third, fourth, and fifth parts of the book. What is successively established is the insufficiency of the natural order, the absolute necessity of remaining open to the divine action, whatever it may be, and finally the necessity of taking seriously the idea of the supernatural order defined by Christianity.

Once one pays close attention to this gradual advance and to the distinctive character of each step, most of the objections occasioned by Blondel's thesis disappear. Actually, few of the commentators have observed this, or, if they have noticed it, they have not been sufficiently careful in drawing the logical conclusion. This provides one more reason for analyzing the progression with some care.

*First Step.*    The first part of *L'Action*, it may be recalled, established through a critique of dilettantism that the problem of destiny cannot be avoided. The second part showed through a critique of pessimism that one cannot stop with a negative solution, that the will for nothingness implies a contradiction. There is something. "On the basis of this datum, once consented to, there will rise up, through a secret initiative that will be more and more apparent, the entire sensible, scientific, moral, and social order. . . . And by following the *élan* of the will to the term of its exigencies, we shall learn whether the action of man can be defined by and limited to the natural realm."[64] Such is the object of the third part of the work entitled: "The Phenomenon of Action."

Here, as in the preceding parts, the author tries successively to define human action within the limits that various philosophical doctrines presume to impose on it. And, with each attempt, he shows that these limits are inevitably transcended even by those who try or pretend to try to stop there. "Man can limit his destiny neither to the pleasures of the senses, nor to the conquests of the positive sciences, nor to the development of individual life, nor to the expansion of the family or society, nor to the conceptions of metaphysics or independent moral theory, nor to the superstitions that he invents to complete and consecrate his life."[65] It thus appears, because of the constant lack of adequation between the *volonté voulue* and the *volonté voulante*, that man cannot limit himself to the natural order.

It is of primary importance to understand well what Blondel understands here by the natural order. In the language of modern theologians, this expression most often refers to the order of creation, including the fundamental relation of the creature to the Creator as well as the knowledge of this relation by the natural light of the mind. In the Trilogy Blondel conforms to this usage. But, in *L'Action* of 1893 and the other writings of this period, he adheres to the usage sanctioned in modern philosophy through the development of the physical and natural sciences and which was consecrated by the appearance of positivism. We are informed of this from the very start of the third part:

> The ambition of the modern mind is to bring within the ambit of the field of knowledge and human powers everything that at first seems least accessible . . . , to found individual or social life on Science alone. . . . In its desire for universal conquest, it wants the phenomenon to be, and to be just as it knows it and uses it; it holds that to ascertain the facts and their relationships is to explain them completely; it regards as already half proved any hypothesis that permits it to avoid the intervention of the First Cause. Is not the fear of metaphysics the beginning of wisdom?[66]

Such is the stance that Blondel calls "the declared will to limit and contain man within the natural order of facts."[67] In addressing himself to the philosophers who are his contemporaries, he gives the same meaning they do to the expression he uses as they do: The term "natural order," far from including the fundamental relation of the world and man to the First Cause, systematically abstracts from it; it simply refers to the field of human activity.

We can therefore presume that when the author of *L'Action* comes to the conclusion that man cannot limit himself to the natural order, all he is saying is that man cannot be content by merely exercising the dominion of his knowledge and power over the world. We may also presume, although this will have to be verified later on, that to affirm the necessity of the supernatural is to say, first of all, not that the order of creation calls for an order of grace, but that "the natural order" in the last analysis should be considered to be a created order, that man cannot dispense with God, and that he ought to recognize this dependence by a religious attitude.

But let us leave aside this preview and return to the advance that the insufficiency of the natural order gradually reveals. Space will not allow us to follow it from beginning to end; so we shall concentrate on the final stages.

Human life, says Blondel, inevitably gives rise to a utilitarian morality.[68] Since this leads beyond itself, we meet with the necessary generation of a metaphysics that is at least implicit:[69] "The notion of an ideal order that is founded relatively on universal reality, seems to ground it absolutely even while going beyond it."[70] Metaphysics, in its turn, becomes pro-moving, that is, it requires something that is beyond it, an action that is specifically moral, one that implies the absolute of duty.[71] The analysis of the conditions for moral activity thus leads to this conclusion: "The term from which reflective action seems to have an imperious need to be suspended is an absolute, something independent and definitive which is outside the chain of phenomena, a real outside the real, something divine."[72]

In the attempt to achieve his action and be perfected, man tries to absorb the divine, to manufacture a god after his own image, and to appropriate by his own power the wherewithal to suffice. This is the phenomenon of superstition.[73] It extends beyond the cult of idols. Blondel discerns it in many practices of civilized man, in diverse forms of mysticism. Kantian moralism does not appear to him to be exempt from it, and the metaphysician who imagines that by natural religion he is going to take hold of the transcendent Being also appears in his own way to be an idolater.[74] For it is always superstition to place the infinite and the absolute in an object available to man, be it only in the domain of thought.

Such an attitude, says Blondel, involves a contradiction. For it consists in turning back to this or that phenomenon in order to make of it something more than it is. The unfolding of the dialectic of action has showed that none of them is sufficient to match the amplitude of the will; yet one pretends there is no need to seek elsewhere an object for one's infinite attachment.

> After all these explorations what emerges is this conclusion, more imperative than ever: It is impossible not to recognize the insufficiency of any natural order and not to experience a further need; it is impossible to find within oneself the means of assuaging this religious need. *It is necessary;* and *it is impracticable.* There, bluntly, are the conclusions of the determinism of human action.[75]

Necessary, yet impossible for man. Farther along Blondel will say that this is the notion of the supernatural. But it is important to remark that he does not—and cannot—say it here. Not having as yet witnessed the appearance of the thought of God,[76] he cannot use the term that qualifies the divine action. He restricts himself therefore to announcing in a terminology that is as indeterminate as possible the apparently negative result of his inquiry: The necessary condition for the achievement of human action is *inaccessible* to human action.

**Second Step.** The dialectic thus begun will, by a further unfolding, lead us to the idea of "the unique necessary," and through it to "the supreme option which is the great and unique concern of man."[77] This "necessary," which is inaccessible, will then receive the name supernatural. But, as will be seen, this term will be at first understood in a very general sense and not as specifically Christian. This second step of the demonstration occupies the third part of the work and is entitled, "The Necessary Being of Action."

The fact that man claims to find his sufficiency in the natural order and does not succeed constitutes a crisis for him. This crisis not only appears at the heart of his various projects; it is immanent to his very condition. The fact is that man wills, but he has not willed to will. In what he wills he recognizes everywhere an obstacle and suffering. In what he does do, incurable weaknesses and faults slip in, for whose consequences he cannot make reparation. Finally, death comes to put the final seal on all these failures. Nevertheless, this apparent miscarriage of willed action manifests the indestructibility of voluntary action; for I would not be conscious of this miscarriage, were there not in me a will superior to the contradictions of life. Such is my condition: I cannot escape the necessity of willing myself, and it is impossible for me to attain directly what is my true self. I can neither stop, nor go back, nor advance alone. Is there any exit from this crisis, this internal conflict?[78]

Blondel goes on to say:

It is this conflict which explains the inescapable presence in my consciousness of a new affirmation; it is the reality of this necessary presence that makes consciousness of this conflict possible within us. There is a "unique necessary." All the movement of the determinism leads us to this term; for it is from it that this very determinism takes its origin and its whole meaning is to lead us back to it.[79]

Arising necessarily from the dynamism of the interior life, the idea of God necessarily produces there an effect. By its presence, which is silently at work in souls, "voluntary life forcibly takes on a transcendent character. The conflict, then, is resolved in an alternative which . . . requires a supreme option and alone permits the will to will itself freely just as it wishes to be forever."[80]

Yes or no, is [man] going to will to live, even to the point of dying of it, if one may speak this way, by consenting to be supplanted by God? Or will he pretend to suffice without him, profiting by his necessary presence without making it voluntary, borrowing from him the strength to get along without him and willing infinitely without willing the infinite? . . . Not that this tragic opposition is revealed to all with this precision and rigor. But if the thought that there is something to be done with life" is offered to all, this is enough to indicate that even the most crude are also called to resolve the question of the great affair, the unique necessary.[81]

Blondel then examines the alternative with a view to making explicit the inevitable consequences of each of the two possible options. Voluntary action, we have seen, is not set in equation in consciousness, unless one recognizes in it the presence and assistance of the *Unique Necessary*. A first thesis results immediately:

To suppose that one finds in one's self the truth necessary for one's conscience, energy for its action, and success for its destiny, is not only to deprive oneself of a free and gratuitous gift, which, even though rejected and disdained, will not thereby compromise the happiness of an average life; it is to give the lie to one's own aspiration and, under pretext of loving only oneself, to hate and destroy oneself.[82]

To destroy oneself, without escaping from oneself, and for all eternity: This is the death of action.

So man cannot live save by opening himself to an action other than his own. He must "allow the First Cause to resume the first place"[83] in his action. How is one to go about this?

Since act cannot be brought to its full achievement unless God gives himself to us, how can we in some way substitute his action for ours? How is it possible, without even knowing that he has spoken or perhaps without even knowing him distinctly, to participate in his secret mediation? How . . . prepare oneself for a clearer revelation of human destiny, if indeed there is such a revelation?[84]

To this question, which is unique in its various forms, Blondel replies in three points which define the dispositions of a will that is entirely good and consistent. Let man do all that he thinks is good in a spirit of submission and detachment because he discerns in this the order of a will to which he ought to subordinate himself. Let him accept suffering, sacrifice, mortification, with love. And finally, "after having done everything as though expecting nothing from God, one must still await all from God as though one had done nothing by oneself."[85]

This third point is of special importance here, since it is through it that the author succeeds in naming the supernatural. "It seemed that the supreme effort of the will was to sacrifice all that it has and all that it is, but now it appears that even this effort is insufficient as long as one attributes merit for it to oneself or regards it as efficacious."[86] What man bears within him "is nothing without consciousness of natural powerlessness, of the very impossibility of man to attain his necessary end by his own power."[87]

> Absolutely impossible and absolutely necessary for man, that is the proper notion of the supernatural: The action of man carries beyond man, and every effort of reason is to see that he cannot, that he should not come to a halt. Cordial expectancy for the unknown messiah, baptism of desire that human science cannot provoke because even this need is a gift. . . .[88]

This is one of the texts that have most embarrassed benevolent readers. Is it not formally contrary to Christian dogma to include in the notion of the supernatural the idea that it is "absolutely necessary for man"? Must we not admit that here an excessively elliptical expression has betrayed the author's thought? One can explain by indicating that the man for whom the supernatural is necessary is not man in his state of nature, but man situated in a transnatural state. Or one can insist on a declaration often repeated by Blondel: Only faith knows the reality of the supernatural; the necessity established by philosophy remains on the ideal plane; it is only hypothetical.

It is our opinion that explanations of this kind do not suffice to legitimate the text we are considering here, if by the gift of the supernatural one must be understood to mean the gift God has made of himself to men in Jesus Christ. And it is precisely this interpretation that would be incorrect. Too much occupied with determining the sense of the words "man" and "necessary," many interpreters have failed to examine the word "supernatural."[89] It has not been sufficiently remarked that Blondel, in determining the genesis of the idea of the supernatural, proceeds by steps, that here he has reached the end of the second step, and that he has not yet formally introduced, as he will at the beginning of the third step, the idea proposed by Christianity. He is still dealing with a more general idea, stripped of all positive and particular determination.

Here the word "supernatural" simply refers to the divine action which, in every man, is at the origin of the voluntary movement that each one, at least implicitly, should recognize as such, if he wants this movement to reach its term. This, in fact, is the point at issue throughout the entire section dealing with "the alternative." Let us gather together out of those final pages several sharply defined propositions:

> Even when it is a question of our desire for good desires, we must
> situate beyond us the origin of this voluntary movement. . . . To man's
> absolute initiative, it is necessary to substitute, freely, even as it is
> necessary, the absolute initiative of God. . . . Our role is to make God
> be in us completely just as he is thereby himself, and to recover at
> the source of our consent to his sovereign action his efficacious pres-
> ence.[90]

In other words, it is necessary that in his thought and conduct the
spiritual creature recognize freely his inevitable dependence with respect
to the Creator: Man cannot enter into communion with God save by the
initiative of God and his sovereign action. This sovereign action of God
is what is "absolutely impossible and absolutely necessary for man," and
it expresses what is meant here by the word supernatural.

To speak of *absolute* necessity in such a context is not only admissible
but required, demanded by the essential relation of the creature to the
Creator, or, in the still more general terms that Blondel prefers to use here,
required by the essential relation of the human will to its principle. Suppose
Christian revelation did not exist but that man were nevertheless desirous
of entering into communion with God: He would have to recognize that
such a communion (whatever be its nature) would be possible only through
the initiative and action of God.

After having exposed the impossibility of man's attaining his necessary end by his own power, Blondel adds: "Aristotle had a sense of this
when he said: There is in man a life better than man, and it is not man who
can encompass it; something of the divine must dwell within him."[91] It has
not been sufficiently observed that this phrase immediately precedes the
passage which speaks of the absolute necessity of the supernatural. If it is
conceded that the author certainly did not attribute to Aristotle an explicit
knowledge of the Christian supernatural, it appears that he is not here
considering the supernatural in its specifically Christian form.

What he sees arising from this determinism of human action is the idea
of an indeterminate supernatural, that is, of the infinite that every man,
even the one who knows nothing of Christianity, obscurely wills but which
is not acquired as a thing: In other words, it is the idea of "the unique
necessary" that is won only by total abandonment to it, the idea of the
divine action to which one ought to remain open, no matter what may be
the form under which it is presented. At this stage the need of the supernatural is none other than the thirst for the Absolute, but the Absolute recognized, through abnegation, in its sovereign freedom.

It will perhaps be objected that the acknowledgement of human powerlessness is immediately called "baptism of desire," "cordial expectancy for the unknown messiah."[92] This language is undoubtedly borrowed from Christian theology, and it eases one into the following step. But it only signifies here an avowal of reason. No doubt, the author stipulates that human science (that is, philosophy) is powerless to elicit this avowal because the latter is itself a gift.[93] But it is nevertheless true that it shows its necessity and establishes that its effective emergence can only be a gift. Thus, in spite of the use of terms borrowed from Christian theology, we are still well within the limits of an indeterminate supernatural.

Shall we say that Blondel has provisionally given to the "supernatural" the simple meaning expressed by the term "transcendent," following a common usage of philosophers and even of theologians of former times?[94] This is quite possible, and it is a fact that in *L'Action* and the *Letter* he manages to use the two terms as synonyms.[95]

But we should not conclude that he regards them as rigorously equivalent even when he limits himself to the philosophical notion of the supernatural and does not have in view the specifically Christian notion. He will explain later that "in its rational aspect the word supernatural refers to what, in the transcendent, is essentially inaccessible to us."[96] It has therefore a more restricted meaning than the word transcendent, although it does not yet encompass the Christian notion.[97] This intermediate situation can be accounted for if it is remembered that, after all, Blondel wants to assist at the genesis of the Christian idea of the supernatural. In the course of his progressive advance, he first sees a very general idea arising, allied to the idea of transcendence. But because it is on the way to the Christian idea of which it offers a presentiment, it is already more than the common idea of transcendence without, as yet, being the positively determined idea that Christian teaching will offer.

*Third Step.* The unequivocal introduction of the Christian notion characterizes the third step of the demonstration. It is introduced at the start of the fifth part of *L'Action* which is entitled "The Achievement of Action." It is evident from the first pages that it is now a question of the specifically Christian idea and no longer the indeterminate idea available to every man. Speaking here of the living witnesses of the faith,[98] Blondel declares that it is not "scientific to study the letter and spirit of every cult but one,"[99] and he states that he will consider dogmas, viewed as hypotheses.[100] The supernatural order, whose necessity he wants to demonstrate from this point on, is explicitly the one "that, from without, dogmas propose to us."[101] Note well the words "from without." It is not from within himself that the philosopher here brings forth the idea of the supernatural order; he takes up, in order to examine it, the idea proposed by historic Christianity.[102]

No doubt, in order to define the conditions for a free opening to a divine initiative that was as yet indeterminate, Blondel allowed himself to be guided by the teachings of Christian spirituality. He admits this himself,[103] and we shall have occasion later on to emphasize the point. But in the earlier section the guidance remained exterior; it was not introduced into the movement of the analysis under the form of a hypothesis to be examined.

To those who would choose to ignore the Christian idea of the supernatural or push it aside without examination, Blondel replies that this is contrary to the philosophical spirit. As a matter of fact, the progressive advance of reflection has resulted so far "in leading us to a consciousness of an incurable disproportion between the *élan* of the will and the term of human action."[104] We have seen how man cannot achieve his fullness "except by being open to an action other than his own."[105] It would be unreasonable, then, to turn away from an examination of the Christian notion of the revealed supernatural. Conscious of its own powerlessness and exigencies, philosophy should ask whether this notion is not in conformity with the primordial aim of the human will.[106]

It is not a question of reconstructing rationally the supernatural order: This would contradict the very idea one wants to examine. According to Christian doctrine itself, it is not legitimate "to claim to discover by reason alone what must be revealed in order to be known."[107] By wanting to determine the content of Revelation, the philosopher would destroy its character as divine revelation. "In its principle, object, and end, revelation, if it is to be what it must be if it is to be at all, must escape reason, and no effort of man purely man can penetrate its essence."[108] In its essence the revealed supernatural is the mystery of the inner life of the trinitarian God, communicated to man through grace and received in faith and charity.[109] It is, then, "a truth impenetrable to every philosophical view, a good superior to every aspiration of the will."[110]

But if it is forbidden to want to discover this mystery other than through revelation, it is legitimate, says Blondel, to push philosophical research

> to the point where we feel that we ought to desire interiorly something analogous to that which, from without, dogmas propose to us. It is legitimate to regard dogmas not as primarily revealed, but as revealing. This means confronting them with the deep exigencies of the will and discovering there, if it is to be found, the image of our real needs

and the expected response. It is legitimate to accept them, as hypotheses, as geometricians do when they suppose the problem resolved and verify the fictitious solution by means of analysis.[111]

This text best defines the advance Blondel makes in this third step of the demonstrations. It consists in putting into parentheses the existence and reality of the supernatural proclaimed and defined by Christian preaching, retaining only the idea and using it as an eventual revealer of the exigencies of the will, or as a screen which enables us to decipher our needs. If the attempt succeeds, if it appears that the acceptance of the supernatural is the indispensable condition for the achievement of human action, then the idea that was the focus of attention at the start as a hypothesis will appear from now on as a *necessary* hypothesis.[112] By itself this is not sufficient to establish the reality of the supernatural in question, because to affirm that it is does not come from man alone, nor does it pertain to philosophy.[113] There will not even be any need to establish its intrinsic possibility,[114] since its essence as well as its existence escapes human reason left to itself. But one will have made it possible to see how "something analogous to what dogmas propose" (observe the prudence of the expression) seems necessary to the human will if its action is to be set in equation in consciousness. Or, what comes down to the same thing, one will have established the practical obligation of welcoming the supernatural proclaimed by the Gospel, should it be effectively manifested to us as a supernatural reality.

It is by such a method and within these limits that Blondel wants to show that the Christian notion of the supernatural is "necessarily engendered."[115] But since this expression is open to equivocation, it is helpful, once again, to clarify its meaning by means of a comparison based on an analogous movement.

In an earlier chapter of *L'Action*, which describes the origin of organic feeling and the consciousness of muscular effort, the author explains, among other things, "how the original notion of the agent's own body is generated."[116] It is a question of ascertaining where the body appears in consciousness and where passivity enters into action, the point where the sense of the organism arises. Without having to leave itself, says Blondel, the acting subject finds in his depths a passivity which is not impenetrable to action but not immediately available. There is something within me which is mine without being I, and which appears to me at first under the guise of material resistance or of a term of exterior unfolding. This perception of the organism implies, on the one hand, consciousness of a subjective initiative, a consciousness which, were it lacking, would make it impossible ever to attribute the result of operation to oneself. On the other hand, it implies that the new element should appear to consciousness as something foreign, even at the very moment when it makes progress possible.[117] By means of this analysis, Blondel hopes to have showed how the notion of the agent's body is generated. Continuing his description, he indicates how the consciousness of organic effort is a complexus of very intricate data, all tributary to the initiative of conscious action. He concludes:

> The preliminary notion of effort is like a frame of reference prepared to receive all the exact lessons of effective experience. What is afferent in real perception is only perceived as such after an initiative which is still indeterminate and thanks to the *a priori* hospitality of an expected *a posteriori*. Depending on whether one has in view the form or the content of organic sensation, one must state with equal emphasis that all is the effect of the subjective initiative or that everything involved expresses the passive impression of the bodily reaction.[118]

This genesis of the notion of the body and of organic effort would seem to throw light on the genesis of the notion of the supernatural. Blondel no more accords to reflection the power of generating the essence and existence of the human body than he accords to philosophy the power to generate the essence and historical existence of the Christian supernatural. All he does is to explain how their notions are generated in consciousness. In both cases this genesis implies two correlative elements: one *a priori* and the other *a posteriori*, an as yet indeterminate subjective initiative and a deliverance which appears foreign to consciousness. The first determines the form of the notion; the second, its content. The difference between the two geneses lies in the fact that in the genesis of the notion of the body or of organic effort, ths new deliverance, being mine (although it is not I), arises within me; whereas in the genesis of the Christian notion of the supernatural, the new factor does not come from myself, but is transmitted by a tradition which proposes it to me as revelation and as a communication from God. But within this difference there is a similarity: "What is afferent in real perception is only perceived as such after an initiative which is still indeterminate." Similarly, what Christian tradition presents to me as divine revelation will appear as such to me only if I see in it the expected response to an as yet indeterminate subjective initiative. That is why one can say: "it is from an internal initiative that this notion [of revelation] springs forth."[119]

To show how the notion of the supernatural is necessarily generated is to show that the supernatural order defined by Christian dogmas corresponds to the indeterminate expectancy of the human will and, by this very fact, succeeds in determining it. In establishing this correspondence in the ideal order, philosophy itself proclaims the inaccessibility and absolute independence of the Christian supernatural, since it appears necessary in the eyes of philosophy, yet is inaccessible to human action.

Blondel allows two chapters to demonstrate this. He begins by outlining the formal characteristics that divine revelation ought to have, if indeed there is such a thing.[120] He next determines, and this is a matter of paramount importance, what conditions are required if revealed truth and the divine life are to be received as they should be: What are needed are the first step of faith and religious practice.[121] To carry out this study, there is no need, the author notes, to admit the truth of dogma and the reality of the divine gift; it is sufficient to set forth this gift in the guise of a hypothesis in order that we may study the intrinsic relations and appropriateness of such a hypothesis.[122] "Once again the reality of this gift remains, it is true, beyond the grasp of man and philosophy; but it is reason's essential work to see its necessity and determine the natural coherence that governs the chain of supernatural truths themselves."[123]

When Blondel suggests that the idea of divine revelation implies the idea of a mediator, of an intercessor, and of a savior,[124] he is only delineating, within the scope of a hypothesis, a series of formal conditions. Thus, the Christian notion of the supernatural retains a purely categorical sense; it does not point to an effective reality. As distinguished from the manner of the theologian who conceives this notion in terms of the person of Christ and of salvation history, the philosopher puts aside all questions of fact or person in order to define what is meant by the notion. Only at the end, toward the close of the last chapter of *L'Action*, does he bring to the fore the need for the concrete reality of the Incarnate Word, and we shall see later on how circumspect he is.[125]

*Relation among the Three Steps.* Let us now go back and cast a glance over the three steps that have lined the route so far in order to see them as a whole. To begin with, Blondel has established the insufficiency of the natural order; he has showed that the *indispensable* condition for the achievement of human action is *inaccessible* to this action. This dialectic of the inaccessible indispensable, or of the impossible necessary, governs and provides the cadence for the next step. It is always a question of demonstrating that the exigency of the will goes beyond its power. From this arises the idea of the necessity of the supernatural. It is revealed in two steps: In the first the necessity is absolute, but the supernatural is indeterminate; in the second, the necessity is hypothetical, but the hypothesis includes the Christian supernatural order. What is evident in the first step is the absolute necessity of opening oneself to the action of God, whatever it may turn out to be. What appears in the second is the necessity of welcoming the positive revelation of God, if it is manifested to the subject through the Christian Gospel. The first is an invitation to a kind of faith of reason which involves generosity of the heart; the second is an invitation to theological faith.

We must not suppose, however, that Blondel superimposes two stages of the supernatural. The second notion is a further determination of the first. And it is a necessary determination in the sense that some such determination is required, but not in the sense that it is virtually included in the first notion. The passage from the indeterminate supernatural to the Christian supernatural is not analytic but synthetic. There is progress from the same to the other by the other of the same.[126] Again, we must indicate here that "the other of the same" is the determination of an essential historicity by a contingent history. We have already said that, if one abstracts from Christian revelation, man has no other choice but to open freely to the initiative of God as principle of his life, if he is to attain his necessary end. The supernatural order which history bears witness to answers in the exterior realm to this essential historicity, so that human freedom, without being able to produce it, finds itself obliged to welcome it when it is manifested. Clearly, the link which binds the Christian supernatural to the indeterminate supernatural is not a natural necessity, but, to use Blondel's term, a "practical necessity,"[127] which is unveiled to freedom, but to a freedom inserted into history.

Of the three steps that the philosopher distinguishes in the genesis of the idea of the supernatural, the most important is not the third, but the second. It is important to insist on this point, which controversy has often misunderstood or caused to be misunderstood.

For a philosopher to expose the necessity of dogmas and religious practice was enough to produce consternation among his rationalist colleagues. To show that the supernatural order, as defined by Christianity, is indispensable for the achievement of human action, was bound to disturb theologians. Inevitably, Blondel's readers concentrated their attention on this part of the work;[128] and this made it appear the more important, so that it gave rise to an error in perspective. While this part is, assuredly, the most novel section in some respects, it represents what is very nearly the term of the dialectic of *L'Action*. But it is not central, nor does it constitute the decisive point in the demonstration of the necessity of the supernatural.

The decisive step is the one in which the idea of God which has arisen out of the interior conflict of the will sets conscience before an alternative and imposes on it the necessity of opting for or against opening up to the divine action, for or against welcoming an as yet indeterminate supernatural.[129] In case anyone has failed to note this in the course of his development, Blondel repeats it toward the end of the conclusion.

> The unique affair is lodged entirely in this necessary conflict which is born at the heart of the human will and which imposes on it the necessity of opting practically between the terms of an inevitable alternative, of an alternative such that man either seeks to remain his own master and remain entirely within himself or delivers himself over to the divine order more or less obscurely revealed to his consciousness.[130]

This is clear enough, and it is important to remember it whenever Blondel mentions the necessity of the supernatural without calling to mind the distinction between the steps, a thing that happens often enough in the last chapter and conclusion of *L'Action* or in the *Letter*. Unless the immediate context provides some indication to the contrary, one should presume that it is a question of the supernatural in the indeterminate sense as discerned first of all by philosophers, not of the supernatural as historically determined by Christianity and specifically defined by Christian theology.

This simple observation should suffice to dispel certain difficulties. Take, for example, this formula that shocked or embarrassed so many readers: "It is impossible for the supernatural order to be without the natural order to which it is necessary, and impossible that it not be since the entire natural order guarantees it by demanding it."[131] It has been customary to understand here by "supernatural order" the order of grace that appeared in Jesus Christ insofar as it is distinguished from the order of creation. So understood, the Blondelian formula is evidently hard to accept. The least one can say is that it constitutes an "equivocal abridgement."[132] But now let us understand by "natural order" the world as the field of human activity. We have seen that this is the meaning of the word in *L'Action* of 1893. Then, let us understand by "supernatural order" the relation of man and the world to "the unique necessary" which absolutely transcends the world and human activity. Then the questionable formula simply means that the world cannot get along without God and that man cannot realize his own achievement without opening to the action of the One who created him. In a word, it proclaims directly nothing more than is to be found in Blondel's proofs for the existence of God.

Will anyone say that this interpretation excessively tortures Blondel's text? Then please refer to the pages of *L'Action* where the classical proofs for God are explicitly taken up. One will find there expressions that are almost identical with those we are commenting on and bearing the very same sense we have just proposed. "The proof for 'the unique necessary' borrows its force and value from the entire order of phenomena. Without it, all is nothing, and nothing can be. All that we will, supposes that it is; all that we are, requires that it be."[133] "Thus, the entire order of nature is for us a compelling guarantee for what is beyond it. . . . Visible things, human sciences, the phenomena of consciousness, art, and endeavor, . . . everything in us and outside us requires 'the unique necessary.' And if, to bear it up, these shadows of being are a solid foundation, it is because he [God] is its invisible support."[134] It is easy to see that the relation here defined between the order of phenomena and "the unique necessary" is identical with the relationship established in the other passage between the natural order and the supernatural order. If this last term says more than what we are to understand by the unique necessary, it is because there has been added to it the idea of a relation of man to God that is consented to. It evokes, not the explicit object of Christian faith, but the choice of an alternative imposed on every man, "the divine order more or less obscurely revealed to consciousness."[135]

It should be noted that Blondel does not limit his vision to this indeterminate supernatural. We have already noted that, for him, it is only a stage, an approach; he always looks beyond. But he does know that he cannot tackle the Christian idea of the supernatural, as a philosopher, unless he passes through this approach on each and every occasion. For the philosopher as such, there is no other mode of access.

To throw into relief the function of this intermediate step is to justify the authentically philosophical character of Blondel's undertaking and the self-imposed caution it requires when confronted with the Christian fact. Henry Duméry might have used this as an argument in favor of his position. But he does not do so. In his demonstration of the necessity of the supernatural he distinguishes two moments: a philosophy of insufficiency and, grafted onto it, a philosophy of a possible increment which would establish the hypothetical necessity of the supernatural proclaimed by the Christian Gospel.[136] The intermediate moment, which appears to us to play a decisive role, he assigns to the first or to the third stage. He thus loses sight of its character.

In his book on *The Philosophy of Action*, written two decades ago, Duméry merges this intermediate moment with the first stage. Joined to the critique of superstitious action, mentioned in passing, it constitutes with it, and going even beyond it, this philosophy of insufficiency.[137] We are told that the pages in which Blondel outlines the dispositions of an entirely good and consistent will[138] do little more than develop "the last exigency of the theistic affirmation,"[139] "the classical thesis of religious expectancy and even of the inefficacious call to the supernatural."[140]

This philosophy of insufficiency, continues Duméry, "is insufficient in its turn"; it is "only a necessary prelude to the philosophy of religion."[141] Blondel does not halt on the plane of essential necessities but views man in situation, that is, in his historic context; he takes into account the fact that the influence of positive religions, notably Christianity, has expanded human reason. In this precise context he no longer hesitates to speak of the necessity of the supernatural. Duméry cites here the phrase we have already introduced: "Absolutely impossible and absolutely necessary for man, that is the proper notion of the supernatural."[142] After this, he declares: "Clearly, this can only be a conditional or hypothetical necessity."[143] And he sets for himself the task of showing that this is the case by an analysis of texts, taken for the most part from the last part of *L'Action.*

That the reader may grasp the evidence proposed, it would be necessary to explain to him on what basis Blondel could declare that a hypothetical necessity is absolute ("absolutely necessary"). Second, we do not see why this declaration should be taken out of the sphere of simple religious expectancy when the following sentence is retained in which the avowal of this necessity is identified with the "cordial expectancy for the unknown messiah."[144] The fact that this expectancy is itself a gift[145] need not prevent it from being an expectancy. It is our opinion that the interpreter has not determined precisely the exact aim of the pages that are found at the close of the fourth part of *L'Action.* The absolute necessity whose avowal constitutes religious expectancy is the necessity of a divine action; it is not yet a question of the supernatural order defined by Christianity. It is only at the start of the fifth part that Blondel introduces the specifically Christian notion of the supernatural.

In Duméry's critical essay on the *Letter* of 1896, one finds the same imprecision in the several pages[146] devoted to the dialectic of *L'Action,* although the form is slightly different. According to this text, the philosophy of insufficiency consists essentially in the reflection that overcomes the temptation of superstition and it shows that this reflection bears witness to, beyond every undertaking in the natural order, an increment of aspiration, a surplus of exigency.[147] What follows the critique of the superstitious act in *L'Action* seems to be no longer attached here to the philosophy of insufficiency but related already to the necessity of conceiving the hypothesis of the supernatural. This, at least, is what seems to be the burden of a page in which the linking of ideas appears to be unsatisfactory.[148] In any case, this obscurity is itself significant. The necessity of posing the religious problem and the necessity of making a place for the hypothesis of the Christian supernatural are not distinguished. There is no mention made of the fact that, according to Blondel, an alternative is imposed on every man, even on one who knows nothing about the Christian notion of the supernatural, and requires him to opt for or against openness to a divine action that is as yet indeterminate in his eyes. As we shall see in a moment, it is precisely this thesis that comes to the fore in the *Letter* of 1896.

In each of these essays Duméry asserts that in Blondel's philosophy the necessity of the supernatural is always hypothetical, even when it is said to be absolute. In one sense this is correct.[149] In fact, the author of *L'Action* declares in the course of the last chapter when he embraces in a retrospective view the series of conditions that have appeared to be necessary to constitute action little by little: "In spite of the great diversity of elements that make up the series, all, sense intuition or positive truths as well as the conditions for individual, social, or religious life, share in a single and same hypothetical necessity."[150] We have no reason to withdraw from the series the idea of the supernatural, even at the stage when it still remains indeterminate. As we shall indicate later, in a passage of the *Letter* where it is precisely a question of the indeterminate idea, Blondel expressly says that the necessity he is speaking about is a "hypothetical necessity."[151] In the preceding sentence he has even called attention to the meaning of this designation:

> Here, as in every instance where, from the point of view of method, there is question of scientific necessity, the reality, or better, the realization of what is proposed as necessary, is subordinate to another element which remains foreign to science: Only effective practice in life cuts through for each one in secret to the question of the relation between the soul and God.[152]

In the course of the next chapter it will be seen that this is in full conformity with the general doctrine of *L'Action*: "The science of practice establishes that there is no substitute for practice."[153] We can thus conclude that if the necessity of remaining open to an indeterminte divine action is absolute within the ideal series of the conditions for action, it participates, nevertheless, in the hypothetical character of the entire series as long as effective practice has not given it realization. Under this heading, it is of the same order as the necessity of the specifically Christian supernatural.

But beware. After having affirmed that, in the chain of conditions necessary for action, everything is continuous and of the same order,[154] Blondel adds: "Each intermediate link participates in the solidity of the whole and exists as a world apart. . . . In the total solidarity and universal continuity, each particular synthesis appears with a quality of absolute heterogeneity and entire originality."[155] In other words, at the heart of the very same necessary sequence of needs for practice, at the heart of this very same ideal order of hypothetical necessities, types of necessity appear, each one of which is original and heterogeneous with respect to the others. The passage from superstition to the idea of God is not of the same type as the passage from sensation to science, or from the family to the fatherland. All are necessary, but all are different.

The same is true when there is question of the supernatural. The passage to the general and indeterminate idea does not have the same character as the passage to the specifically Christian idea. In the two cases, the necessity is not identical, or at least is not unfolded in the same way. The first expresses the way the necessity is inevitably manifested to every man, at least in an implicit way. The second is such that its exact determination can appear only to one who knows Christian dogma and is willing to view it, hypothetically, as revealing the profound exigencies of the will. Surely, the two necessities are hypothetical in the sense that only effective practice can bring about the realization of what reflection proposes as necessary. But at the very heart of and within the series of ideal bonds, the second is also hypothetical for an added reason: It cannot unfold without the hypothesis of revealed dogma.

The difference between these two modes of necessity is sharply defined for the attentive reader of *L'Action*. But in the *Letter* it is hard to discern. Blondel, as we shall show, concentrates in the second work on the first mode; the second he only touches in function of the first and in a marginal way. Duméry, then, cannot be blamed for not having found the distinction in his interpretation of the *Letter*. But neither did he note it in his commentary on *L'Action*.[156] In both cases he blurs over the distinction between the two types of necessity and the two degrees of hypothesis. We shall see in a moment the mischief this introduces when he comes to interpret the *Letter*.

***Echoes of* L'Action *in the* Letter.** It is virtually impossible to understand what the *Letter* is saying about the necessity of the supernatural, if the various passages are not referred to the corresponding steps in *L'Action*. Since the author neglected doing this explicitly,[157] the interpreter must supply for this by comparing the two texts; he must perceive that *L'Action* is reflected in the *Letter*.

He will remark, then, that the center of gravity of the second work, as in the first, is the indeterminate notion of the supernatural. This appears in a key passage with which we must begin our examination.

After having explained that the method of immanence considers the supernatural "not as real under its historic form, not as simply possible as though it were an arbitrary hypothesis," but "as indispensable at the same time that it is inaccessible to man,"[158] the author of the *Letter* poses the crucial question: "Does not speaking of necessity mean throwing a rash and hasty bridge between the two orders, making even the freedom of the divine gift enter illegitimately into the determinism of human action?"[159] And to justify his negative reply, he clarifies the sense in which the word "necessary" is used here.

> What is necessary is that, under a form whose exact and concrete definition cannot be established for each individual, the thoughts and acts of each person constitute in their totality a drama whose outcome is not realized unless the decisive question arises sooner or later. Each one, simply availing himself of the light that enlightens every man coming into the world and by the use of his own powers, is called upon to declare himself regarding the problem of his salvation. For, in order to make the simplest reflective affirmation about the reality of the objects that make up our thoughts, to produce deliberately the most elementary acts that enter into the determinism of our will, we must implicitly pass through the point where the option becomes possible or where, in the absence of any other light, it becomes necessary to choose between the solicitations of the hidden God and those of an always evident egoism.[160]

Citing the first two sentences of this passage, Duméry holds that they affirm "the necessity of taking the notion of the supernatural as a hypothesis," and by this he means the Christian notion, the one Blondel finds in the catechism.[161] "What is necessary," he says, "is the summons to take a stand on religious grounds. The supernatural is necessary because it is impossible to escape it as a possible solution."[162] This interpretation does not seem to take the context into account. Far from considering here the necessity of taking the Christian notion of the supernatural as a hypothesis, Blondel includes in his view men who cannot assume it as a hypothesis because they have no explicit knowledge of it. What he has in mind is a summons which, under a form which cannot be defined for each individual, inevitably arises in every consciousness. Each man, he says, even one ignorant of Christian revelation, is led to declare himself on the problem of his salvation in the sense that the internal logic of action makes him inevitably pass through the point where the option becomes necessary as a choice between the solicitations of the hidden God and those of egoism. This is obviously a summary of the central development of the fourth part of *L'Action*, entitled, *"The Conflict*, Third Moment."[163]

But let us continue with the *Letter*. Analyzing the "drama" just indicated, Blondel says that the philosopher will show that

> the progress of our will forces us to the avowal of our insufficiency, leads us to a felt need for an increase, gives us the aptitude, not to produce or define it, but to recognize and receive it and, in a word, opens to us by a kind of prevenient grace that baptism of desire which, on the supposition that there has already been a secret touch of God, remains always accessible and necessary, quite independent of all explicit revelation and which, in revelation itself, is like the human sacrament immanent to the divine operation.[164]

We have already made acquaintance with the words "baptism of desire" in the last section of the fourth part of *L'Action*.[165] If one will take the trouble of comparing these two fragments, it will be seen that, in a more precise and explicit form, the second repeats the contents of the first. It will be easier to understand, then, what was already apparent when only the earlier text was being examined: The need for an increase that Blondel claims to discover in every man is not yet clothed here with the specific and positively determined form defined by Christian revelation. What is referred to is the necessity of opening oneself to an as yet indeterminate divine action. The avowal of our insufficiency, which constitutes the baptism of desire, is accessible, says the author, "outside all explicit revelation."[166] It is a call of the "unknown mediator."[167] Of course, this call "ceases to be efficacious," "if one is closed to the revealed Savior,"[168] and in the revelation itself it is "like the human sacrament immanent to the divine operation."[169] But in itself it is essentially an aptitude for "recognizing" and "receiving"[170] an increase which has not yet been determined.

To say that this passage in the *Letter* concerns the necessity of taking the Christian notion of the supernatural as a hypothesis, is to alter the movement of Blondel's thought.[171] This necessity can only be introduced later.

To show that every man is summoned to opt "between the solicitations of the hidden God and those of an always evident egoism," does not force the freedom of the divine gift into the determinism of human action. All it does is to designate the point of insertion of this free gift. That is why Blondel can speak of the "natural exigencies of the soul"[172] immediately after having reminded us that the supernatural order always remains beyond "the exigencies of our nature and even of every conceivable nature."[173] For by "the natural exigencies of the soul" he means "that secret exigency that forces all to recognize the elements of the problem and the means for resolving it."[174] It is unfortunate that the use of the word "exigency" creates an ambiguity that proves to be a stumbling block for many readers. We have to observe the context carefully. Here the meaning is clearly expressed: The natural exigencies of the soul are a "whetstone," a "prepared point of insertion."[175] With respect to the supernatural order that constitutes "an ineffable and unforeseen increase,"[176] they give us "the aptitude, not to produce or define it, but to recognize and receive it."[177]

However, this last formula does not mean that Blondel only intended to determine "the conditions without which it would not be capable of being assimilated by us."[178] The philosopher's intention is broader than this. It is a question of defining "the *necessity* that binds together the two heterogeneous orders without misunderstanding their independence."[179] From the philosophical point of view this necessity is to be found in the logic of action in virtue of which it becomes apparent to every man under one form or another that it is inevitably necessary to opt for or against the opening of action to God.[180]

> Without this aspect of internal necessity, which, in expressing the ultimatum we are subject to in acting, at the same time defines our true responsibility, the rigors of the sanction could not be justified. As a consequence, every philosophy, save the one we are talking about here, must be put on its guard against affirming that there is something necessary in the moral and religious life or against admitting the sanctions of present and future life without violating every notion of equity and goodness.[181]

We see here how Blondel answers the question presented him by the meeting of philosophy and Christianity. If it is true that welcoming the Christian supernatural is obligatory under pain of eternal loss, there must be, he says, a trace of this exigency in man and an echo of it in philosophy.[182] This trace and echo, as we now know, is reflected in the logic of action the moment it sets every man before the inexorable alternative: whether to opt for or against opening to the as yet indeterminate supernatural with a confused consciousness of the inevitable consequences of this option. It is this logic, this necessity interior to action, that justifies the rigors of the sanction against those who refuse the light of faith. And it is this logic that constitutes the *a priori* in virtue of which we can recognize that Christian preaching is our concern.

Thus, at the decisive point, the author of the *Letter* concentrates on the notion of the supernatural defined in the fourth part of *L'Action*: a notion as yet indeterminate but which prepares the mind to grasp the sense of the specifications offered by Christian dogma.

Moreover, the author analyzes this relationship as he had already done in the fifth part of *L'Action*. By showing that man suffers a positive failure when he closes himself to the superior life whose source is not in himself, philosophy, says Blondel, provides new light not only on the doctrine of perdition, but also on the question of Christ's "vicarious satisfaction."[183] This can be related to the passage on the notion of dogmas and it takes up a theme from the last chapter that we chall comment on later: "It seems that, in requiring for the conception of the effective realization of the integral order of things an element that is both distinct from nature and from God as its author, philosophy justifies from its own point of view what is perhaps an implicit dogma, namely, Emmanuel, the final cause of the creative plan."[184]

However, in the *Letter* Blondel lays stress on the reservations he had already carefully outlined in *L'Action*. "In determining the genesis of the idea of revelation or in indicating the necessity of dogmas or of revealed precepts, we do nothing more than trace out the shape of empty frames of reference within which nothing that is strictly ours can establish reality or fill out the abstract design."[185] Why this multiplication of precautions?

We know that it was the fifth part of *L'Action* that led rationalist philosophers and Christian apologists to misunderstand (each in his own way) the strictly philosophical intention of the work. Here Blondel wants to stress this intention and show that he distinguishes most clearly the realms of reason and faith. With this in mind he is led, on the one hand, to emphasize the general notion of the supernatural which every man can sense, even when he knows nothing of Christianity and, on the other hand, to recognize that the attempt to set forth the exigencies of the will by means of Christian dogmas entails some risk of confusion for the reader.

Thus, he acknowledges that "This spectacle [of dogmas and precepts] is undoubtedly most instructive, if we are to determine with precision the insufficiency of our nature and if we are to trace to the end the demands of reason and the prayerful aspirations of life; but we must all the more beware of the temptation to confuse domains and fields of competence and to rediscover more than can be discovered."[186] The first part of the sentence outlines what Blondel clearly wanted to do in the fifth part of *L'Action*. The second part is a warning given to Christian apologists who failed to see how he distinguishes the two domains and who confused his intention and method with those of other thinkers.[187]

He adds this significant statement which vigorously expresses the point of impact and limits of philosophical reflection when it touches Christian dogmas and precepts: "Philosophy is applicable to Christianity to the extent that Christianity has radical empire and judgment over men, even over those who do not know it or exclude it."[188] In other words, the Christian notion of the supernatural order relates to philosophy only to the degree that it appears as the ultimate determination of the indeterminate idea of the supernatural that arises in every man, even when beyond the reach of Christian teaching. It is always through the prism of this indeterminate idea that philosophy has access to the formal sense of the Christian notion. That is why Blondel can say: "Philosophy considers the supernatural only to the extent that the notion is immanent to us."[189]

But having said this, he also knows that "beyond the already divine drama that is enacted in the consciousness of every man, there is inserted even now, for believing and living souls, a new mystery of grace which can be partially unveiled only by revelation."[190] When the author of the *Letter* speaks of the drama that takes place in every man, he has in mind the supernatural in a very general sense and not, as yet, the "new mystery of grace" which only revelation can unveil. Correlatively, the mystery of grace that believers live by is a novelty that lies beyond the idea of the supernatural immanent to every man.

**Gratuity of the Supernatural.** Evidently one cannot neglect these remarks if one hopes to understand how the Blondelian thesis of the necessity of the supernatural safeguards the gratuity and strictly supernatural character of the divine gift proclaimed by Christian preaching.

It might at first seem that the author of the *Letter* took little care to make his point. He seems to appeal exclusively to a different consideration that we shall analyze in the next chapter: the idea that philosophy is pure phenomenology, that it discloses the necessary relations among phenomena without making any pronouncement on real being. The method of immanence, he says, shows that "our thoughts are inevitably organized into a tightly knit system," "underlying the use of freedom itself."[191] The necessity it manifests is hypothetical: "The legitimate scope of philosophical conclusions stops at the threshold of real operation in which alone the human act and the divine act, nature and grace, can be united."[192] It is because of this reservation that philosophy can show the necessity of the supernatural without implying any real continuity between the world of reason and that of faith. "The immanent affirmation of the transcendent, even of the supernatural, in no way prejudices the transcendent reality of the immanent affirmation."[193] The passage that immediately precedes this declaration shows that the author means by "immanent affirmations" both the necessity of revealed beliefs and practices as well as the necessary and efficacious idea of God. It would seem, then, that the distinction established in *L'Action* does not interest him here, that he has no need of it to make it clear that Christian revelation and faith are a gift of God, and that all he needs to establish this is rigorously to maintain the distinction between the formal plane of reflection and the real plane of action.

Since the aim of the *Letter* was to define the nature, scope, and limits of the method of immanence, it was only natural that it should insist on this aspect. But that does not entitle us to neglect the distinction between the successive steps of *L'Action*, a distinction whose traces the alert reader can find in the *Letter*.

Let us gather together here several propositions by means of which the principal work not only seems to respect but even to set in bold relief the transcendence and gratuity of the supernatural.

1. The immanent notion of the supernatural is generated in a negative way: that is, by man's failure to realize his achievement in the natural order, namely, in the objects his activity is concerned with. Before having even been named, the supernatural appears to the philosopher "as indispensable at the very moment it is seen to be inaccessible to man."[194] The second characteristic is as essential as the first: "the supernatural will not remain conformed to the idea we conceive of it save to the extent that it continues to be, on our own admission, beyond human grasp."[195]

2. This negative idea receives further determination when confronted with Christian dogmas viewed as hypotheses. In proceeding in this fashion, there is a recognition of the fact that the content of revelation cannot be generated within consciousness, that it comes from without, that it has an historical origin.

3. Finally, in establishing that the science of action cannot supply for action, we are helped to understand that only the experience of faith can discern in the Christian message the gift of God, in its unprecedented novelty, in its ineffable gratuity.

Thanks to these various distinctions that Blondel introduces into his development in the course of *L'Action* of 1893, he can show a need for the supernatural in man without establishing by this demonstration any real continuity between the world of reason and that of faith, without making the supernatural order itself enter into the determinism of action. Once again, his philosophy does not require that God reveal himself; it unveils the *a priori* in terms of which the exigencies of revelation can be grasped and admitted.

## THEOLOGY AND THE NECESSITY OF THE SUPERNATURAL

Can Blondel justify his perspective when interrogated or criticized by theologians, especially when they throw doubt on or contest our ability to establish in philosophy the necessity of the supernatural, without at the same time naturalizing it or making its absolute gratuity disappear? In the beginning, he will do this in perfect conformity with what he expressed in *L'Action* and the *Letter*. This can be showed by a brief indication given to Dom Delatte in a letter, dated August 31, 1894.[196] It can also be seen in another document we shall examine. But a little later Blondel will explain his thought in another way, and he will progressively modify it.

   ***First Explanation.*** On July 14, 1896, at the very time the last of the six articles that make up the *Letter* had just been published in *Annales de Philosophie Chrétienne*, an Italian Barnabite, Father Semeria, wrote to Blondel,[197] submitting to him an account of the difficulty that his reading of these articles had occasioned in his mind. "If the supernatural is necessary to human nature (viewed in the light of reason as it is in itself), it ceases to be supernatural and becomes natural." Certainly, this consequence can be avoided, he explains, if with "the Thomists" one holds that human nature in its present state is corrupted, "that is, lowered beneath the level of a hypothetical pure nature." The supernatural would then appear to be indispensable as a remedy for the positive deficiencies caused by sin. But such an idea of corruption complicates in a singular manner the doctrine of original sin. "The non-Thomists judge that our present nature is *de facto* a state of pure nature, even while it is also *de jure* a fallen nature by reason of the historical antecedents of our present condition."[198] From this point of view

> it appears hard to see how a supernatural in the authentic sense of the word would be necessary, that is, indispensable for us. For supernatural means something superior, not only to our own powers, but also to the exigencies of human nature. Granted that this nature is *de facto* integral now, an element it would have *need* of would consequently become (or could become) natural.

The only thing that can be demonstrated is that the supernatural is not in opposition to nature, that, on the contrary, it favors it. If one believes in the possibility of establishing that something is lacking in human nature altered by sin, this in itself would not prove that this something is truly supernatural.

After having explained his difficulty, Father Semeria concludes:

> I would like to know how you, honorable Sir, understand this matter. For, on the one hand, I do not believe that you would accept the Thomist interpretation of human nature (a conception that to me seems to be contrary to the idea of divine justice and goodness) and, on the other hand, I do not see how, in terms of the hypothesis of the non-Thomists, one can save a true necessity and a true supernaturality. If the supernatural is a true supernatural, it seems to me that it cannot be necessary, except in a very vague and broad sense. If, in the true sense of the word, it is necessary for a nature that is not intrinsically corrupted by original sin, I do not see how it can remain truly and properly supernatural.

Blondel's reply, dated August 19, 1896, provides us with a document that is remarkable in its precision. Without reproducing it in its entirety, since it is long, it is worth citing it extensively by way of résumé and commentary. As far as the necessity of the supernatural is concerned, it confirms the interpretation already offered of *L'Action* and the *Letter.* Blondel writes:

> My reply is very simple and I summarize it in two propositions: (I) Among the different theological doctrines that define the relation between the supernatural and natural orders and among which you ask that I take a stand, I have no need to choose, because (2) when it comes to speaking of a relation of necessity between these two orders, I take my stand on completely different grounds, and the relation I refer to has a completely different meaning and a scope quite different from the one discussed by theologians.

Faced with the problem that consumed the energies of the various theological schools, Blondel remarks that he is not competent to treat them and that his own problematic is quite different. On the first point he has this to say:

> Indeed, I say that I am incompetent (and in my thinking every philosophy is equally incompetent) to determine the positive content and concrete nature of the supernatural, to consider it in the absolute and under its ontological aspect, and to speculate on the nature of the bonds by which God joins it to the natural order. In a word, I do not begin by taking this supernatural in itself or in God in order to study it in relation to ourselves or in ourselves. Only theology, based on revelation, can examine it with authority.

> Let me add that I do not even consider human nature in itself as a fixed entity or as a reality known in its depth, and that I have no

obligation, on this basis, to define the disturbance caused in it by original sin, nor to inquire into the sense in which our present nature postulates or requires a complement superior to its own power. . . .

Thus, I do not situate myself at the point of view of a supernatural which, by divine degree, is imposed on our nature, nor at the point of view of an absolutely determined human nature which would require a supernatural order. The different hypotheses that you offer me all fall into one or the other of these categories. But my whole effort has been to demonstrate that philosophy, if it is what it ought to be, has no need to pronounce for or against doctrines that remain in the exclusive ambit of theology.

What, then, is the peculiar problematic of Blondel? He tells us immediately:

> According to the exigencies and limits of the method of immanence, I restrict my study to the chain of phenomena which, in us, constitute "subjective faith" or which, in the absence of a known and defined credo, open to every man of good will, under an indeterminable form, that "baptism of desire" which remains always possible and necessary for salvation. . . . I seek only to describe the subjective dispositions and the practical attitude of a sincere mind, of a soul consistent with itself.[199] And if we already have knowledge of what I have called "objective faith," that is, revealed truth defined by the authority of the Church, philosophy has no right on this account to avail itself of this knowledge so as to introduce it into the series of autonomous affirmations. It can only ascertain that these data whose terms we cannot invent do indeed correspond to its call and needs.—Since philosophy should be applicable to every reason and to every human will, it must speak of this supernatural in a sense that is "broad" enough and "vague" enough so that no one is absolutely prevented from participating in it;—and if it should make those who have an obligation to adhere to it understand the nature of this obligation, it must rigorously define this necessity that makes our adherence indispensable for salvation;—and if it should not invoke any revealed dogma, it must leave in suspense the question of an original fall and the disorders of our present nature.

These last statements are especially favorable to our interpretation. Philosophy does not arrive at the explicit notion of the Christian supernatural except through the indeterminate idea which arises in every man. The passage from one idea to the other is not analytic: Philosophy cannot invent the terms of the Christian notion. It can only ascertain that this notion, known exteriorly, corresponds to the other with incomparable precision. If it claims to find in this correspondence a quality of necessity, this is because it is supposed to make the one who knows Christian revelation understand his obligation to adhere to it. But its function ends here.

Philosophy cannot go so far as to define the ontological relation that unites the supernatural, considered in itself, to human nature (even actual human nature) considered in itself. This relationship is only perceived by theology on the basis of revelation.

So when Blondel says that the natural order requires the supernatural order, the necessity he expounds does not tie together the two realities which are, in the eyes of the theologian, nature and grace, but only the two postures of the spirit which are, in the eyes of the philosopher, the logic of action and the exigencies proclaimed by the Gospel. That is why Blondel maintains that he has no need to take sides among the different theological doctrines that have attempted to define the relation between nature and the supernatural.

However, at the end of the letter to Father Semeria, he indicates in a few words how his way of viewing the problem is "compatible with theological teaching which considers it under a very different aspect." He points out certain correspondences between the implications of his method and the doctrine of the original fault or that of a supernatural vocation. This reply which is directed to the query of the theologian who questions him is somewhat cursory. But this is not the issue here since the reply is extrinsic to the movement of the philosopher's thought.

*Second Explanation.* We are a bit surprised to discover another attitude in a letter to the same correspondent, dated November 26, 1900. To a question asking "how by a spontaneous exigency we can require or postulate the supernatural without this supernatural ceasing to be gratuitous and, of itself, inaccessible to man," Blondel replies this time in a notably different manner. He explains that he takes his position *in concreto* before a man of flesh and bone, and that tries to make him aware of the divine call, of being the instrument of prevenient grace. "Be careful," he says to this man. "If it is God's hour, if grace places in you a supernatural motion, you cannot imprudently withdraw from this vocation; . . . for just as the natural gift of reason creates in you a positive moral duty from which you cannot escape without betraying your own will and without a failure of your interior sincerity, similarly, the gift of prevenient grace incorporated into your being, without being merged with your nature, since it brings you something that is incommunicable and non-naturalizable, establishes in you a religious duty, a debt. So, in the supposition that, *hic et nunc,* you are acted on by grace, I say that the integral development of your being requires the complement of the divine life as proposed *ab extrinseco* by Christianity as a consequence of the original touch *ab intrinseco.*"

Language like this leaves nothing to be desired from the point of view of orthodoxy; but it is the language of a preacher or spiritual director rather than of a philosopher. Did Blondel conclude that his correspondent could understand nothing less than this ? It could be, but his later publications indicate, nonetheless, that the change of perspective from one letter to the next was not purely *ad hominem.*

What happened between August, 1896, and 1900? It should be recalled that the savage attack of Père Schwalm appeared in September, 1896, that two months later the Abbé Gayraud took up the cudgel, and that both were to be supported by many others. Blondel was nonplussed by what, to him, could only appear to be a radical lack of understanding. Accused of practicing the Kantian method pushed to its final phenomenalist consequences, he was less and less daring and soon would no longer dare at all in his attempt to justify the phenomenological nature of his philosophy. Accused, from another quarter, of naturalism, he believed that he was obliged to appeal to theology in his own defense.

In 1897 Laberthonnière came to his defense with an article entitled "Le Problème religieux," published in *Annales de Philosophie Chrétienne.*[200] According to Laberthonnière, Blondel, as one doing philosophy, set out from the natural order in order to inspect from the bottom up the relations between this order and the supernatural. But one might take the opposite tack and, supposing the religious problem solved and Christianity admitted, seek from this point of view the conditions for a solution that would be within the competence of philosophy. And one might be surprised to see how, looking at things from the top down, "the conclusions M. Blondel reached by his free investigation are spontaneously rediscovered by means of an analytic regression."[201]

It was in this way that Laberthonnière came to grips with the thesis on the necessity of the supernatural.

> Since a supernatural order does exist and since every man *de facto*—we do not say *de jure*—is called to live supernaturally, then it follows that God acts by his grace on the heart of every man and penetrates it with his charity; that action itself which fundamentally constitutes our life is, in fact, supernaturally informed by God. . . . That is how exigencies for the supernatural can be found in nature and, indeed, are found. These exigencies do not belong to nature, *qua* nature, but they appear to nature insofar as it is already penetrated and invaded by grace. . . . Consequently, in fashioning the science of action, since this action is at the same time ours and God's, we ought to be able to find in it the supernatural element that enters into its constitution.[202]

Although Blondel quickly became aware of elements that distinguished his thought from Laberthonnière's, he adopted[203] and for a long time maintained this system of defense (and the theologians who were his friends or who wanted to benefit by his work often assumed the same point of view). One reads, for example, in his well known study on *History and Dogma*, published in 1904, "that the state of nature remains a pure abstraction which does not exist and never has existed, and that, in studying our human nature as man as it actually is, it is not this state of nature that we can know in knowing ourselves, any more than we can, by living, withdraw ourselves from that radical and universal penetration of something which will always prevent man from finding his equilibrium in the human order."[204] Blondel asks in a footnote that he not be accused here of "a confusion between *the supernatural life,* as constituted in us by baptism and habitual grace, and *the supernatural state* in which man is situated before realizing and in order to realize this life of grace."[205] In order to emphasize this distinction better, he would soon create a new term, "the transnatural."

We find this term in the articles of 1909–1910 on *La Semaine Sociale de Bordeaux.* Here is how he takes up the same theme again: "It is because of an undeniable error that one can reason as though the natural state of the unbeliever, of the one who is ignorant, of the apostate, were the state of 'pure nature,' that state which undoubtedly could have been, but is not and has never been, and whose real conditions we cannot even define with precision." All men have in fact a supernatural vocation. "That state which is neither the state of nature nor of grace and which we may abbreviate by calling it a *transnatural* state, in order to indicate the disequilibrium of a destiny afflicted by a fall and touched by an inner summons," could only be erroneously thought of as one which "translates nothing on the plane of consciousness" of the disequilibrium.[206]

The aim of these remarks is to justify the Blondelian enterprise in the eyes of theologians. The author was asked to situate his problematic in terms of the classic doctrine of the various states of humanity. His task was to make clear that, without denying the possibility of a state of pure nature, he had in view real man, actually called to the supernatural life in spite of his failure.

But it was one thing to situate the problematic of the philosopher with respect to a theological doctrine and quite another to allow it to be transformed in the process, even to the point of confusing perspectives. It can be asked whether Blondel did not slip somewhat in this direction. In the *Letter,* it will be recalled, his problem was the following: If it is true, as

Christian preaching claims, that welcoming the supernatural is necessary for all men, there must be some trace of this necessity in the logic of human action. During the period we are now discussing, the problem often seems to become the following: Since, according the theology, real man, although a sinner, retains his supernatural vocation, he ought to have some consciousness of this first grace that perpetually solicits him. The difference is clear: Instead of seeking a bond between two postures of the spirit, Blondel seems to be looking for a reflection of grace in psychological consciousness. He states:

> Surely, the grace remains secret, veiled, ineffable; it is not known and recognized from within under its true name, by definition, in its specific being. But it determines psychological facts that are recognizable as such, verifiable and employable facts, facts that entail a responsibility and whose science can be established, whose concatenation determined, and use guided. In default of this conscious element, though still anonymous, the correspondence of the intelligent and free will to the divine call would lose all reasonable and moral character.[207]

We see here that the transformation of the first problematic reenforces that "psychologism" that has sometimes laid the language of *L'Action* open to reproach. There, we have pointed out, the fault was corrected by explicit indications and by the general movement of the thought. But the tendency is no longer corrected in as precise a way in the text we have just cited or in others written around the same period.

What happened was that Blondel was at this time borrowing some of his language from the work of Cardinal Dechamps whose existence he had learned about in 1904 and who provided him with an authority and with arguments for guaranteeing the orthodoxy of his philosophical apologetics. If one reads the articles he devoted to this work and which were published in 1905–1906 under the signature of Abbé Mallet, it will be seen that his psychologistic vocabulary derives from Cardinal Dechamps' disquisitions on the "interior fact."[208] Blondel himself remarks that Dechamps protests that "the supernatural is first present to us as a fact of consciousness, that it is discernible not in itself, *ut est*, but in its internal effects, *ut agit*, not so as to be defined but to be welcomed, even though this might be under a pseudonym."[209]

Blondel, to be sure, does observe that this psychological fact consists primarily, according to Dechamps, in the conscious realization of the insufficiency of philosophy to resolve the essential problems of thought and human life.[210] On the other hand, he is wary of a "certain philosophical unsteadiness" in the work he is commenting on.[211] This warrants our thinking that he was not (or, at least, not always) deceived by the psychologistic language. But many readers, less alert, have been deceived by it.

Whatever the case may be on this point, our philosopher found in Dechamps, as he had already found in Laberthonnière, the idea that in the present state of humanity each man bears within himself "the anonymous presence of an immanent supernatural,"[212] and that this latter is translated on the level of consciousness in the form of an insufficiency, of a need. Now, among theologians, the immanent supernatural that informs every human life was understood in a directly theological sense, according to the way in which Christian tradition affirms the supernatural vocation of every man and prevenient grace. In adopting this perspective, Blondel was abandoning the philosophical notion of an indeterminate supernatural which had served as an intermediary step in the movement of *L'Action*.

It is important to note this carefully. Laberthonnière, for whom Christianity was *the* philosophy, could attach no value to this intermediate notion. Dechamps did not have to bring it in. For, after having showed that "the interior fact is the need that reason incontestably experiences for a divine teaching authority in religion," it was sufficient for him to show that the exterior fact that corresponds to it is this very authority, namely, the Catholic Church whose marks are "invincibly demonstrative of their origin."[214] In borrowing this way of handling the correspondence between an internal fact, as bearing witness to an immanent supernatural, and an external fact, as revealing the supernatural, Blondel in his turn no longer had any need for an intermediate step. And he no longer mentions it.[214] The supreme thesis of philosophy, he writes, is "the knowledge of a real void, so to speak, of a void that by ourselves we can neither suppress, nor fill, nor forget."[215] "It is this void that is, in us, the place reserved for the supernatural because it has already been prepared and hollowed out by grace."[216]

Later on Blondel will remark that this way of presenting matters was less appropriate for a philosopher than for a theologian-philosopher expounding his method for apologetics. When revising, in 1932, the series of articles devoted to the work of Cardinal Dechamps, he will call attention to this defect in several notes. "Much remains to be done," he wrote, "to make precise and justify the philosophical theses that serve as *praeambula* for theological perspectives."[217] There is room for tying down "what philosophy ought to present as necessary in every hypothesis and what it can recognize and organize in the concrete order and on the basis of the experience that may be ours."[218] The author announces that he will do just this in his Trilogy.[219] And in fact we find in the second edition of *L'Action* a rehandling of the philosophical idea of the supernatural, but in another context and under a form other than that of the first edition.

*A New Element.* In *Le problème de la philosophie catholique*, which, besides the articles on Dechamps, reproduces extracts from the *Letter*, Blondel points out that "what no doubt gave rise to so much misunderstanding and confusion was the mixture, in theory and in controversy, of different states that are actually united in reality, but which must be distinguished in the scientific knowledge that we should have of them."[220] Thus, there is a state of nature, a state of original justice, a fallen state, a transnatural state, and a supernatural life.[221] As a matter of fact, beginning at least with 1905, Blondel distinguished them very well in principle. But he maintained that as a philosopher he only had in mind the transnatural state; and he considered the real void that philosophy manifests in man as the mark of the supernatural vocation which pertains to a fallen and redeemed humanity.

As indicated in the preceding section, from now on he wants also and above all to keep in view the state of nature that could have been realized, even though it never existed in the historic and concrete order.

> Although observable data are lacking that could offer support for a scientific knowledge (and such a knowledge always requires in the case of living realities an experimental fulcrum), it is, however, possible, legitimate, and useful to examine what, in any state, is included in or required by a spiritual being capable of affirming by reason that God exists, that he is first cause, last end, unique source of an infinitely desirable beatitude and perfection.[222]

This study will reveal in the spirit a *desiderium naturale videndi et habendi Deum*, an inefficacious desire, but one open to the idea of an order that transcends every conceivable nature and which thus marks out the place for the supernatural in philosophy itself.[223] Blondel explicitly says that he is taking up the thesis expounded in 1924 by Father de Broglie in his article, "On the Place of the Supernatural in the Philosophy of St. Thomas." This doctrine seemed to confirm and justify his consistent aim. "It serves," he says, "as a kind of geometrical locus for the meeting of rational speculation, revealed teaching, and historical and moral facts."[224] It is this doctrine that will enable him to distinguish and bind together the universal and necessary condition of the spirit—and the states realized in the historic and concrete order. It will be the guide for all that will be said about the supernatural in the Trilogy. It will provide an introduction to the consideration of the historic states of humanity (including the transnatural state) that will be taken up in a still later work, *La philosophie et l'esprit chrétien.*

We have no intention of studying this whole collection of works. Let us consider only the second volume of the second edition of *L'Action,* a work notably different from the early work of 1893 bearing the same title, and let us ask what form the genesis of the idea of the supernatural takes there.

The first thing to note is that the third step has disappeared, having been consigned to the work that was to follow. It consisted, it will be recalled, in examining from a philosophical point of view, as hypotheses, the dogmas and practices of Christianity in order to discover their intrinsic relations and their correspondence to the exigencies of the will. At the end of the second edition of *L'Action* the author announces that this examination will be the object of *La philosophie et l'esprit chrétien.* It will be in this work that one can inquire into whether the Gospel message offers "a unity that is intrinsically coherent and compatible with a rational organism."[225] The same thing is indicated in the course of this latter work.[226] This is repeated in the last publication prepared by Blondel, *Exigences philosophiques du Christianisme.* Explaining there why he set the study on philosophy and the Christian spirit apart from the Trilogy, he defines the subject matter in the very same terms used in 1893 for defining the same subject as it appeared in the fifth part of *L'Action.*[227] Thus he clearly indicates where we ought to look for the equivalent of what was then the third step in the genesis of the idea of the supernatural.

Can we also find the equivalent of the first two stages? Since the new edition of *L'Action* is divided in a way that is different from the earlier work and since the titles of the parts (and even of the chapters) are different, a glance at the table of contents is not enough to enable us to get our bearings. But upon reading the work it becomes quickly apparent that the concatenation of themes is the same and that correspondences can be found.

In *L'Action* of 1893, it will be recalled, the third part established the insufficiency of the natural order. The same demonstration can be found in the text of 1937, where it occupies parts III, IV, and V—with this difference that the words "natural order" have been constantly replaced by "immanent order," because the former is to be reserved henceforth for what theologians call the order of pure nature.[228] After the critique of pessimism had brought forth the affirmation, "there is something," the author states that, beginning with this admission, he will unfold the objects of willing, and that the supreme question will thus be little by little prepared: "Yes or no, is there for one who limits himself to the immanent

order agreement between the *volonté voulante* and the *volonté voulue?*" [229]
Or again: "It is a question of knowing whether consciousness and the will
to act would even be possible if the term of thought and action were to be
found only in the objects that make up the immanent becoming of this
world." [230]

The reply is given in the critique of superstition, which concludes with
a double impossibility and a double necessity:

> It is impossible not to recognize, not to experience the inadequacy of
> every immanent order wherein our action unfolds in relation to the
> capacity, to the exigencies of our willing and acting. Therefore, it is
> necessary to seek beyond for the true and supreme end to which every
> human effort tends.—It is impossible, if we are to be consistent with
> the indestructible *volonté voulante*, to find in ourselves and in our
> *volontés voulues* the satisfaction to which we necessarily aspire and
> have freely pursued. . . . Indeclinable, impracticable: Faced with
> transcendence, these are the two qualities that are apparently im-
> posed on us actually and simultaneously for our action to follow its
> course. . . . [231]

Thus, we find once again, at the same stage of development, the same
conclusion that was reached in the first work: the insufficiency of the
natural order (called from now on the immanent order).

In like manner we also find the second conclusion, that is, the second
step: the absolute necessity of opening to the divine action, whatever it may
be. But, whereas the demonstration formed a continuous and homogeneous block in the 1893 text (the whole of the fourth part), it is now split, in
the 1937 text, into two distinct elements.

Immediately after having established the inadequacy of the immanent
order when compared with the exigencies of our willing, the author shows
how it imposes on us the necessity of affirming the transcendent God, how
the idea of God sets us before an alternative that has to be resolved no
matter what the consequences of one solution or the other, what spiritual
dispositions we should have if, faithful to the total *élan* of our aspiration,
we want to form our will according to the divine will and thus belong to
God. [232] We easily recognize here the sequence of ideas that were treated
in the fourth part of the first edition. But now they are treated briefly and
simply presented as the last of the concentric waves in which human action
is unfolded. This apparent reduction of what previously constituted the
decisive part is explained by the fact that Blondel, having already expounded the proofs for God and treated the option in *La Pensée* and in
*L'Etre et les êtres*, is content with offering only a summary here. Another
difference is much more important; it is the one that is in clear evidence

at the end of the development in the definition of religious expectancy.

Throughout, we wind up with the same conclusion that it is impossible for man "to attain his necessary end by his own powers,"[233] that "the term to which he is obliged to tend," remains "inaccessible to the most generously confident action."[234] But in *L'Action* of 1893 the idea of this end "absolutely impossible and absolutely necessary for man" is called the "notion of the supernatural."[235] In *L'Action* of 1937 the idea of this "more than human destiny" which belongs to man[236] is called the "feeling of a transcendence,"[237] or the "very rational notion of the transcendent";[238] and it is a further advance of thought that makes us add to this notion "the very human idea and the very religious feeling of a supernatural,"[239] "the philosophical hypothesis of a completely gratuitous gift,"[240] a "rational conception of the supernatural."[241] Thus, the absolute necessity of opening to the divine action, whatever it may be, is established in two steps: opening to transcendence, opening to a hypothetical supernatural. The original demonstration is split. Or rather, its earlier scope is reduced, and a new element leads it to its term.

Why? Because, yielding to the demands of theologians, Blondel wanted to inscribe in the very fabric of his philosophical development the possibility of a state of pure nature. In *L'Etre et les êtres* he had insisted on this point: "One primary datum must be maintained: A state of pure nature is conceivable and effectively realizable."[242] "Yes, in the eyes of reason, as well as in terms of the possibilities and exigencies of nature, this state of incompleteness is conceivable without there having to intervene any internal necessity, any just demand."[243] "It would already be a very exalted destiny, this role of seeking God indefinitely without finding the infinite, in a humble, courageous, and unquenchable generosity in accord with that maxim of Malebranche: 'to tend to the perfect without laying any claim to it.'"[244] Such is exactly the idea Blondel restates at the point we have reached in the second *L'Action*:

> It would be a fine destiny to affirm the mystery of God, to humbly adore the inviolate secret whose indirect light, without being unveiled, would illumine every man coming into this world, conferring on him the power to dominate things and be master of himself. Let no one say, then, that in the natural order human life would be unworthy of being lived.[245]

However, adds the author, philosophy can and should open another perspective: the hyposthesis of a complement offered, of an increase gratuitously provided, of a gift that human nature cannot demand but which it could be prepared to receive and which it could welcome, without doing violence to itself, because it would be the culmination of its aspirations.[246] This is the subject matter of the sixth part of the work. This hypothetical gift, explains Blondel, would proceed directly from a divine initiative; it would have an absolute originality and would in no wise derive from the primitive gift that constitutes reasonable nature and the will that is essentially proper to man.[247] Such a hypothesis is metaphysically possible and appropriate because it is called for by the disproportion between the indefiniteness of the religious aspiration and the infinity of the object to which it :ends.[248] Besides, it offers a positive likelihood when one considers the miseries and blemishes man would like to liberate himself from and which make him feel the need for a redeemer.[249]

Observe that, in spite of a certain analogy, the thought process here is distinct from that of the last part of the 1893 work. There, Blondel had in view Christian dogma as hypothesis for the purpose of examining its correspondence with human aspirations. Here, he abstracts from dogma,[250] for the purpose of showing that, even in its absence, human aspirations lead one to form the hypothesis of a gratuitous supernatural order. It is only in *La philosophie et l'esprit chrétien*, we have said, that he takes up the earlier point of view again. There he will show how the Christian mysteries resolve the enigmas of philosophy. For the moment, he limits himself to what philosophy can derive from the simple analysis of human willing. He does not go beyond the term reached in the fourth part of his first work, that is, the second step in the genesis of the idea of the supernatural.

As is now more clear, the essential difference consists in advancing in two steps. He first shows that every human will implicitly bears within it the natural and inefficacious desire to reach God. Then he explains how this desire would remain "vague, irrational, or even unreasonable if it were not shown at the same time how the act of willing gives rise to the hypothesis of a sublime and gratuitous pouring out of divine charity."[251] From this, there results an obligation to inquire whether such a hypothesis may have been realized; whereupon we are led to the philosophical examination of Christianity itself (which examination will lead to an invitation to engage in a personal and active verification from which no one can be dispensed).

We shall not examine here the equivalent of the third step. It would take too long to analyze likenesses and differences between the fifth part of the first *L'Action* and the much more expanded contents of *La philosophie et l'esprit chrétien*. Suffice it to note that in the final work Blondel avoids certain expressions that had shocked theologians. He no longer says that the result of his investigation is to propose "as a necessary hypothesis, the supernatural order as a scientific postulate."[252] But he does maintain that his study terminates in considering Christianity "as the crowning of the universal edifice and the only solution to the complete problem of destiny."[253]

As we see, Blondel expended considerable effort in his later works to keep in view the objections theologians had for a long time addressed to him. This effort had its reward. If *La Pensée* drew some criticism, the works that followed it were judged to be compatible with even the most classic theology. Whether one accepts or rejects what he has to say about the supernatural, there is no question about his orthodoxy.

But among philosophers or theologians who had been favorable to the first writings, a double current appeared. Some applauded the Trilogy as reflecting a ripening and balanced flowering of the early findings. Others were disappointed to see Blondel inserting into his philosophical work theological elements that seemed to them to blur the original clean-cut development. We shall not examine here the question of whether the Thomistic thesis of the natural desire to see God should be understood as Blondel understands it, following Father de Broglie, or whether there is not some other way, as indeed there must be, of scuttling the idea that God could not create beings endowed with intelligence without ordering and calling them to the beatific vision. Within the limits of this study we cannot undertake a sufficiently careful exegesis of the thought of St. Thomas nor treat the theological problem it raises. We simply propose the following question: In the supposition that the theological doctrine adopted by Blondel is, on every point, a requirement for believers, is it necessary to introduce it at the very heart of a development that claims to be purely philosophical? Isn't there something inappropriate about this procedure?

The idea of pure nature—like that of integral nature, fallen nature, the transnatural state, or supernatural life—is a theological concept. To the extent that the philosopher abstracts from Christian teaching, he does not encounter it. He can speak of human nature, but he has no competence for situating it with relation to the salvation history that Christian preaching bears witness to. Now, in the Trilogy, as we have seen, Blondel explicitly declares that he wants to abstract from Christian teaching. So it seems that he should avoid reference to the idea of a state of pure nature and withhold consideration of it until he comes to *La philosophie et l'esprit chrétien.* Yet he does take it into consideration, although he recognizes that he could not have thought it up had he not been instructed by Christian theology.[254] He even recognizes that this procedure might raise an eyebrow. "In a sense our procedure might appear to be the work of artifice since it pretends we are in ignorance of what we know from another source and thus permits us to discover what we could not have discerned did we not already possess what we seem to master."[255] Then he immediately adds, in order to defend himself against the charge of perpetrating a crafty fiction or of a rash claim: "It is one thing to discover an unknown, the possibility of whose existence we do not even have the right to know, and quite another to study the intrinsically intelligible organization of a hypothetical reality regarding which we possess certain lights capable of guiding our intellectual analysis without embarrassment to the sincerity of the critique."[256] This remark would seem in our opinion to justify the developments found in *La philosophie et l'esprit chrétien* more than those which anticipate it in the Trilogy.

As a matter of fact, this anticipation offers a serious difficulty: It brings two different perspectives into constant collision in such a way that the reader becomes lost. Blondel, the philosopher, considering the universal and necessary condition of the human spirit, abstracting from all Christian teaching, wants to show that every man bears in his being, thought, and will something which obliges him to take seriously the Gospel message regarding a gratuitous gift of God. Blondel, at the feet of theologians, declares that man, though desirous of this gift, could have managed to get along without it. Certainly, the two perspectives are on different planes, and to this extent the author does not contradict himself. On the one hand, he wants to direct the unbelieving philosopher toward Christianity; on the other, he wants to show the theologian that this philosophical procedure is compatible with theological teaching. But the exposition would have been clearer if the two programs had been treated separately. Their constant interplay in the same passages risks bewildering the reader. It is almost as though the writer, in an embarrassed shell game, takes back on one page what was granted on another. He could have helped the reader, had he remained faithful to the end to the plan and method of the Trilogy (which claims to abstract from Christian teaching), and if he had, consequently, reserved for the final work all treatment of the state of pure nature.

Perhaps it will be said that he had necessarily to have it in view, even in the Trilogy, since he claimed to be examining what would be required in any hypothesis or situation by a spiritual being capable of knowing by reason that God is his final end. It is our opinion that the concern to limit the examination to what is necessary, regardless of the circumstances, was sufficiently indicated by the explicit determination to abstract from Christian teaching. When he approaches the notion of the supernatural, the author of the Trilogy declares again that he is limiting himself to "the strictly philosophical aspect,"[257] that is, to what can be known in an "indeterminate way" by "every mind conscious of its innate powers."[258] That should apparently suffice in making it clear that philosophy is limited to what is necessary in any hypothesis.

The same reservation was indicated in the *L'Action* of 1893 by the fact that Blondel there distinguished sharply, on the one hand, the indeterminate idea of the supernatural, an idea accessible to every man in a confused way and which even the philosopher ignorant of Christianity can discover and, on the other hand, the determinate, positive, and specific notion of the Christian supernatural, a notion which only the Gospel message makes known. The real reason for the misunderstandings occasioned by this work and by the *Letter* of 1896 is not the fact that the author makes no explicit mention of the possibility of a state of pure nature; the reason is that many failed to observe the important distinction we have stressed. They did not see that the author approached the idea of the supernatural in a way familiar to philosophers and not according to the assumptions of theologians. The key words were not sufficiently noted: Natural order, necessity, exigency, etc., all had under his pen a very different meaning from the meaning theologians were accustomed to. Swept along by the current of the theological debates, Blondel himself modified his language and perspective instead of developing his first exposition.

It was certainly indispensable for him to show the compatability of his enterprise with theological teaching. But he could have done it without introducing this encounter into the very heart of his philosophical development. It was also indispensable for him to edit out, or at least explain, certain expressions which were equivocal in the eyes of theologians. But he might have done it without also adopting their language in a work that wished to remain philosophical.

### *Need of the Supernatural and the Natural Desire to See God.*

Even if Blondel had understood the Thomistic thesis on the natural desire to see God in some fashion other than the one he chose, could he have adopted it without modifying his original thought to some extent? No doubt, he does transform the idea that he incorporates, bending it to the movement of his own thought. However, he thinks that he has held on to what is essential and judges that this essential is identical with the idea of a need for the supernatural he had always held. But this identification was absent from the first works, and it can be asked whether it corresponds exactly to their content.

First of all, the Thomistic idea of a *desiderium naturale videndi Deum* is not even mentioned in *L'Action* of 1893. Nor is the beatific vision ever

treated there. This absence is the more striking in that what is contrary to this vision, hell, receives considerable treatment. Seeking to justify the idea of eternal damnation, which is a scandal for many, the author set out to demonstrate that the pain of damnation is an inevitable consequence of the haughty self-sufficiency of a solitary will which refuses to open to God and has placed its all where there is nothing to fulfill it.[259] He also defines "the death of action," which is the term of the negative option. But when he passes to "the life of action," he leaves the term of this option in the background and is content with simply defining that without which it cannot be attained. "No one sees God without dying. Nothing touches God that is not brought back to life again; for no will is good unless it has gone out from itself in order to make way completely for the total invasion of God's will."[260] So it is in an incidental and furtive fashion that the beatific vision is even hinted at. What moves the dialectic of *L'Action* is not the attraction of this future vision but the original *élan* of the act of willing. And the conclusion of this dialectic is not the necessity or even the possibility of this vision, but the duty imposed on every man to will what God wills.

It will be recalled that the first work of Blondel is really a science of practice. When he treats "the life of action," this consists in showing what the "substitutes and preparations for perfect action"[261] are, namely, the generous accomplishment of duty, willing acceptance of suffering and mortification, recognition of the divine initiative. When he comes to speak of the Christian supernatural order, he devotes himself principally to explaining what ought to be the nature of the human cooperation appropriate to the divine action: necessity of the step of faith, necessity of some religious practice. At the term of each development the conclusion is the same: "Man, by his own deliberate intention, does not equal the fullness of his spontaneous aspiration save on condition of annihilating his own will by installing within himself a contrary and mortifying will."[262] "When we will fully, it is [God], his will, that we will. . . . Our true will is to have no other but his. . . . When, by this free substitution, we recognize that he does all in us, then he grants us the boon of having done all. . . . We achieve independence only by abnegation."[263] In his report on Blondel's thesis Emile Boutroux had noted well: "According to him, what we definitively will, whether we advert to it or ignore it, is the substitution within us of the divine will for our own will."

This differs significantly from a natural desire for the beatific vision. To begin with, the whole perspective is different. Blondel is considering the conduct that man ought to adopt in the course of this life, not the beatitude he can hope for in a future life. Even when he speaks of eternal life, he is thinking mainly of the life we enjoy in this world through explicit or implicit faith.[264] But there is an even more important difference, situated at the very heart of willing and of the desire in question.

To be sure, the willing that the dialectic of *L'Action* reveals at the source of every human activity is a willing of the infinite. Even more exactly, it expresses, indeed it is, the fundamental and necessary relation of man to God. In this sense, it has some affinity with the natural desire for God which St. Thomas and his disciples speak about. So it is not implausible for Blondel and his friends to appeal to the Thomistic idea in order to show the traditional character of the thesis expounded in *L'Action* of 1893. However, the two ideas bear only a partial resemblance with one another.

In St. Thomas the natural desire to see God aims directly at its term, as do all natural appetites, without any internal opposition. In Blondel, on the contrary, the act of willing the infinite or the need for the supernatural has for its object the substitution in us of the divine will for our will; so it cannot aim at its term except through the acceptance of a kind of death. St. Thomas shows that our will can only be fulfilled by God himself when he communicates himself to us. In the course of the dialectic that establishes an analogous conclusion, Blondel adds that man can only open to this divine action through a passive purification, by constant mortification, by sacrificing that tendency that leads him, in the words of Claudel, to fall back "on his essential difference." Blondel not only shows that our action requires more of us than we can do alone; but he leads us to the admission that "the natural order does not suffice for our nature which, nevertheless, repels the supernatural."[265] Thus, he discerns at the heart of finite being (and not just of fallen being) two antagonistic tendencies, equally natural and equally radical: a desire for the supernatural and a repugnance against it, so that the former can neither receive satisfaction nor even be recognized without a profound sacrifice. That is why the "need of the supernatural" that the dialectic of *Action* reveals is cut from a different cloth than the "natural desire to see God" which is manifested in the *Summa Theologica* or in the *Summa Contra Gentes*.

Because of this difference, Blondel's idea lets us see in a more immediate way that the supernatural will not bring man's willing to fulfillment without submitting it to a reversal. It thus offers a more direct preparation for understanding, in faith, the transcendence of the divine life whose communication the Gospel proclaims.

In the Trilogy Blondel did not discard the characteristics that distinguished his idea from that of St. Thomas. But he did obscure them by wanting to identify the two ideas. His early thought was more precise.

In expressing our preference for the early thought, we do not mean that there is nothing useful in the clarifications introduced in the Trilogy or in the work on the Christian spirit. Nor does the sympathy with which we speak of *L'Action* and the *Letter* signify that they have, in our eyes, uttered the last word on the place of the idea of the supernatural in philosophy. I repeat it again; I make no profession of being a Blondelian. A Christian's only master is the Gospel interpreted by the Church; a true philosopher is not tied to any particular philosophy. But can one refuse to hear the suggestions offered by a great work to the extent that they are coherent and provide an introduction to the Gospel? Even though it were necessary to prefer another approach and to speak, therefore, simply as a historian, it would still be an obligation to understand sympathetically and exactly the thought one interprets.

# CHAPTER THREE

# The Ontological Affirmation and the Religious Option

After having established the necessity of the supernatural, of dogmas, and of religious practice, the author of *L'Action* states that a final link is to be added to the series of relations bound together in consciousness under the constraint of practical necessities. He wants to show "how there is inevitably formed in us the idea of objective existence; how we invincibly affirm the reality of the objects of our knowledge; what exactly is the necessary sense of this objective existence; on what conditions this reality, necessarily conceived and affirmed, is in fact, real."[1]

> What appeared up to now in a regressive analysis as a series of necessary conditions and means successively required to constitute action little by little, will henceforth, by a synthetic view, be revealed as a system of real truths and simultaneously ordered beings. . . . Whereas action appeared to be primary and being derived, it is truth and being that will appear to be primary but without ceasing to have their subsistence and nature determined by the action that finds in them its rule as well as its sanction.[2]

It is a question, then, of showing how the science of action restores ontology by renewing it. This is the object of the last chapter of the work, "The Bond of Knowledge and Action in Being."

We know that this chapter was not included in the thesis defended at the Sorbonne on June 7, 1893. It was added after the defense in the copies of the commercial edition that were offered for sale in November of the same year. For practical reasons Blondel had postponed the definitive rewriting of the work.[3] What is not generally known is that an earlier version of this chapter situated in the same place was contained in the manuscript deposited by the author at the Sorbonne in May, 1892, for the purpose of securing permission to have the book printed. The text was much shorter and had a different orientation. It was called "The Universal and Eternal Consistency of Action." It purported to show that, when one supposes him elevated to the divine life through grace and the sacraments, the human person is the total bond of things and their veritable *raison d'être.* He made no formal claim, as in the text published in 1893, of justifying the idea of objective existence and of constituting an ontology.

What made the author decide to make this change? We are inclined to believe that it was the result of an objection his friend, Victor Delbos, made after a reading of the thesis in May, 1893. Delbos wrote:

> It seems to me that you give metaphysics a rather restricted treatment: According to you, it makes its appearance as a moment in the development of action, and you consider it more in terms of its efficacy than according to its intrinsic nature. Like you, I am inclined to be on guard against a metaphysics that would be erected into religion; but it does seem that it has something more to do than to elevate action or prepare it. It could be considered as consecrating it, or better, as justifying it.[4] . . . I feel that what you have marvelously showed are the necessities that action requires, postulates, lives by. Would it not be logical to confer on them, through metaphysics, a value and a sort of absolute objectivity?[5]

To respond to this invitation, it would appear that Blondel modified the original orientation of his last chapter, that he makes of it "a kind of metaphysics of the second power,"[6] destined to justify "the exterior subsistence of the truth interior to man,"[7] the objective being of all that has appeared as a condition for action.

The text is renowned for its obscurity. This has been explained by the fact that the author had to write rapidly without having the time to mature his thought sufficiently. This is true. But one can be even more precise after reconstituting the history of the editing with the help of the documents preserved in the Blondel archives.[8] The author of *L'Action* wanted to incorporate into the definitive text of the last chapter what he had written earlier. In vain did he drastically modify it; he could not edit out elements that manifestly had a different aim. Moreover, after having laden with revisions the manuscript destined for the printer, he inserted into the proofs numerous and often very long additions which seriously affected the development of certain parts of the argument. As a whole it is not sufficiently welded together. Thus, the reader must pay close attention and even reread certain parts if he is to discern the thread of the development.

In spite of these defects, the chapter in question is one of the most remarkable to come from Blondel's hand. Since it has occasioned many misunderstandings, as indicated above, we should like to analyze it here in a precise and continuous fashion, set in relief the main structure, and explain the meaning and connection between the various theses that he juxtaposes and which often interfere with one another and with a linear development. In this way it will be possible to see the very special sense in which the author understood the connection between the ontological affirmation and the religious option. It will be remarked, we hope, that shining through the occasional awkwardness of a thought still in search of itself, profound insights will make their appearance. Perhaps it will be concluded that it behooves us to retain some of them, even when it is judged that certain reservations should be maintained and that what is best could be expressed more felicitously in some other way.

## THEORETICAL AND PRACTICAL KNOWLEDGE

In approaching the ontological question at the end of the last chapter of *L'Action*, the author indicates that he has reserved the question until this point had been reached. He had analyzed the dialectic of action as it appeared to consciousness; he had exposed to reflection the series of conditions necessary for the unfolding and achievement of human action; he had unrolled a chain of practical necessities. But, "although contrary habits of mind may have persuaded the reader,"[9] he had not affirmed the objective existence of any of these conditions.

Thus, Blondel "phenomenizes," so to speak, all the previous developments. This procedure has served to disconcert many readers. It is good to know that the author himself seriously questioned whether it would not have been better to introduce the ontological question earlier, or not to have raised it at all. This comes out in the correspondence exchanged with Delbos.

After having revised his text, Blondel, still hesitating about inserting the new version, consulted his friend. Delbos approved the addition of the chapter and replied as follows to the questions Blondel raised: "In view of your way of understanding action, I do not think you can handle or even raise these problems except at the end. . . . This chapter serves to link *your* philosophical way of treating *your* subject with the general fashion of understanding the philosophical problem."[10]

More significant still is a letter Blondel wrote several months after the appearance of his book, asking Delbos for his final judgment on "the place, role, and validity of this last chapter."

> You recall your old metaphysical criticisms; you also know that I hesitated for a long time about inserting this last chapter without managing perhaps to justify it. It still seems to me, now more so than a year ago, that the problem of objective reality can only be usefully taken up after the unfolding of the integral determinism of action, up to and including the specified conditions for a truly religious life. Only at this price, it seems to me, can the transposition of the old ontology be complete and efficacious.[11]

Here we see clearly that Blondel's perplexity was concerned in a particular way with the place where the ontological problem would be most appropriately treated. It is also clear that, while his hesitation had not completely disappeared, he was more secure in his position.

He will become completely reassured, it seems, over a period of years, prior to the change in outlook that will be reflected in the Trilogy. We read, for example, in "L'Illusion idéaliste,"[12] an article dating from 1898, and summarizing to some extent the last chapter of *L'Action*: "Before setting out to inquire into the value of our thought, we must know what we actually do think. . . . The first task for all philosophical research is to unroll as integrally as possible the continuous chain of thought, without any realist or idealist prejudice."[13] It is in this way that we shall make apparent "the only effective way of affirming or denying being."[14]

This suggests that, in spite of Blondel's hesitation, we should take seriously the reason why he finally decided to tackle the ontological problem only after having unfolded the integral dialectic of action. Recalled again in "L'Illusion idéaliste," this reason has already been exposed and repeated in the course of the last chapter and in the conclusion of the principal work.

> To pose the problem of the knowledge of being with precision and scientific competence, one must have previously determined the complete system of relations that falls between the two extremes: From the voluntary to the deliberately willed, from the ideal as conceived to the real as operative, and from the efficient to the final cause, all the intermediate steps ought to be covered before one has the right to turn around and see in the fleeting succession of phenomena the very solidity of being.[15]

To situate being or the absolute in one or other of the intermediary objects, is "to fall into the idolatry of the understanding."[16] Blondel asks whether all philosophical doctrines have not yielded more or less to this temptation.[17] One is tempted to seek the absolute of truth and being in sense data, in positive science, in an exclusive determinism of freedom, in a metaphysics closed in on itself, or in an ethics that refuses all further research. One thus sets up doctrines that are mutually exclusive.[18] In order to extract from what is controversial what cannot be controverted, it is first necessary to suspend the ontological affirmation, to consider the objects of knowledge as they appear, that is, as heterogeneous and connected (and not as excluding one another), and not seek in an order of phenomena the truth of another order, but assume that each ought to have its own truth and solidarity.[19] Thus, the moment one poses the ontological question, one is in a position to affirm the reality of the totality of the objects of knowledge.[20]

In order to avoid all misunderstanding, it should be noted that it is on the level of philosophical science and in terms of the necessities of the regressive analysis that Blondel suspends the ontological affirmation until the term of his reflection. By this method he will show that spontaneous knowledge included it from the start. The role and strength of reflective knowledge is to force upon us "the acknowledgement of the truth that is in us before it is in reflective knowledge and which it does not attain except at the term even though we live by it from the beginning."[21] "All the movement of the interior life leads to the necessary affirmation of being because this movement is founded on this very necessity."[22] This is what the science of action will show at its term.

There too, the author says, this science will proceed by regressive analysis; it continues to unfold the series of necessary conditions, the inevitable sequence of the needs of practice.[23] At first it seems "only to deal with the internal relations that make all phenomena unified in our consciousness; but at the term these same phenomena will be found to constitute the being of things. The practical necessity of posing the ontological problem leads us necessarily to the ontological solution of the practical problem."[24]

The last chapter of *L'Action* establishes at the outset two theses in the course of an alternating deduction advancing by successive ascending levels. On the one hand, it shows "that in us there is a certain knowledge of being from which we cannot escape," and even "that there is between being and knowledge an absolute correspondence and a perfect reciprocity."[25] On the other hand, he shows "that between knowledge and being there remains a radical heterogeneity, that between the vision and possession of being the distance remains infinite, and that, if there is a necessary being of action, action does not necessarily have being in itself."[26] By this distinction, says the author, the problem of knowledge and being assumes a new meaning; the method and the solution are transformed.[27]

To establish the first thesis Blondel shows how, on the plane of reflection and by a phenomenological analysis, the idea of real or objective existence is necessarily generated in us, and then how we inevitably affirm the reality of the objects of our knowledge and the ends of our action.

Here, first of all, is how the deduction of the idea of objective existence is handled. It is expressed by a simple manifestation of what the integral dialectic of action implies, as it has been described thus far. "Whatever we think and whatever we want, from the fact that we think and want, the universal order of the determinism follows. In vain do we try to deny it or interrupt it; by the effort made to destroy it or withdraw oneself from it, we affirm it and ratify it."[28] It always appears to us, then, as independent of our deliberate will and reflective thought; for us it is a nature. Moreover, since its role is to impose an alternative on our freedom, we see that this determinism, although it is ours because of the spontaneous production of thought, it is at the same time outside us as a term for willed operation.[29] Thus, "the nature of things appears to us as an objective reality because it is imposed on us by the unity of the determinism and because it imposes a free option on us."[30]

By this we see that the intellectual problem of being is posed at the same time as the moral problem of our being. Correlative and irreducible, the series of objects linked before the understanding and the system of ends offered to the will are equally implicated in the genesis of the idea of real existence. This bond of the determinism and of finality justifies our inevitable belief before the eyes of reflection: "There is an affirmation of being anterior and interior to every attempt at negation, even when it is complete."[31] "We are, incurably, and things are incurably for us."[32]

This is nothing else, says Blondel, but the abstract and general notion of objective existence. But, he adds, the inevitable movement of reflection makes it immediately apparent that it is necessarily realized in concrete objects. Indeed, the chain of the determinism only exists by reason of what it links together and determines. So, in affirming the reality of the system, we necessarily affirm that of the objects that constitute it and without which it would not be.[33]

We affirm each object in its singular nature and irreducible quality. "Its nature and truth is to be what is heterogeneous and individual: this is how it is given in intuition, and this is how it is. And what remains to be discovered in it that is anterior or ulterior is the new object of an ulterior or anterior investigation that will reveal the distinct nature of other syntheses that are equally irreducible."[34] Let us not seek the truth of sensation behind sensation nor, in a general way, the reality of the phenomenon in a substratum placed behind it, or in a more remote phenomenon. There is no privileged phenomenon, no phenomenon to be eliminated. Each bears within itself its own truth and individual reality.

> But, at the same time, each term without ceasing to be heterogeneous with respect to all the others is bound to them by a solidarity such that one cannot know or affirm one without implying all. The objects this determinism links together are neither more nor less real in one point of the series than in a neighboring point; neither is it necessary to look for the secret of one in some other, nor believe that one can be admitted without the other.[35]

This necessity of affirming the reality of all the phenomena (that is, of all the objects of knowing and willing) in their original irreducibility and in their unbreakable solidarity, is a leitmotif in the last chapter of *L'Action*. The author repeats it at each successive level of his deduction. We find it reappearing when he wants to maintain against criticism the identity or reciprocity of knowledge and being. But he first brings it in to show that this necessary identity is always realized in conjunction with a possible heterogeneity, that knowledge is "living or dead, depending on whether the being whose necessary presence it bears within it lies there as a dead weight or reigns by reason of a free adherence."[36] Thus, before developing all its consequences and in order to unfold them, the first thesis gives rise to the second. From the fact that there abides a necessary presence of reality in thought, it does not necessarily follow that reality is present to thought. And this second thesis, far from destroying the first, goes a long way to confirm it.

Here is how this genesis takes place. Among the phenomena that the dialectic of action makes inevitably appear to consciousness before it embraces them all in the necessary affirmation of being, we encounter, it will be recalled, the great alternative which requires every man to opt for or against welcoming the divine will and action, as well as the idea of the vitalizing or death-dealing consequences of this option. Now if it is true, as we have seen, that we cannot establish any object in being without thereby establishing the whole series, it follows that we cannot affirm the reality of any phenomenon without passing by the point where we are compelled to open to the divine initiative or fold back in upon ourselves. And since it has been made clear that, depending on the choice, human action lives or dies of the necessary being it bears within itself, it is also apparent now that, depending on the same option, the necessary knowledge of being is living or dead, possessive or privative. The ontological affirmation is thus found to be affected in some way by the option which is the great affair of life.

This thesis is so subtle that it is worthwhile citing the whole passage in which Blondel expresses it. After having explained that the ontological affirmation necessarily bears on the entire series of heterogeneous and connected objects which the dialectic of action links together in solidarity, he continues in these terms:

> There is, then, no object whose reality can be conceived and affirmed without our having embraced in an act of thought the total series, without our actually submitting ourselves to the exigencies of the alternative it imposes on us, in a word, without passing through the point where there shines forth the truth of the Being who illumines every reason and before which every will must take a stand. We have the idea of an objective reality; we affirm the reality of objects. But to do so we must implicitly pose the problem of our destiny and subordinate to an option all that we are and all that is for us. We do not reach being and beings save by passing through this alternative; depending on the way we decide, the sense of being is inevitably changed. The knowledge of being implicates the necessity of the option; being in knowledge is not before but after the freedom of choice.[37]

We have already pointed out and briefly discussed the complaints that this thesis stirred up earlier, at the time of the great controversies. Here we must examine it in greater detail, keeping in mind more recent interpretations.

Let us first clear away a serious confusion shared by several early interpreters and by some today. The option Blondel speaks about in this chapter is not the option concerning Christianity but the option concerning the unique necessary. It is not a question of the Christian faith, which would suppose an explicit knowledge of revelation, but the act of opening to "the Being who illumines every reason and before which every will must take a stand." This is what the text we have just cited says and later on we shall come upon analogous expressions. Surely, anyone who knows Christianity and understands it to be God's revelation, cannot open to the Word which illumines every reason without believing in the Word Incarnate. But that is not what Blondel has in mind here. He only speaks directly of the *religious* option whose ineluctable character has been shown in the fourth part of *L'Action*. He leaves at the perimeter the explicitly *Christian* option whose necessity had been shown in the fifth part of *L'Action*. He will return to it only at the end of the Conclusion.

So it is the religious option, considered under its indeterminate expression, which first affects the ontological affirmation. Even with this clarification many find the thesis difficult to accept. Almost as though the author took pleasure in disconcerting them, he insists: "What we cannot dispense ourselves from thinking and affirming, is, from all appearances, what is most real and sure outside us. Be undeceived: . . . it is in what can be received or refused that we must see the true reality of objects imposed on consciousness."[38] Many readers believe that in *L'Action* Blondel subordinated the objective value of knowledge to an existential choice. Is it not clear that he gives them reason here for such a belief? To find a legitimate sense in his declarations, must we not restrict somewhat their literal sense? In spite of an apparent irrationalism, it may be sufficient to read carefully what he says in order to discern a profound truth.

"The knowledge which, before the option, was simply subjective and propulsive becomes after it privative and constitutive of being."[39] This proposition, which repeats the preceding ones under another form, has the advantage of enunciating directly the double distinction introduced by Blondel. Before the option, there is a "subjective knowledge of truth,"[40] a necessary knowledge whose effect is to propose for us an inevitable alternative.[41] After the option, there is, in addition, an "objective knowledge of reality."[42] Depending on whether the option is negative or positive, this objective knowledge is privative or possessive of being.

Let us glance first at the distinction between what is before and what comes afterwards. Several interpreters have thought that the temporal sequence should be minimized. Thus, in his essay on the philosophy of action, Henry Duméry says that for Blondel the option is coextensive with knowledge and intervenes not only "at the end of the program, but at every instant and when confronted with each singular reality."[43] Indeed, it is only "the recognition of the normative *a priori* and an identification with its movement."[44] In other words, all it does is ratify the ontological judgment which is operative throughout the regressive analysis and not only at its term.[45] "It becomes constitutive of being because, in a Plotinian fashion, it finds being to be a trace of the One."[46] Blondel's statements on the role of the option signify but a single thing:

> . . . the purely hypothetical scope of the analytic determinism and consequently the necessity, in applying it to the real, of including in it the ontological judgment. Now, whether the option is good or bad, the mutual immanence of the two dialectics remains inseparable, even unknown, even misunderstood. Thus, there never exists, even by way of abstraction, a knowledge that is purely subjective followed by a second objective knowledge.[47]

When the author of *L'Action* seems to assert the contrary, the exigencies of the double dialectic require that he not be taken literally. It should be remarked that "the expression spreads out in a temporal sequence what is, on the contrary, simultaneous in the unity of an act of several dimensions."[48]

We have more than one reservation regarding the general tenor of this interpretation. On the one hand, it seems to Plotinize Blondel's thought, and, on the other, to confuse the perspective of the first *L'Action* and that of the Trilogy. But the only question that interests us directly here is to know to what extent it is proper to minimize the temporal significance of the distinction between the knowledge that is anterior to and consequent the the option.[49]

This same reduction has been proposed, although from a more general and quite different point of view (not Plotinian) by Father Albert Cartier. It is only on the plane of reflection, he says, that "subjective knowledge," knowledge of the necessary conditions for action, can be said to exist "before the option." In reality, it is not a complete act of knowledge, but "the thinking aspect of thought, which is nothing outside the concrete option that opposes it or conforms with it." "In this meeting with the *volonté voulue*—whatever it may be—it becomes 'objective knowledge,' the necessary movement toward being, but, depending on the choice, ending in self-fulfillment or privation."[50] In other words, "it is only by an artifice of method that action intervenes only at the term to give consistency to an evanescent phenomenon; . . . in fact, on the transcendental plane, it is in every sense contemporary with being and truth."[51]

This interpretation, like that of Duméry, contains a remark that is quite correct and another that, in our opinion, is less so. It is true that it would be to misunderstand Blondel's thought were one to believe that it is his opinion that in concrete life and thought the option only intervenes at the term of a complete analytic reflection, like the one that philosophy must unfold. The subjective knowledge that is prior to the option does not represent the slope of a mountain that must be climbed to its summit in order that we may stand suddenly and definitively on the opposite slope of objective knowledge. The crest which the option expresses can be crossed in the twinkling of an eye. The option is available throughout the course of life. So knowledge is always both prior to one option and subsequent to another. In this sense it is always both subjective and objective.

But this does not mean that the option (at least if one means, as Blondel usually does, the option before the unique necessary) is in every respect contemporary with or coextensive with knowledge,[52] that there could never be, whether by abstraction or artifice of method, a subjective knowledge followed by an objective knowledge. Knowledge and option alternate: The first prepares the second and the second enriches the first. In this sense, knowledge which is first subjective becomes objective, that is, possession of known being.

Blondel's thought has two correlative and complementary aspects which must be simultaneously maintained. He indicated this himself to one of his correspondents:

> It is the necessity of the analysis that forces us to reunite in a single block and then split into two symmetrical parts what precedes and follows action. In reality the rhythm of knowledge and practice is an infinitesimal progression; and since we act without cessation in order to know and know without ceasing in order to act, speculation never remains purely speculative. . . . We should not reason as though knowledge had no support in an implicit but real possession of being. I only say that this knowledge, once disengaged by reflection, is not an end in itself, a halting place, but a means, an invitation to act, and by this very fact to obtain still more being.[53]

Blondel, we see, explains his thought in two assertions: On the one hand, he recognizes that there is "an artifice in the method which consists in examining in opposing groups what precedes action and what proceeds from action";[54] on the other hand, he declares that there must be in the course of life a permanent alternation of knowledge and action. He holds both that "we have to go to being" and that "we are already and always in it,"[55] without either of these propositions destroying the other.

Thus, it is not possible to eliminate entirely the temporal implication of his distinction between a subjective knowledge, which precedes and prepares the option, and an objective knowledge, which follows and depends upon it. If we are to find an "acceptable sense,"[56] a "legitimate sense"[57] for this distinction, it will have to be in some other way. For the moment, we still have to face the apparent scandal: a subjective knowledge which becomes objective through an existential choice. But perhaps it will disappear if we pay attention to the particular sense given here to the words "subjective" and "objective."

In everyday language, when we distinguish a subjective knowledge from an objective knowledge, we mean that the first is affected by dispositions that are peculiar to the individual, so that the discourse which expresses what is subjective cannot be universally recognized as an adequate expression of truth. In the language of the last chapter of *L'Action*, the subjective knowledge that precedes and prepares the option is imposed universally and necessarily on every subject, no matter what may be his individual dispositions and even though he may exert an effort to contest it. It is a "subjective disposition,"[58] but of the universal subject and not of the individual subject. What is called "purely subjective" is what is "necessarily present to thought,"[59] what proceeds inevitably from the internal dynamism of the spirit, in a word, in the logic of action whose term is the idea necessarily generated in every man "that the objects of his thought and the conditions of his action are necessarily real."[60] Subjective knowledge, then, is knowledge "of the truth,"[61] and even "necessary knowledge of the truth."[62] Blondel repeats this in many ways: It is a "representation of the object in the subject,"[63] "vision of the true,"[64] "knowledge of being,"[65] "vision of being."[66] In us it constitutes that "certain knowledge of being from which we cannot escape,"[67] a knowledge "coextensive with its object,"[68] so that "there is between being and knowing an absolute correspondence and a perfect reciprocity."[69] Could one ask for more precise declarations? What Blondel calls a "subjective knowledge of truth,"[70] is identically what is called in everyday language objective knowledge and which is accorded an ontological scope both by the Aristotelian and scholastic tradition.

Why, then, does he write that it "is still only a representation of the object in the subject"?[71] Why does he declare it to be "purely" subjective?[72] Why does he oppose it to the "objective knowledge of reality"?[73] The answer lies in this very simple sentence: "The necessary knowledge of truth is still only a means for acquiring or losing possession of reality."[74] To say that it is purely subjective does not mean that it is a completely subjective representation of being, but that it does not have being in itself, that it does not put us in possession of authentic reality. Reciprocally, the knowledge that Blondel calls "objective" is not more objective than the first, in the ordinary sense of the word,[75] but it "unites to the vision of truth the full possession of the real"[76] or its "positive privation."[77] "Instead of putting us in the presence of what is to be done, it recovers in what is done that which is."[78] The two knowledges are not opposed in virtue of the absence or presence of adequation with their object; they differ as a view and possession (or privation) of being. It is in this precise sense that Blondel places between them "an intellectual difference,"[79] saying of the first when it becomes the second: "Without changing object, it changes its nature."[80]

Once this has been made clear, we can readily admit that the author's language was equivocal. To call the knowledge of being prior to the option "purely subjective" is to run the risk of bewildering readers. Blondel would soon become aware of their hesitations or misunderstandings. Beginning with 1897, his correspondence reflects a change of language. In "L'Illusion idéaliste" (1898), which is a reworking of the last chapter of *L'Action*, the term "subjective knowledge" is avoided. After that we read in its place: "speculative knowledge," "speculation," or "abstract idea." And in order to avoid any appearance of giving a univocal sense to the word "objective," he calls the knowledge that follows upon the option "effective."[81]

The possibility of this transposition already made its appearance in the conclusion of *L'Action*.[82] There, the author distinguishes the "science of practice" and "practical science." The first is explicitly identified with the logic of action,[83] as developed throughout the course of the work; its final affirmation is that there is no substitute for practice. The second which, on the contrary, can suffice unto itself results from the experience expressed in generosity, sacrifice, and openness to God in one who has opted for the unique necessary.[84] An effect of the option, this "practical science" is evidently what was called "objective knowledge of reality" in the preceding chapter. Similarly, the "science of practice" is the unfolding of what was named "subjective knowledge of truth." We speak of unfolding in order to indicate a distinction within an identity. The subjective knowledge which prepares for the option can remain rudimentary; but in this case it implicitly contains all that is unfolded in the science of practice, which is science only if it is integral. At one and the same time Blondel holds that "we implicate in our choice the totality of what speculation attempts to determine" but that "we have no need to possess this explicit knowledge to be subject to responsibility."[85] Keeping these clarifications in mind, we can say that the "subjective knowledge of truth" is identical with the "science of action" which is theoretical or speculative knowledge, distinct from practical or experimental knowledge by which the reality known becomes reality possessed.

At this period the "science of action" is for Blondel "philosophy" par excellence.[86] So we have authority for thinking that if the necessary affirmation of being, uncovered by this science at its term, is called "purely subjective," it must be understood in the sense in which the author defines the limits of philosophy. And this invites us to seek in the *Letter* of 1896 the reason for a thesis that scandalized or embarrassed so many readers.

We read in the *Letter* that "philosophy's function is to determine the contents of thought and the postulates of action, without ever furnishing the being whose notion it studies; laying hold of life whose exigencies it analyzes, sufficing for a realm whose sufficient conditions it establishes, realizing the very thing concerning which it must say that it conceives it necessarily as real."[87]

This is the very thesis that the last chapter of *L'Action* develops. But here it makes its appearance at the conclusion of a paragraph which explains its historical development. Ancient thought, says Blondel, "had naïve faith in its unique sovereignty and in its own sufficiency."[88] Its tacit posutlate was "the divinity of Reason, not only in the sense that God is Logos or that the Word is God, but in the sense that our speculative knowledge encloses the supreme virtue and, of itself, consummates in us the divine work."[89] In Aristotle it is rational contemplation that constitutes *the divine life* in man, an act which has its origin and term in us; "and it is metaphysics which is the full science of being, which procures being and, if one may say it, salvation itself."[90] In Spinoza modern philosophy reveals its ambition to absolute hegemony in wanting to secularize religion and "lead man to beatitude by its own powers."[91] However, under the misunderstood or rejected action of the Christian idea, modern thought is becoming transformed little by little; it is progressively led to renounce autosufficiency.[92] Finally, philosophy comes to understand that it cannot "realize the very thing concerning which it must say that it conceives it necessarily as real."

We see now what this proposition is saying. The science of being does not suffice to procure being in the sense that the latter is salvation and beatitude for man, the divine life in him. The word being here (*l'être*) clearly does not signify "being" in the crude sense of empirical existence; it refers to what suffices unto itself, the absolute. It has in view something like Spinoza's "substance." Its signification appears clearly when we set side by side two parallel propositions. A few pages later Blondel says that philosophy does not have to "furnish the being whose notion it studies,"[93] and that it does not have "to furnish the absolute of substantial and salutary truth even when it should inquire after its conditions."[94] For him, then, philosophy ought to recognize that it is incapable of putting us in possession of the absolute, incapable of consummating the divine work in us.

However, philosophy could never attain consciousness of this incapacity and insufficiency, unless it had the notion of the absolute and conceived it necessarily as real. According to Blondel, it is at the very moment when it discloses in man the necessary affirmation of being that it recognizes speculation's inability to put man in possession of being. It cannot proclaim its own insufficiency for fully resolving the ontological problem save to the extent that it contributes on its part to the solution. Therefore, it inevitably recognizes an ontological dimension to the solution.

But, as theoretical knowledge, it is not as yet vivifying and possessing knowledge. It is in this sense, and only in this sense, that it does not suffice unto itself and we do not suffice unto ourselves. Blondel does not intend to arraign philosophy as such but separated philosophy. He shows that, since the appearance of Christianity, rational contemplation can no longer lay claim to the autosufficiency it arrogated to itself in Hellenic thought. It should lead to something other than itself. For a Greek thinker, as we know, the knowledge of truth is contemplation (*theôria*) of what is manifest (*alétheia*). According to the Gospel and the Bible, this knowledge is communion (covenant) with what is firm (God and his work). Blondel develops the first to the point where it appears to invoke the second; he thus establishes a philosophical bond between the patrimony of Greek thought that has been preserved and the heritage of evangelical thought that can be accepted or refused. Consequently, when he declares that the philosophical solution of the ontological problem is "subjective and immanent," that it does not have an "objective or absolute value,"[95] one must understand simply that human theory about being does not suffice to put man in communion with the absolute.

This is what the author of *L'Action* is saying when, in the last chapter, he maintains that the necessary knowledge of truth is "purely subjective," and that "being in knowledge" depends on the religious option. Far from being deprived of all ontological scope or dimension, this "subjective knowledge" itself generates on the plane of its own reflection the necessary affirmation of being, and it does this because it is itself founded on this very necessity. If it is called "purely subjective," it is to point out that it does not put us in possession of the reality it conceives.

Blondel explained this himself in several letters to Father Auguste Valensin.

> I had to bring separated philosophy to court. I wanted to go on record against the thesis that purely speculative and exclusively rational and natural knowledge provides a satisfying science and a sufficient solution. I wanted to insist on two capital truths: On the one hand, to attain, to possess, the reality of beings and especially of The Being, it is not enough to know (in the weak or theoretical sense). On the other hand, knowledge (in the strong or Johannine sense) implies a depth of vision which shows forth the solidarity of things, the secret of their dependence, the meaning of our present and eternal destiny. It is for this reason that I insist so much on the two kinds of knowledge (the whole of this long chapter has this distinction as its leitmotif), the one which precedes, proposes, and point by point imposes the Option; the other which results from the attitude we have taken and which, at the limit, is the revelation itself which will deliver us to death and God's judgment.[96]

For Blondel the science of action is the theoretical knowledge that opens the mind to knowledge in the strong, Johannine, and biblical sense. "Applying itself to action, reason discovers more than in applying itself to reason itself, without ceasing to be rational."[97] It manifests what, in fact, the logic of human life implies: "Everything depends on the attitude taken before the unique necessary, since it is the principle of the entire series, and since the sequence of the whole determinism has as its effect to lead us surely to it. Without being, there can be no other beings in us; with it, all are present."[98]

We now understand the sense in which Blondel proposes this thesis, which, at first reading, could seem shocking or at least enigmatic: "The knowledge of being implies the necessity of the option; being in knowledge is not before but after the freedom of choice."[99]

After having considered principally the necessary knowledge of being insofar as it prepares the subject for the option and, consequently, for practical knowledge, we must now consider this practical knowledge insofar as it achieves or fulfills necessary knowledge in a positive or negative way. What Blondel is saying in substance is that, depending on whether one chooses to open up or remain closed to the exigencies of the unique necessary, the original knowledge of being becomes possessive or privative of being. But—and there should be no mistake about this—the being that is possessed or rejected in practical knowledge is the same being that is affirmed in original knowledge; so the being that is necessarily conceived sustains both the knowledge that possesses and the knowledge that refuses it.

Let us first take a look at possessive knowledge where this relation is easier to grasp. Blondel puts it thus: "So that truth may reside really in the knowledge we have of it, we must will, in what is necessary in this knowledge, that which is able not to be willed, and we must equal the free adherence it demands with the inevitable light it imposes."[100] One might object that this thesis confuses matters and "attributes to knowledge a quality which is not strictly intellectual, since it appears to be subordinated to a voluntary act."[101] The author, who anticipates this objection himself, replies immediately, and his explanation includes exactly the point we want to stress.

> It is not a question, when willing, of making reality subsist in us because an arbitrary decree has created it in us; it is a question, when willing, of making it be in us because it is and as it is in itself. This act of the will does not make it depend on us; it makes us depend on it.

The role of this necessary knowledge that precedes and prepares the option is to be an inflexible rule. But the moment what is necessarily voluntary in it is freely willed, it does not, on that account, cease being a knowledge. On the contrary, it now has the advantage of bearing really within itself, the being of which it only had a representation.[102]

In thus showing that, by the subject's free adherence to the exigencies of the unique necessary, the knowledge of being does not cease to be a knowledge but on the contrary becomes "fulfilled"[103] knowledge, Blondel at the same time gives expression to this important idea: The being that fulfills knowledge after the option is the same being whose necessary affirmation appeared at the term of theoretical knowledge as the truth by which we secretly live from the start. In other words, the being that a free adherence puts us in possession of is the same being that we necessarily affirm. That is why the positive option does not generate a reality which would not have existed without it, but simply makes reality be in us as it is in itself. "The universal order is real in our knowledge only to the extent that we fully accept what is necessary in it."[104]

As in the case of possessive knowledge, privative knowledge is sustained by the necessary affirmation of being. This is clear from the passage in which Blondel explains that the negative option, although it deprives us of the possession of known reality, does not on that account suppress the knowledge of reality. This knowledge of reality, he says,

> retains within it all that is necessary; it loses all that should have been voluntary, but it does not suppress the effects. It was on the way to being in order to fulfill the knowledge of reality that it presented for a free adherence; it is still on the way to being, but in order to empty knowledge of this reality that it continues to require by a necessary exigency.[105]

It follows from this that privative knowledge is "truly an objective knowledge." For it is "conscious of a real lacuna and, so to speak, of a positive privation."[106] What one denies and excludes in closing oneself to the exigencies of thought is being. "Truth for the one who repels and refuses to live by it is undoubtedly not the same as for the one who feeds on it, but it is just the same; although entirely different in the two cases, its dominion is not affected more in one case than in the other."[107]

Finally, it is from the being that has been refused that privative knowledge derives the sanction for the act that repels it.

> In the man who acts as though beings were without The Being and who accepts the means without directing them toward his end, the will continues to produce the exigency for all the being needed for knowl-

edge, and knowledge shows all the being that has been excluded but
which is still necessary for the will: For the one who has denied it, it
affirms the infinite that we need, but it does this in such a way that it
refuses to the one who denies all that knowledge affirms for him.
Beyond every manner of error and deviation, there subsists a truth
. . . which, with all the precision and rigor of necessity, maintains its
sovereign rights over every reason and freedom.[108]

We can now measure the error of those early interpreters according
to whom the religious option was supposed to confer an objective value on
theoretical knowledge and an ontological dimension on philosophy, both
of which they completely lacked of themselves. But, as we have seen,
Blondel's view was that philosophy itself demonstrates that there is a
necessary affirmation of being, that is proposes an inevitable alternative,
that the possession or privation of being depends on our option, and that
the original affirmation, like a judge and a two-edged sword, remains in
force amid this choice. If, in saying all this, philosophy was not also
conscious of saying "being," its discourse would be empty and meaning-
less. But being here is of such a nature that saying it and possessing it are
two different things. It is this gap or distinction that is stressed when it is
declared: "It is in what is capable of being accepted or refused that we must
see the true reality of the objects imposed on knowledge."[109]


## THE CONSISTENCY OF THE KNOWN

The development that follows the above analysis has as its aim to explain
what practical adherence adds to the being that is necessarily conceived;
in other words, how perfect action consummates all that has served to
constitute it. It unfolds the various implications of the two correlative
theses so far established. It describes a kind of helix where each level of
the spiral introduces the same themes on successive planes. But the curve
of thought is even more difficult to grasp than in what has preceded. For,
beginning at this point,[110] Blondel incorporated the former text already
referred to, whose aim was quite different. It was also in the course of this
development that he introduced into the page proofs his longest additions,
so long in fact that he had to divide the single section originally planned
into three parts,[111] where the content of the thought becomes exceedingly
involved. To follow this exposition in all its complexity would be a futile
and unprofitable pursuit. It will be more useful to limit ourselves to an
outline of the general movement and to establish the coordinates for certain crucial points.

"Since knowledge needs to be completed and, as it were, fulfilled by a free adherence . . ., what must be welcomed in oneself in order to place oneself in this knowledge? How is this plenitude of the object inserted into the subject?"[112] Blondel replies:

> The universal order is only real in our knowledge to the extent that we fully accept what is necessary in it. Now, we cannot accept all things, we cannot accept ourselves, without passing through the 'unique necessary' where we have seen the principle of the total determinism. If our own will prevents us from attaining our true will, nothing can really be in us as long as we have not put off this solitude of egoism by a substitution of the divine will for the self-love that loses all in wanting to gain. So we must understand this double truth: We cannot reach God, affirm him truly, act as though he existed and make him exist in reality, and have him within us, save by belonging to him and by sacrificing all the rest to him. All the rest communicates with us only through this mediator, and the only way to obtain the all-to-all is to begin by the alone-to-the-alone with him.[113]

We see that this statement applies to knowledge what was said of action in the pages dealing with the unique necessary and the great alternative.[114] As in the case of action, knowledge becomes possessive of being, depending on whether or not man opens up to the exigencies of the unique necessary. The fact that we are referred to the fourth part of the work, rather than to the fifth, confirms what we have already noted: The option which, according to Blondel, fulfills knowledge is not directly an explicit faith in Christianity; it lies in adherence to the unique necessary of which every man has, at least, a confused knowledge. On the other hand, the same reference will be of assistance later on in showing that, by exalting practical knowledge of God through sacrifice, Blondel does not mean to depreciate theoretical knowledge.

Let us follow, for the moment, the chain of ideas in the passage just cited.

We are told that to know God really, we must love him to the point of belonging entirely to him and by sacrificing all the rest to him. But, because God is the first cause of all being, we find in this abnegation our own interior consistency and universal communion with all men.[115]

It is by the love of charity, including abnegation, that we know another deeply. It is through this love that others are in us and for us what they are in and for themselves.[116] "Love and the 'science' of men are one and the same."[117] Thus, to love all men, to love God, is the same thing: "and without this active love of the members of the human race for one another, there is no God for man." And again, "in the common practice of life, in the secret logic of consciousness, without God there is no man for man."[118]

In thus making the frontiers of egoism disappear, do we not expose the individual or the person to becoming lost in universal confusion? Blondel replies that universal communion is, on the contrary, the unique means for possession and perfect distinction, "the only way to realize the human person and, through him, to constitute all the rest."[119] Indeed, communion with others implies that they be themselves in themselves and that we remain ourselves in ourselves.

> And these two conditions are inseparable: For if we realize ourselves only by participating in what they are, we are real and distinct only to the extent that they are also. There is, then, a necessity to found the exterior reality of exterior objects, so that seen from without the things outside may have a real consistency: The truth of the objective without is indispensable for maintaining the subjective within of beings.[120]

Thus, "the truth of subjective intercommunion requires that the being-in-itself of the individual person be affirmed and, by it, the being-in-itself of the entire phenomenon."[121]

Similarly, the truth of communion with God requires that man remain a distinct person, that he not cease to be an individual. But, for this, communion must be realized through material and sensible nature. "The entire natural order is, between God and man, like a bond and an obstacle, like a necessary means for union and a necessary means for distinction."[122] Thus, the necessity of loving God, like that of loving man, leads to the necessity of affirming the being in itself of the phenomenon.

We must now see what this affirmation implies. Blondel first asks what *being* signifies when one speaks of objective existence. That which is truly real and objective in our knowledge, he explains, is what serves as intermediary between necessary knowledge and voluntary knowledge. This intermediary is the entire order of phenomena whose concatenation the science of action has unrolled and in which our action seeks its ends. In other words, they are "those heterogeneous and unified syntheses that have appeared to us as natural intermediaries between what we will, because we are not yet this, and what we are to be, because we shall have willed it."[123] No one of these syntheses ought to hold a privileged position: "Reality is not in one of the terms more than in the others, not in one without the others; it lies in the multiplicity of the reciprocal relations which give solidity and unity to all of them; it is this very complexus."[124] Thus, "objects must be what they appear to be, and their reality must consist, not in some inaccessible recess, but in what is precisely determined in them and exactly knowable. . . . To be, for them, is to subsist, independent of the failures of action and human knowledge, just as they are known and willed by us."[125]

One wonders what mirage could have made certain interpreters see in the philosopher who wrote such words a phenomenalist or a subjectivist. Astonishment increases when we see the same author explain the objectivity of sense phenomena by the double immanence of reason in the sensible and of the sensible in reason.[126] The surprise is complete when we see him explicitly rejecting that subjective idealism to which several readers were to reduce his thought. "A fully consistent idealism," he wrote, "makes all the distinctions that separate it from realism vanish and suppresses what is artificial in the poorly posed question it pretended to resolve."[127]

Blondel invites us to understand "how what we know is real, just as we know it, but without our personal knowledge being absolutely essential to the relations that only appear to exist in function of it."[128] With this in view, he calls attention to the fact that we have no true personal thought except through the presence in us of a necessary and impersonal truth, which is therefore independent of us.[129] Clearly, this is the classic idea.

The only serious complaint that might be lodged against these pages, as also against many others in the same chapter, is that they are too involved. It is difficult to pick up the thread if one has not already grasped elsewhere the relations they aim to set forth. We shall not take time here to develop ideas that are still not ripe for meditation.

One idea, however, does merit consideration because it will always hold an important place in Blondel's thought and because later repetitions help in our understanding of a statement that is still obscure as it appears here. At this point the author of *L'Action* asks on what conditions it will be possible to found absolutely the objective reality of what we necessarily affirm; and he finds that meditation on the Word Incarnate provides the foundation.

To understand Blondel's problematic and language we must recall that from the earliest dawn of philosophical reflection in his mind, he sought in the Christian notion of the incarnation of the Word the keystone of an integral metaphysics, including cosmology.[130] It was this concern that soon led him to study the curious Leibnizian theory of the *vinculum substantiale*, which historians, in general, scarcely take seriously. But it seemed to Blondel that Leibniz had perceived a real problem without being able to offer a satisfactory solution since he failed to realize that the substantial bond of beings was the Universal Mediator, the Incarnate Word.[131] For his part Blondel thought he had found the solution in the Christology of St. Bernard, who remarks that God-made-man understands or knows mercy by his divinity in a way that differs from his mode of knowing by his humanity.[132] In a free citation Blondel gives this affirmation a general character: "Quod sciebat ab aeterno per divinitatem, aliter temporali didicit experimento per carnem."[133] Christ the Mediator thus appears as the universal "binder." He is truly that "substantial bond" Leibniz would seek without knowing where to find it.

Neither St. Bernard nor Leibniz is named in the passage of *L'Action* under discussion. But once alerted, it is easy to see what factors were operative in Blondel's approach and why, in order to avoid arousing the prejudices of unbelieving philosophers, he chose to leave the scope of certain affirmations undetermined.

He begins the development by recalling one of Bossuet's theses (though he is not named either[134]): Things are because God sees them. This position is inadequate, says Blondel, because, merely as seen by God, things are primarily passive of his creative action and, as it were, inexistent in themselves.

> If things are active and truly real, they subsist in their objective aspect; in a word, if they exist, it is because God views them through the eyes of the creature, not insofar as he creates them, but insofar as they are created and their author makes himself passive with respect to their action. . . . Their reality stems from the fact that, linked to universal science and the divine omnipotence, there is a knowledge, both total and singular, of all the partial syntheses gathered by all the centers of sensibility and of reason scattered in the world.[135]

Careful not to seem to subject God to any necessity, Blondel adds: "Perhaps, destined to receive in himself divine life, man could have played this role of universal bond and sufficed for this creative mediation, because God's immanence in us would be like a magnetic center that would bind together all things."[136] "But also," he continues,

> . . . in order that, in spite of all, the mediation be total, permanent, voluntary, . . . perhaps a Mediator was necessary who would make himself patient of this integral reality and be like the Amen of the universe. . . . Perhaps it was necessary that, having become flesh himself, he should become, by a passion that was simultaneously necessary and voluntary, the reality of what is an apparent determinism in nature and of the coercive knowledge of the objective phenomenon, the reality of voluntary failures and of the privative knowledge which is their sanction, the reality of religious action and

of the sublime destiny reserved for man when he is fully consistent with his own willing. It is he who is the measure of all things.[137]

"Perhaps it was necessary," says Blondel. His language is sometimes less circumspect. For example, he wrote to Father Auguste Valensin: "Our knowledge is only objective and the objective is only real by Emmanuel, and if the Word is incarnated. Unless we go this far, the problem of objectivity seems to me to be radically insoluble."[138] One might believe the author of these lines subordinates the objectivity of human knowledge to a truth of faith, and simultaneously affirms the inconsistency of the natural order and the absolute necessity of the incarnation.

But we should not be deceived by such an abbreviation of his thought. Blondel established at the outset that we necessarily have an objective knowledge of reality, that is, the objects known by us are real just as we know them. Only later does he look for the ultimate foundation and last justification for this objective reality. Before discovering this foundation, and even were one to fail to discover it, the existence of the ontological affirmation is incontrovertible. In any hypothesis, human knowledge is valid and reality is imposed. If there is reason for seeking a further justification for it, it is because, at each step, knowledge implies a constant union of disparate aspects, a constant mediation which is inaccessible to the natural light of the mind. To the Christian thinker, the Incarnate Word appears to be the connecting link joining these unified aspects.[139] To conclude that the mystery of the incarnation resolves the philosophical enigma is not to require the incarnation but to profit by the light that the notion provides and that has not been found anywhere else.[140]

This subtle scheme of thought has been retraced by the author himself in a letter written in 1897: "There is a natural knowledge of objects, an inevitable affirmation of their reality which, in fact, remains independent of the explicit and total justification that can be furnished." He then invites his correspondent to meditate on these lines in which every word has been carefully weighed:

> *Speculatively* we cannot, to my way of thinking, justify absolutely the objective reality of all we necessarily affirm as objectively real without passing through Emmanuel; yet, there is in this no trace of ontologism, for I do not say that things are *known* in God but that we cannot fully explain that they *are* as we know them except by making use of a datum whose secret pure philosophy will never command. Nor is there any trace of agnosticism in this because I recognize that philosophy has the power *both* to show the legitimacy or necessity of these objective affirmations even while not justifying them fully, *and* to explain certain consequences that result from this compulsory objec-

tification, *as well as* to perceive that here it cannot even claim autarcheia.[141]

We now understand in what sense and with what nuances Blondel finds in the incarnation of the Eternal Word the substantial bond of things and the ultimate foundation of their objective reality.

Is this thesis, which he held to the end of his career, absolutely convincing? From the philosophical point of view we have seen that Blondel himself leaves another possibility open: His deduction, then, makes no more claim to rigor than an argument based on plausibility. But since he undertakes this deduction by arranging a confrontation between a philosophical enigma and a "theological opinion"[142] which is not a dogma, the question is to determine what value this opinion has and what we can conclude from it. More exactly, what is the cosmological scope of the meditation on the Incarnate Word? What is the exact significance of the famous declaration of St. Paul which inspired Blondel's theological choice: "Omnia in Ipso constant"? Neither exegesis nor theology seems to have clarified this point sufficiently.

Blondel's "Pan-Christism"[143] includes two other aspects more classic than this particular theory. In *L'Action*, before the final chapter, in the discussion of the notion of revealed dogmas, we have seen the discrete introduction of the notion of mediator, intercessor, redeemer.[144] These same themes are taken up in a more extended and explicit fashion in *La philosophie et l'esprit chrétien*. They are all grouped together, linked to the notion of dogma, in a passage of the celebrated *Letter* of 1896.[145] We shall have occasion to return to it.

The author of *L'Action* has showed, so far, how we are necessarily led to conceive and affirm an objective existence, to propose the reality of objects conceived and ends pursued, and to suppose the conditions required for the subsistence of this reality. All this, he reminds us, "only expresses the inevitable exigencies of thought and practice. That is why it is a system of scientific relations before appearing as a chain of real truths."[146] To expose to reflection the entire collection of these necessary relations, "is simply to unveil what we cannot prevent ourselves from admitting in order to think and affirming in order to act."[147]

But now, in virtue of the same necessity, all this is transformed into a system of truths that are regulative for action. "What is unable not to be immanent to thought, we are unable not to tend to make immanent within us by practice."[148] This last discovery is the link that joins the two ends of the chain and closes the circle of the dialectic.

"When all the conditions of thought and action are defined, when the content of life is reintegrated into consciousness, whether one likes it or not, one must think that it is; that is why we must act as though it were."[149] The theoretical impossibility of doubt entails the practical affirmation of reality. Shall we say, conversely, that the practical possibility of negation entails the theoretical impossibility of certitude? This is only provisional: "Sooner or later what ought to be will be, since it is what already is; and the deviations, faults, and illusory phenomena will remain forever founded in the truth that will one day reveal their error and present deficiency."[150] If theoretical knowledge cannot infallibly distinguish reality from a permanent illusion, practice is sure: "in acting as though it were, it alone possesses what is, if it truly is."[151] So nothing can substitute for practice: "We do not resolve the problem of life without living; and never to speak or prove does not dispense from doing and being. Thus, the role of action is absolutely justified by science itself: The science of practice proves that there is no substitute for practice."[152]

Having reached this point, Blondel gathers together the results:

> It is a necessity to suppose the truth of the natural order, of the supernatural order, of the divine intermediary who is their substantial bond and subsistence. It is a necessity, once again, to be unable to seek confirmation anywhere else but in effective practice or to fail to find it there. Let us suppose that action has provided it. Then the link that connects the two ends of the chain has been perfectly inserted: It was necessary that the two ends be joined; they are joined. It was necessary that the necessity of the total determinism be gathered up in a free act of the will; it has been entirely gathered up. It was necessary that the mediating role of action be absolutely justified and founded; it has been. It was necessary that this mediation be a principle of unity and distinction, and it is: We are beings in The Being. Appearances, duration, all the unstable forms of individual life, far from being abolished, share in the absolute truth of the divine knowledge of the Mediator.[153]

Perhaps one will be tempted to think that here Blondel subordinates the possession of being to explicit Christian faith. He does nothing of the kind. For, according to him, reality can be possessed without any explicit knowledge of Christ or even of God. The option that provides this reality can be made on the basis of a confused grasp of the unique necessary. Only the Christian knows that such an option involves an implicit meeting with the Incarnate Word.

Nor do we believe that Blondel refuses knowledge of truth to the man whose religious option is negative. For he holds, as we have seen, that privative knowledge is still an objective knowledge which never ceases bearing within itself necessary knowledge of truth. "The true can be known without God being possessed."[154]

The moment the science of practice concludes with the necessity of action and the religious option, by this fact it proclaims the reign of truth. In fact, it announces that "what we require in order to act is first required of us,"[155] and that the conditions necessarily implicated in every action, while we can revolt against them, "do not cease to be realized in us."[156] In the process of its development science registers the inevitable; there is nothing imperious about it.

> But once it is complete, it commands, and by the very sovereignty of what is, it exercises its judicial role. Once the chain is linked together, the entire determinism, which appeared as the phenomenon of the human will in the understanding, henceforth appears at the same time as an absolute reality that understanding imposes on the will. As a consequence, to the truth of the primacy of action, . . . there corresponds the great affirmation of the equal primacy of truty. . . . This reign of truth is entirely outside us and will never have its scepter of iron taken from it; but this reign of truth is entirely within us since we produce within us all its despotic exigencies.[157]

## PHENOMENOLOGY AND ONTOLOGY

As we can see, the whole chapter just reviewed has as its object and result the establishment of the "exterior subsistence of the truth that is interior to man."[158] Under this rubric it describes a metaphysics which Blondel defines as a "metaphysics of the second power which founds, not simply what a first metaphysics that was still subjective presented erroneously as the very reality of being, whereas it was a simple mental view or speculative phenomenon, but the entire determinism of nature, life, and thought."[159]

As we announced at the start, what is proposed is a restoration of ontology. The originality of this treatment rests on the negation from which it starts, the affirmation it promotes, and the method it utilizes.

Concerned about saying something that would have relevance for his contemporaries, Blondel could not repeat a scholastic type of ontology that most regarded as passé. At the time he was writing *L'Action*, positivism, phenomenism, and critical philosophy constrained the majority of thinkers to stand firm against every metaphysics or at least to entertain a profound mistrust of it. He had to begin with this attitude. As in the case of every position he examined, he wanted here also to take his position on his adversaries' grounds, adopt their language, and provisionally accept their problematic in order to show the inconsistency of the system and the necessity of rising to a higher view. The concern to establish contact with doctrines that were current in those days explains the frequent use, a bit excessive in our estimation, of terms like "science" (when referring to philosophy), determinism (for necessary implications), and phenomenon (to designate the given, the object of knowledge as such). It also explains the peculiar play of oppositions between subjective and objective, phenomenon and being, in short, concerning the exterior form the ontological problem assumes here and its treatment. Because the theses argued by the author are no longer living issues or only survive in different forms, his language and the outer aspect of his problematic are dated. Some pages are no longer relevant and we cannot even succeed in understanding them without an effort of historical reconstruction. This is the price one pays for having been timely, once the hour has passed. But in certain respects Blondel's timeliness was and still remains a force; for by proceeding as he did he was certainly saying something to someone. He treated living problems, problems that gripped a whole generation. And because he cut to the quick, he uncovered an insight that is still illuminating for us today.

The fact is that Blondel, by treating contemporary problems, revived a question that is as enduring as man himself, the question of the absolute. By declaring that it was his intention to go beyond idealism, or critical philosophy, in order to consider subjective necessities, it might have been concluded that, beginning with the subject taken in isolation, he wanted to establish the exterior existence of the objects represented in consciousness; in other words, that he wanted to solve the problem of the value of knowledge formulated in the most shallow and artificial way. He was justified in protesting against such an interpretation: "I do not begin by taking my position within the subject (which would suppose a conceptual distinction and the work of intellectual surgery). I take my position prior to this dichotomy, in the action that is immediation, synthesis of subject and object, real and prospective operation, but not yet analytic and reflective."[160]

When he states that he is analyzing the total content of consciousness, that he is studying the chain of internal phenomena or of subjective facts, it must not be supposed, in spite of certain ambiguous expressions, that he intends to undertake a psychological analysis of subjective states, of states of consciousness. At times he even indicates this himself: "By striving to equate what is distinctly thought by us with what thinks, what lives, and is in us, we are in fact led from condition after condition and from discovery after discovery to unroll the entire series of our representations and constitute the science of the conscious interior as well as of the apparent exterior."[161] Internal phenomena or the contents of consciousness are for him intentional objects; he submits them to phenomenological analysis. When he asks the question regarding their "objective existence" or "real existence" or "objective reality," when he tries to establish the "exterior subsistence of the truth interior to man," it is not a question of knowing whether something exterior corresponds to our internal representations, but of knowing whether the objects of our knowledge and the needs of our will carry within them something absolute and on what conditions we might, through them, enter into possession of this absolute. We have seen that for Blondel objective existence is synonymous with being, while being is synonymous with the absolute. One can regret the ambiguity of the first quasi-identification and the frequent equivocations of the author's vocabulary, but if one reads him attentively the thought is clear: The problem of objective existence, as treated in the last chapter of *L'Action*, is not a pseudocritical problem; it is the ontological problem insofar as it concerns the absolute.

This throws light on a statement which scandalized, when it did not fascinate, many readers:

> To believe that one can reach being and legitimately affirm any reality at all without having come to the term of the series that begins with the first sense intuition and leads to the necessity of God and religious practice, is to court illusion: We cannot stop at an intermediate object and make an absolute truth of it without falling into the idolatry of the understanding. . . .[162]

Many imagined that the author of these lines was questioning the solidity of human knowledge, the reality of the physical world, and the certitudes of metaphysics in order to make them depend on the Christian faith. This is to read him at cross-purposes. While recognizing that these words, which appear at the start of the chapter in anticipation of later developments, are not immediately clear, the rest of the chapter, which offers an abundant commentary on them, leaves no doubt as to their meaning. They do not question the value of our knowledge, even when it is fragmentary, but indicate the way in which human knowledge can take hold of itself reflexively as a knowledge of the absolute and become an actual possession of the absolute. What is condemned here as idolatry of the understanding is not confidence in intelligence but premature and exclusive assertions purporting to discover being in a substratum back of every phenomenon or identifying being either with some particular phenomenon or with the totality of phenomena considered in themselves. First among doctrines which "people the intellectual world with idols," Blondel places phenomenism and positivism,[163] that is, doctrines which restrict the power of the mind in relation to the absolute. It is precisely to avoid this kind of restriction that the author postpones his treatment of the ontological problem until he has completed the integral analysis of the datum implied in human action in general.

By provisionally remaining neutral regarding the being of the datum, every possibility of contradiction interior to this datum is eliminated. From now on phenomena are to be taken for what they are: heterogeneous and solidary. Philosophy thus assumes the character of a scientific description.[164] But its integral unfolding will necessarily lead to the option before the unique necessary; and this option will everywhere re-establish being which, from the beginning, was secretly everywhere.

To philosophy thus conceived, Blondel gives the name "phenomenism" or "phenomenology." These names do not appear in *L'Action*,[165] but they are found in the report of the defense of the thesis,[166] in the letter of 1894 addressed to the *Revue de Métaphysique et de Morale*,[167] in the *Letter* of 1896 published in *Annales de Philosophie Chrétienne* in several installments,[168] and in the correspondence of this period. A few years later the author will remark that the term "phenomenism" was ambiguous and that "phenomenology" is to be preferred.[169]

Whatever be the word used, Blondel feels at this time that philosophy "is limited to studying the chain of internal phenomena and the development of our inevitable exigencies."[170] In a passage of *L'Action* which recalls the principal steps of the work, he writes:

> All that we have called sense data, positive truths, subjective science, organic growth, social expansion, moral and metaphysical concepts, certitude about the unique necessary, inevitable alternative, death-dealing or life-giving option, supernatural fulfillment of action, affirmation of the real existence of objects and the conditions of practice, all these are still only phenomena in the same sense.[171]

All these elements, he says a few pages later, "share in one and the same hypothetical necessity,"[172] "are still only forms of the same interior need,"[173] that is, of the exigencies of action. Thus, throughout the course of its development, philosophy is limited to the consideration of what appears, what is manifested to consciousness, with a view to establishing necessary relations. Even when it finally broaches the ontological problem, it still registers a single necessity. Philosophy does not affirm being, says the author; it shows that we necessarily affirm it and indicates under what conditions we affirm it adequately. At the heart of ontology, philosophy remains a phenomenology.

There is no reason to believe that these limitations of philosophy are the result of impotence. If it does not posit anything in being, it is because it discovers that the ontological affirmation was already there spontaneously before it began its work of reflection, and will be there voluntarily when it shall have completed it.

"I am a phenomenist," wrote Blondel, "in the sense that I regard philosophy as a partial and subordinated form of activity, that it contributes to clarifying and directing this activity without substituting for it."[174] It is in this strictly defined sense, which is in no way agnostic, that he refuses to attribute "to the speculative work of philosophy the power to reach the real."[175] If the language used in disclosing the immanent necessities remains phenomenological to the very heart of ontology, it is not because it is powerless to pronounce the word being, but because saying it already reflects a prior spontaneity and prepares an option that words cannot replace.

It is interesting to follow the discussion carried on between Blondel and Delbos on how to conceive philosophy. We have indicated how, in the definitive draft of the last chapter, the author of *L'Action* took into account his friend's observation when the latter reproached him for having given metaphysics too restricted a role. We have also quoted the letter of September 25, 1895, in which Blondel asked Delbos for his most recent impressions on this chapter. Delbos must have reiterated his criticism, for we find Blondel justifying himself in still another letter, written a few days later (October 1).

> I think that the traditional idea of metaphysics which strives to envelop the total content of thought and reality is correct, as an idea. I even think that thought, based on its proper principles, can constitute a closed system, an integral system, and it is precisely for this reason that I have set forth, not as symbols but as definite postulates, the natural conditions of religious life and the complete determinism of action. Only, instead of juxtaposing, as you would like to do following Schelling, the philosophy of essence and the philosophy of existence, I try to show that they overlap and compenetrate one another everywhere, without being confused or allowing of substitution anywhere. . . . If one limits oneself to juxtaposing dialectic and practice, an irreducible and irrational element is left outside metaphysics, and this is contrary to the hypothesis; the only way to save integral metaphysics—which you correctly want to maintain without sacrificing

practical life—is to understand that it penetrates life and does not substitute for it.

Blondel concludes, however, by admitting that in his desire to make a strong plea for action he tends to exaggerate, and that his friend does well to remind him of the complementary aspect: "Action enjoys no supremacy over the word; metaphysics is total and also divine, and I often forget this."

In spite of this grudging admission, the author will for a long time defend the concept outlined in *L'Action* and systematized in the *Letter* of 1896. But Delbos will persistently prod him to maintain and strengthen the specifically rational aspect of his endeavor, providing him with the scientific and metaphysical basis it requires.[176] And Blondel will allow himself to be convinced. As already indicated, the Trilogy will be presented as "a speculative philosophy,"[177] "a technical system of philosophy,"[178] a "metaphysics of the necessary."[179] Without rupturing the bonds between speculation and human action, without losing sight of the problem of destiny, the later work will, nevertheless, introduce a kind of reversal when it widens its view to include the fundamental conditions for the whole created order. Instead of a phenomenology of action, perfected by the genesis of the ontological affirmation, we are offered a metaphysical study of thought, being, and action in general. A "study of action through action,"[180] a concrete philosophy of destiny, will be tacked onto the larger view as a complement with a relative independence.[181] Since this "practicing philosophy"[182] will have been preceded by an ontology, it will be pointless to bring it to completion by a genesis of the idea of being and of the conditions for its affirmation. By the same token there is no longer any reason for methodologically reserving the ontological question for the end or, consequently, for presenting the science of action as a phenomenology.

Later we shall return to the concept of philosophy implied in the early works and then in the later ones. What is important to repeat here is that, even in the early works, Blondel, while exalting the cognitive role of the religious option, does not intend to downgrade speculative knowledge. When he invites us to recognize the insufficiency of philosophy, he does not situate it in the theoretical order but in the order of salvation and beatitude. Furthermore, it is philosophy itself that proclaims its own limits, and in doing so it believes that it simply reflects the limits of the field open to purely human knowledge and action. Similarly, when Blondel states that philosophy only sketches out empty frames, he does not suppose that he is mouthing empty phrases but, depending on the context, that his discourse does not contain divine revelation or is not sufficient to procure salvation.[183] In the second case, where insufficiency is involved, the void is supposed to reflect the void of a life closed to the unique necessary. Indeed, the entire natural order "is only a means of accomplishing a higher destiny. If one does not attain it, the best ordered life remains a well-constructed frame, but empty."[184] Now philosophy can reveal this void only by exposing to view the exigencies of the original affirmation of being. It shows that "there subsists in thought a necessary presence of reality,"[185] even when, in virtue of the negative option, reality is not present to thought. Thus, theoretical knowledge always retains its own value.

It maintains this value even in the affirmation of God, in spite of the close connection Blondel establishes between this affirmation and the religious option. But we cannot be satisfied here with a global demonstration. Several Catholic theologians or philosophers felt that Blondel's thought on this point was incompatible with traditional doctrine on the natural knowledge of God. Even sympathetic interpreters had difficulty finding an acceptable meaning for some statements. Others interpreted them inexactly. These statements must therefore be explained.

## PROOF OF GOD AND AFFIRMATION OF GOD

The reader's plight becomes clear at the beginning of the last chapter of *L'Action*. Blondel states there that when, in the course of previous developments, he encountered the idea of God, he only considered it from the practical point of view: "In showing that this concept, inevitably generated in consciousness, obliges us to affirm, at least implicitly, the living reality of this infinite perfection, there was never a question of concluding to the being of God; it was a question of seeing that this necessary idea of the real God leads us to the supreme alternative upon which will depend the question of whether or not God shall be or not be for us."[186]

One may be tempted to read these lines in the following manner: The logic of action gives rise in consciousness to the idea of God, not as an affirmation but only as an idea; this idea simply entails the necessity of an option; this option alone affirms the existence of God. This is how the thesis of *L'Action* has often been understood. Even a philosopher as sensitive and open to Blondel as Pierre Lachièze-Rey seems to have adopted this interpretation:

> Originally, and this can be observed not only in the first *Action* but especially in the report on the defense of the thesis, M. Blondel took his position exclusively on the phenomenological level. . . . God seemed, therefore, to be only an idea, an idea whose genesis was described when it was shown how it had to arise necessarily at a

certain moment in the process. . . . But when there was question of its ontological value, the idea of God led by its presence only to the necessity of an option, an option which we could in no way escape. The affirmation of God seemed to be a sort of postulate, and M. Blondel's position did not seem far removed from that of Kant. . . . It seems, on the contrary, that henceforth, in the later works, we are directly immersed in being, that the existence of God is no longer the object of an affirmation required by the deliberately willed fulfillment of thought and action, that is, by a decision in favor of this outcome, but that it is immediately experienced in act, that it is regarded as really given in the propulsive movement and that the option now only concerns the intellectual and practical attitude taken by the mind in the presence of this situation. The demonstration is no more than the elucidation of an original possession and it is no longer a question of making an act of rational faith, while running the risk involved in the affirmation, but of consenting to what the search will inevitably reveal.[187]

With Lachièze-Rey we are of the opinion that Blondel comes to ontology in the first *Action* only at the end of a phenomenology and by means of it; while in the Trilogy he takes his position on the ontological plane from the start. But we do not believe that in the first *Action* the relation between phenomenology and ontology, between the idea of God and the affirmation of God, is exactly as the commentator describes it.

If the pages that treat the *Unique Necessary* are consulted, it will be seen that the phenomenology of action generates in consciousness not only the appearance of the simple idea of God but also the affirmation of the existence of God. Thus, Blondel writes:

In my action there is something which I have not yet been able to understand and equal, something which prevents action from falling into nothingness, and which is something only by being nothing of what I have willed up to now. Therefore, what I have voluntarily affirmed can neither be suppressed nor maintained. It is this conflict which explains the coercive presence in consciousness of a new affirmation; and the reality of this necessary presence makes possible within us the consciousness of this very conflict. There is a "unique necessary." All the movement of the determinism leads to this term: For it is from it that this very determinism starts, and its whole meaning is to lead us back to it.[188]

The force of this proof, says Blondel, lies in the fact that it is the result not of a logical construction of the understanding but of the total movement of life. It grasps in voluntary action "precisely what is already there, what consequently is necessarily expressed to consciousness and is always represented there in one form or another."[189]

The dialectical exposition of this spontaneous proof ought to show that it unites into a demonstrative synthesis all the partial arguments which, taken in isolation, remain sterile.[190] Far from criticizing the onto-logical, cosmological, and teleological proofs as Kant did, Blondel shows how they derive a compelling force from the dynamism of action:[191] Thus renewed, the argument which proceeds from contingency "acquires an entirely different character, a greater forcefulness than has ordinarily been accorded it. Instead of seeking the necessary outside the contingent, as though it were a term to be discovered later, the argument shows that it is in the contingent itself as a reality that is already present."[192] As for the ontological argument, it also acquires a new meaning and vigor. For it is legitimate here, and only here, to identify idea and being because "we first find the idea in being and being in action."[193] There can be no doubt that "in order to reach the 'unique necessary' we do not grasp it in itself where we are not; but we set out from it in us where it is in order to see better that it is by understanding to some extent what it is. We are constrained to affirm it insofar as we have an idea of it; for this idea is itself a reality."[194]

These quotations give only a very incomplete view of Blondel's demonstration. But they suffice to show that the author of *L'Action* really wanted to prove the existence of God and wanted to do this by recovering an original affirmation through reflection.[195] For him tracing the genesis of the "necessary idea of God" is identical with disclosing this implicit and spontaneous affirmation. The option imposed by the idea of God could not consist, therefore in "making an act of rational faith while running the risk involved in the affirmation." Its role is of another order: It must substitute in us the divine will for self-love.[196] On this point there is no difference between *L'Action* and the Trilogy.

But what does Blondel mean, then, in the passages of the last chapter cited above? When we had to face the idea of God, "there was never a question of concluding to the being of God."[197] "We could not arrive at God and really affirm him, . . . except by belonging to him and sacrificing all the rest to him."[198]

In order to understand these statements or other similar ones where the language is not always without ambiguity, we must once again refer to the pages which treat the "unique necessary." Immediately after having set forth the proof for God, Blondel indicates why and in what sense the proof calls for something to complement it.

> The thought of God in us depends doubly on our action. On the one hand, it is because, in acting, we discover an infinite disproportion in ourselves that we are constrained to seek the equation between our

action and the infinite. On the other hand, it is because, in affirming absolute perfection, we never succeed in equaling our own affirmation, that we are obliged to seek its complement and commentary in action.[199]

We need only understand this last sentence in order to have the explanation we are looking for. "When we think we know God enough, we no longer know him."[200] Why? Because the idea we have of him, while it originally emanates from his being, is not identical with him. "There is a necessity of always passing beyond because he is always beyond. The moment we no longer stand in awe, as before an ineffable newness, but look upon Him from the outside as an object of knowledge or a simple occasion for speculative study without youthfulness of heart or love's anxiety, the game is over; we have in our hands nothing more than a phantom and an idol."[201] "The living thought we have of him is neither living nor does it remain so unless it is turned to practice, unless we live by it and feed our action on it."[202]

Thus, for Blondel it is God's transcendence in relation to the idea we have of it; in other words, it is our condition as a creature that accounts for the fact that "we are unable to know God without wanting to become him in some fashion."[203] And, Blondel adds, it is this same transcendence that accounts for the fact that we are able to become him only by substituting his will for ours.[204]

It is in this light that we must read what the author says in the last chapter: "We can only reach God, affirm him truly, act as though he were and make him be in reality, we can only have him as our own by belonging to him and by sacrificing to him all the rest."[205] From this point of view the commentary that follows becomes equally intelligible: "To know God really is to bear in oneself his mind, his will, and his love. *Nequaquam plene cognoscitur nisi cum perfecte diligitur.*"[206] By exalting this practical knowledge of God Blondel does not mean to downgrade theoretical knowledge. On the contrary, he shows what exigencies this theoretical knowledge imposes once it has recognized the transcendence of its object.

On the strength of these same exigencies he states that, concerning the proofs for God, he did not claim "to conclude from them to the being of God."[207] Still, as he indicates a few lines later, they are for him "proofs of his existence." Far from invalidating them, he thinks his work has "renewed them, not so much by the form of the argumentation as by the spirit which inspires them and by the nature of the conclusion."[208] If he has reservations about the conclusion which other philosophers have often failed to mention, these reservations in no way touch the theoretical rigor of the arguments. Blondel explicitly reminds us here that the idea of God "inevitably generated in consciousness, forces us to affirm, at least implicitly, the living reality of this infinite perfection."[209] However, as we noted above, since God is beyond the idea that we conceive, "by affirming absolute perfection we never succeed in equaling our own affirmation."[210] Consequently, "we are forced to seek its complement and its commentary in action."[211] But it is evident that the religious option, by which knowledge becomes possessive of being, does not result automatically from the proof. This explains why the proof could not conclude to the being of God. But it does, nevertheless, conclude to his existence by showing that we affirm it necessarily, even when we strive to ignore it. Blondel even prolongs this conclusion by showing the necessity of voluntarily affirming what our thought inevitably implies. Thus, far from impoverishing the theoretical force of the proof, he enriches it.

The author of *L'Action* clearly distinguishes two affirmations of God: One is original and necessary and is implicitly present in every man; the other is voluntary and is included in the positive religious option. It is worth remarking here that he thus makes use of a Pauline idea, and that he is fully aware of what he is doing.[212] As we know, St. Paul says of idolatrous pagans that "they are without excuse, for although they knew God they did not honor him as God or give thanks to him."[213] He holds therefore that idolatry implies an original grasp of the true God, that it is a culpable disregard for what is inevitably known. He thus invites pagans to recognize actively what they know confusedly, and he will then present them with the Christian faith as the true realization of this knowledge that idolatry perverts.[214] So, for St. Paul, the effective recognition of the true God is a free act, and its necessity is prescribed interiorly by our original grasp of this God.

Such is the idea repeated and elaborated by Blondel. He draws from the sources of Christianity itself when he distinguishes between the two affirmations of God and stipulates that real knowledge of God is identical with the religious option through which man turns away from "superstition" to open himself to God's action.

## ENVELOPED AND DEVELOPED ONTOLOGY

Whether it is a question of the being of God or of relative being, in order to understand what the last chapter of *L'Action* says, we often had to appeal to the content of the fourth part of the work where the idea of the unique necessary arises along with the alternative it imposes on every man. This last chapter appeared to be a kind of reduplication of the fourth part. How is such a duplication justified; or, in other words, what relation unites and distinguishes elements that have been repeated?

The question is the more acute in that the object of the fourth part of *L'Action* in its relation to the third part is defined in the same terms as the object of the last chapter in its relation to all that precedes. In the course of the third part, very accurately entitled, "The Phenomenon of Action," Blondel indicates several times that "the ontological question has been put aside and would be premature here,"[215] that he has "relieved" the science of phenomena of all ontology.[216] At the start of the fourth part, entitled, "The Necessary Being of Action," he announces that from now on it will be a question "not of what appears, but of what is." "We shall be drawn forcibly to the affirmation of being, led forcibly to face the alternative it gives rise to, obliged forcibly to opt between two decisions, each of which radically excludes the other."[217] This part seems to have for its object to establish the necessary passage from the science of phenomena to the affirmation of being. But, as we have seen, this is also what the last chapter of the work sought to establish. What is the meaning of this repetition?

Are we to suppose that this fourth part of *L'Action* is already Blondel's ontology and that the chapter subsequently added was appended merely to draw out some corollaries? This would certainly not be correct because, at the beginning of this chapter, Blondel announces, not a series of corollaries or clarifications, but "a supreme advance of thought," "an advance that will serve as guarantee and justification for all the preceding steps."[218] He warns the reader not to yield to the temptation of attributing to previous affirmations "a metaphysical significance which they do not as yet have."[219] Later on he declares that all are still only "phenomena on the same level," including "certitude about the unique necessary, inevitable alternative, lethal or life-giving option"—all those elements, in other words, that go to make up the content of the fourth part of the work.[220]

Are we to conclude, then, that this part has no ontological thrust? This would be contrary to the opening declarations and to what we have gleaned from what is stated in them. It would also require that we concede that Blondel, in editing that last chapter in which he limits the scope of earlier statements, more or less unconsciously modified his own thought. Actually, we are not obliged to get involved in this particular hypothesis because the very chapter in question limits the scope of its own content as well as of earlier affirmations. Thus, in tracing the genesis of the affirmation "of the real existence of objects of thought and conditions for practice," he states that this affirmation, too, is but a phenomenon on the same level as the preceding ones.[221] Once again, then, we find the original thesis repeated: The philosophy of action remains phenomenological from beginning to end, even when it discloses the inevitable affirmation of being. And because the last chapter attributes this quality to it on a universal basis, its statements cannot be used to demonstrate that the fourth part of the work has no ontological dimension.

So we have to take seriously what Blondel states in both places. In each instance we find a genesis of the ontological affirmation and an analysis of its implications. Are we to suppose, then, that the author was proposing two successive ontologies? In this case, what relation would the one have to the other?

Let us keep in mind what is essential in the final ontology: We inevitably conceive the idea of real existence, we invincibly affirm the reality of the objects of our knowledge; but to do so we necessarily pass "through the point from which there shines forth the truth of the Being which illumines every reason and before which every will must take a stand."[222] Depending on our option, the meaning of being will be changed. "It is in what it is possible to accept or refuse that we must see the authentic reality of objects imposed on knowledge."[223]

It is clear here that the ontology of the last chapter of *L'Action* presupposes the findings of the fourth part: It takes them up again, assimilates and applies them to itself. But at the same time it goes beyond them. In the earlier section it was a question of the moral and religious problem of our being; here it is a question of the intellectual problem of being. On the one side, the conditions necessary for the being of action were spelled out; on the other, these conditions invite us to recognize being in its truth. It is only in this latter instance that we have a discussion of being considered for itself. It is only here that ontology is formally set forth. But this ontology rests on the germinal ontology that was contained virtually in the idea of the unique necessary and the inevitable alternative. In short, there is in *L'Action* but a single ontology which is developed dialectically: Proposed *in itself* beginning with the fourth part, it is only expressed *for itself* in the last chapter.

This relationship enables us to understand both why Blondel believed he could present his thesis at the Sorbonne without this chapter and why he also believed that he had to add it later. Without it the work was virtually a totality, but this totality was not formally displayed. The return to the original principle had been effected, but this was not explicit.[224]

After having added the last link to his exposition, Blondel also had to make a place for it in the Conclusion, which summarizes the results of the entire work. With this in view he touched up the text of the thesis after the defense by inserting several additions.[225] It will not be without profit to point out here the most typical modification since this will confirm the interpretation we have just proposed.

In both versions the author reminds us that philosophy should begin by limiting itself to the study of heterogeneous and solidary phenomena without seeking real being in any of them; it will thus assume the neutral quality of science, having suppressed the source of contradictions. After this Blondel continues as follows in the first version:

> But it is possible to establish the neutrality of this zone, where the peace of science ought to reign, only by keeping out the secret principle of divisions, only by manifesting in all its integrity the great and decisive question. In order to avoid seeing it where it is not, it must be seen only where it is. It is not to be found in the controversies between positive science and metaphysics, nor even in the battles between nature and ethics. It lies entirely in this necessary conflict that arises at the heart of the human will and imposes on it the need to opt practically between the terms of an inevitable alternative, of an alternative such that man either seeks to remain his own master and keep himself entirely in himself, or to deliver himself over to the divine order more or less obscurely revealed to consciousness. For us being and life are not in what is to be thought, or believed, or practiced but in what is actually practiced. Man and philosophy must be, as it were, decentered so that this vital center may be situated where it really is, that is, not in intellectual speculation, not in moral prescriptions, but in action; for it is through action that the question of the relations between man and God is necessarily resolved.[226]

This passage is clearly a résumé of the fourth part of the work. As in this fourth part, the above citation shows that access to being is through the religious option. And, as in the same part, it refuses to develop this germ of an ontology into an explicit ontology.

But the second version of this same passage immediately makes a place for this ontology. Instead of harkening back to "the great and decisive question" (the inevitable alternative), the very first sentence (which begins almost the same way) refers us back to the problem of objective existence or of being. It thus introduces a résumé of the last chapter of *L'Action*. This text is worth citing at length in order to make the comparison we are interested in easier, and also because of its unusual density.

> But it is possible to conquer for science this neutral zone where peace ought to reign only by keeping out the secret principle of division, only by knowing how to look for objective existence solely where it can be,

and only by finding being where it is. The necessary knowledge of truth is still only a means for acquiring or losing possession of reality. Although this objective knowledge ought to be identical with its object, there is between the two, nevertheless, all the difference that can separate possession from privation. And objective existence consists in what, in this necessary identity, can and ought to be freely accepted in the constitution of voluntary identity. Thus, the reality of known objects is founded, not on a kind of underlying double, not on the necessary form of their phenomenon, but on what an inevitable option imposes on us; it is realized in mediating action which allows them to be what they appear to be. . . . Things are thus all subordinated to the great and decisive question regarding the employment of life; their justification lies in the fact that they raise this problem for us, and the solution to the problem also justifies them. *Omnia propter unum.* Metaphysics is controverted, but it is not controversial. This is so because the science of what is, without being dependent, is inseparable from the will for what is. This is its originality.[227]

By the fact that he characterizes the essence of metaphysics or of ontology in this way, Blondel reintroduces "the great and decisive question," the question that was the direct object of this passage in the first version. After having reminded us that this question is "the only sign of contradiction that must never disappear," that it is "the unique affair,"[228] he takes up the text of the first version again at the precise point where he had abandoned the question, in order to locate and define it once more.[229]

Thus, a comparison of the two successive drafts of the Conclusion confirms our interpretation of the relation between the last chapter and the fourth part of the work: The "metaphysics of the second power" makes explicit *for itself* (*pour soi*) an ontology that is implied *in itself* (*en soi*) by the decisive question of human destiny, the question of the inevitable option before the unique necessary.

Thus, the ontological dimension of *L'Action* begins considerably before the chapter which has as its specific object the restoration of ontology. In fact, we can now even demonstrate that in certain respects it begins well before the fourth part of the book.

In the course of the second part, the critique of pessimism showed that the solution to the problem could not be negative, that the will for nothingness implies a contradiction. As a result we were led to acknowledge that "in my acts, in the world, in myself, outside myself, somewhere, somehow, there is something."[230] These words, which make no claim to philosophical exactness, "translate the naïve movement of life which becomes enamored of itself and of all that sustains it without knowing what it is."[231] As yet they neither intend nor claim to express the ontological affirmation.[232]

Unfolding the content of action from this point forward, Blondel will initially disclose nothing more than the heterogeneous and solidary phenomena that make up the natural order. It is only when the insufficiency of this order gives rise to the idea of the unique necessary and the necessity of the supreme option that we are led to the affirmation of being; and this first affirmation is still only in an involved state and will only be made explicit in the final ontology. But it is important to observe that this affirmation, which is gradually brought into sharper focus, only expresses through the dialectical process what was already virtually affirmed in the vague admission at the end of the critique of pessimism: "There is something."

Thus, from the very first positive observation to the end, *L'Action* appears to be the progressive justification and the dialectical unfolding of the ontological affirmation. As in Hegel's *Logic*, it sets forth the idea of being, beginning with its most undetermined expression, and ends with the affirmation of the absolute.

But this development seeks to remain phenomenological throughout. Even when the idea of the unique necessary and the supreme option arises, even when the idea of real being or of absolute truth appears in its most explicit form, these ideas make their appearance only as necessary conditions of human action.[233] As we have seen, this in no way implies that philosophical language is incapable of referring to being or to the absolute. It only means that when it does refer to them it remains human discourse and does not become absolute knowing. If God gives utterance of Himself to man, it is not in the language of the philosopher; it can only be through his revelation, received in faith.

## OBSERVATIONS ON TWO INTERPRETATIONS

We thus bring to a close the commentary on the last chapter of *L'Action* and the analysis of the relation between phenomenology and ontology. Along the way we have insisted on two points: On the one hand, the problem of knowledge and of being as Blondel raises it here is not the critical problem as it has very often been conceived by Neo-Scholastics; nor is it the problem of legitimate certitude. It is the ontological problem which is concerned with the relation between human discourse and the absolute. On the other hand, the supreme option which mediates this relation according to Blondel is not, at least directly, to be equated with faith in Christianity; rather, it is the option imposed on every man by the idea of the unique necessary. Had Blondel's adversaries adverted to these two points at the time of the great controversies, they would have had to choose something other than fideism as the burden of their complaint. Oddly enough, even the interpreters who defended him against the charge often failed themselves to keep the two points clearly in mind. Consequently, some of their explanations leave something to be desired.

Yves de Montcheuil's Introduction to Maurice Blondel's *Pages religieuses* is a remarkable text, and it is one of several that contributed greatly to bringing out the true meaning of his thought amid misconceptions. It helped many readers to understand how Blondel, while setting forth the necessity of the supernatural, could still maintain and justify its gratuity, and how he could, without lapsing into fideism, give faith a role in the relation between knowledge and being. But for neither of the two problems could this rather hasty and irregular text dispel all difficulties and provide complete satisfaction.

The following is a typical summary of Blondel's thought as presented by de Montcheuil: "In following the unfolding of the determinism of action to the end, we reach the conclusion that, at the risk of not being able to affirm anything at all, we must affirm the supernatural."[234] This proposition reappears many times in slightly altered form: "no value and no reality can be affirmed without the affirmation of the supernatural";[235] "if the supernatural is not, then nothing can be";[236] "if this (supernatural) end is not given and accepted, we fall back into complete absurdity";[237] "it is impossible, short of accepting the supernatural which requires faith, to accord an absolute value to anything whatsoever."[238]

Statements like this astonished more than one reader. Are they not irreconcilable with Catholic doctrine which affirms the native consistency of knowledge and human values as well as the gratuity of the supernatural? And do they not betray Blondel's thought, at least as he expressed it in his later works?

Taken out of context, it must be admitted that they "sound strange." But set within the movement that gave rise to them, and due allowance being made for the explanations that accompany them, we believe they can be given an acceptable sense which does not betray the content of *L'Action*. But if we are to discover the sense in which they are legitimate and faithful to the text, certain qualifications must be added.

What does Père de Montcheuil mean by "affirm"? Most of the time he uses as synonymous expressions like "to confer the value of being,"[239] "to grant an absolute value,"[240] "to posit in the absolute."[241] Thus, he has correctly understood the sense in which Blondel conceives the ontological problem. Moreover, he accurately explains how abstract knowledge supposes a previous possession of being, how concrete knowledge enables us to possess it in a fuller fashion, whereas the negative option makes us lose it.[242] Clearly these cursory indications cannot do justice to the complexity of the last chapter of *L'Action*; we cannot blame the author for this. It is more regrettable, however, that he sometimes seems to give another meaning to the word "affirm." For example, in the course of an important explanation, he several times uses as synonymous the expression "to have legitimate certitudes."[243] This equivalence is dangerous since it can easily lead one to believe that we are dealing with an epistemological problem, whereas it is always a question of the same problem that Blondel proposed as ontological. It would appear that in this case readers have been misled.

Having adverted to this ambiguity, let us now take up the principal difficulty. We are told that "if we do not affirm the supernatural, we cannot affirm anything at all.[244] In other words, if we do not believe, we cannot attribute an absolute value to anything whatsoever. Is this not complete fideism? Père de Montcheuil asked himself this question.[245] The answer he proposed,[246] if properly understood and unburdened of certain infelicitous expressions,[247] corresponds essentially with Blondel's thought and contains what has to be said to eliminate a fideist meaning. We need not summarize this reply, but we must call attention to a point which the author declares to be "very important" and, as a matter of fact, it is. Thus, he writes:

> Blondel does not say . . . that only those who have explicitly affirmed the supernatural, who have accepted Christian dogmas, have legitimate certitudes. A constantly recurring idea for him is that the option between the rejection and acceptance of the supernatural is imposed on all, although under very different forms, and that it is always the Christian supernatural that is accepted or refused, that is, participation in the divine life, even when it has not been possible to give expression to the terms of the choice. One can explicitly affirm the supernatural, possess it, without knowing how to represent it to oneself.[248]

De Montcheuil, we see, has noted well that for Blondel the option that mediates between the knowledge and possession of being is not necessarily explicit faith in Christianity, but that it is initially the option imposed on every man between opening or closing to the divine action, even though this action may for him remain indeterminate. This single remark should be enough to dispel the charge of fideism. But, to produce its effect on the reader, it should have been given greater emphasis and introduced earlier.

The author did not stress sufficiently his remark because, without confusing the stages of the genesis of the idea of the supernatural in *L'Action*, he did not explicitly distinguish and analyze them. He did not show that for Blondel the idea of the supernatural, to the extent that it is immanent in us, remains indeterminate; that its positive determination comes from historic Christianity; that, consequently, the method of immanence establishes the necessity of the religious option directly, but the necessity of Christian faith only in a mediate way. In the absence of these qualifications, the theologian who hears one of his colleagues repeatedly insisting that without the affirmation of the supernatural nothing at all can be affirmed is naturally inclined to understand him in a fideist sense. And when he is told, only at the very end of the exposition, why this is not the correct interpretation, this fleeting observation, insufficiently prepared, runs the risk of coming too late with too little to reverse the original impression.

Apparently Père de Montcheuil himself recognized how open to misunderstanding some of his formulas were. Almost all the ones that might have smacked of fideism—and we have cited a good number of them —were deleted in the second draft of the text, which, were it not for the misfortunes of war, might have been the only one to have been published.[249] This makes it easier to pass judgment on their deficiencies.

However, even this criticism should be held within bounds that have not always been respected. We can put aside the unjust remarks of some incompetent publicists. But we are more deeply moved by other harsh criticisms; by those, for example, proposed on two occasions by Henry Duméry, even while offering homage to the memory of Père de Montcheuil.

We do not begrudge the author of *La philosophie de l'action* and of *Blondel et la religion* his refusal to subscribe to certain formulas:[250] They are the very ones we have found ambiguous and which disappeared from the second version. Still they should not be given a sense which they never had when they came from de Montcheuil's pen. He never intended to say that the rejection of the supernatural prevents man "from making from that point on the least valid judgment."[251] On the contrary, he explicitly declared that in the order of abstract knowledge (which remains in force even after the negative option), there are "true knowledges and false knowledges."[252] It is equally hard to admit that he presented "the act of faith as the criterion even for natural ontology."[253] What he did write moves in the opposite direction: "If it is meant that it is not praiseworthy for us to think what we please, that there are laws governing the abstract expression of thought, . . . that neglecting them will be injurious not only to our practical interests but also to our spiritual interests, then we are completely right in affirming that conceptual knowledge has an ontological value and scope."[254] This would seem to correspond to the exigency Duméry reminds us of: "Ontology is philosophically valid to the extent that logical and normative order shall have been determined with full rigor."[255] But de Montcheuil adds that conceptual knowledge does not have "by itself the power to give us access to the possession of being," and in this sense it does not have an ontological dimension.[256] And in this he is simply reproducing Blondel's thought. Finally, when it is noted fairly enough that certain statements are open to equivocation, it would be fair also to make reference to what tends to remove it: the distinction between explicit faith and implicit faith.

To explain the source of the equivocations cited, we are told that Père de Montcheuil "repeatedly confuses the formal plane of reflection and the real plane of action," that "he failed to conceive clearly the nature of the relations that hold between the intelligible order and the order of realization."[257] These declarations are the more surprising in view of the fact that de Montcheuil is perhaps the first theologian to emphasize the phenomenological character of *L'Action*. Thus, he writes: "By the analysis of the postulates of action, we unwind a series of conditions connected in such a way that we cannot affirm some without the others, but we affirm the reality neither of the whole nor of any particular condition among them."[258] Couched in different terms, this distinction between "connection" and "affirmation" which he explains[259] and frequently recalls[260] is the very distinction he was chided for not having clearly conceived. But it is precisely by means of this distinction that he defines the relation between abstract and concrete knowledge and discerns an ontological dimension that is peculiar to each type of knowledge.

It is also by means of this distinction that he defines and delimits the scope of philosophy with respect to the supernatural. He says that Blondel shows "that the supernatural is necessary for us," but not "that it is, effectively."[261] Did not de Montcheuil at least neglect this distinction when he wrote that Blondel's thesis "puts into the real spirit an effective need for divinization"?[262] Duméry says that he did neglect it.[263] But we have seen that on many occasions he addresses the same reproach to Blondel himself.[264] Is this not an indication that the commentary he is criticizing is a rather exact reflection of the original? Indeed, it does reflect the original, but at least it does not perpetuate one confusing note; for, as we have seen, Blondel is in no mad rush. And if de Montcheuil in the texts cited does use language that differs from Blondel's in ever so slight a manner, it is because he wants to situate Blondel's thesis with respect to two theological opinions that the author could have had no knowledge of when he was composing *L'Action*. The "real spirit" here is not the spirit that affirms, as distinguished from the spirit that unfolds a series of linked conditions, but our human spirit with the orientation it receives from God as opposed to a possible "pure nature." We have already spoken of the embarrassment involved in any attempt to reconcile the problematic of *L'Action* and that of theology; but we have also had to recognize that circumstances made such an attempt inevitable. Long before de Montcheuil, others made the attempt, Blondel among them.

To sum up then: In spite of its defects, de Montcheuil's published interpretation is more exact than Duméry admits. After having experienced some misgivings when de Montcheuil's text was read to him for the first time, Blondel himself finally praised his penetration after a second reading.[265]

If Duméry has difficulty in seeing how de Montcheuil's interpretation remains faithful, may this not be because his own exegesis departs somewhat from Blondel's thought? Toward the end of his study of the philosophy of action, Duméry wrote: "Some of the statements in the *Letter* which incline in the direction of denying philosophy all ontological scope seem to be somewhat out of harmony with Blondel's spirit and method as we have personally discovered and analyzed it in *L'Action*. "[266] This was to level against the *Letter* one of the complaints lodged against de Montcheuil in the same study. But later Duméry withdrew this charge,[267] saying that he now had "evidence for a complete identity of inspiration" between the *Letter* and *L'Action*,[268] having discovered in the *Letter* itself unity between the plane of reflection and the ontological plane.[269] But does he understand it the way Blondel does?

Let us consider the chapter in the essay on the *Letter*, that deals with the ontological role of the option[270] and which introduces again the complaints against de Montcheuil's interpretation. According to Duméry supernatural and natural values are for Blondel joined together in the action of the Christian without being confused. The former do not annul the latter. Nature maintains its relative autonomy.[271] The observation is correct, but it must be taken out of its restrictive context. It is not only on the level of realization that each value retains what is specific,[272] but also on the level of reflection. We have seen how Blondel never tires of repeating in the last chapter of *L'Action* that all the conditions linked together by his regressive analysis are phenomena that are at once both *heterogeneous* and solidary. To write that in the ideal series of conditions "all is homogeneous," while in the system of obligations (on the real plane of action) "all is heterogeneous,"[273] is to modify his thought. In either case the mind proceeds by leaps; and if its advance, whether it be ideal or real, is always governed by a practical necessity, this necessity which is new at each stage invites the mind each time to proceed beyond the step at which it is tempted to halt. (Besides, how could action diversify a series that reflection could only view as homogeneous?) For Blondel there is a circumincession of the regressive analysis and the progressive movement. The distinction "between the formal plane of reflection and the real plane of action," as Duméry conceives it, or "between the reflexive plane and the ontological plane," atrophies this relation. There is no reason for introducing this distinction in order to differentiate supernatural and natural values because their heterogeneity is made apparent in the regressive analysis itself.

Compared with the other conditions, certitude concerning the unique necessary, the idea of the lethal or life-giving option, or the positive notion of the supernatural, are all phenomena that are simultaneously *heterogeneous* and solidary.[274] "Each order of phenomena is equally original as a distinct synthesis, transcendent with respect to the inferior orders that constitute its antecedent conditions, and irreducible to the orders that are consequent to it and to which each appears to be subordinated."[275] This statement leaves very little room for doubt about its meaning.

Without analyzing it in detail, Père de Montcheuil was clearly aware of Blondel's intention. He notes that the idea of God, which necessarily made its appearance in the course of the dialectic of action, elicits "a kind of change of direction in the dynamism of the will."[276] "After having showed that the individual ought to aspire to become man, it was necessary to show man that he ought to aspire to become God"[277] (by grace). Thus, there is no need to puzzle over how, in de Montcheuil's perspective, we are to conduct ourselves "in order to avoid deducing a real continuity from the formal continuity between nature and supernature."[278] He easily avoids this kind of deduction because he does not propose a formal continuity between human action and divine action but a solidarity as well as a heterogeneity.[279]

But we still have not come to the critical point. A page of the *Letter* on apologetics from which Duméry cites several lines will lead into this subject.

Blondel writes that philosophy "prepares us to understand better and better that we can neither dispense with nature nor stop with it; that the human order partakes in everything and does not have its sufficiency in anything; that our natural being, while it is incapable of self-achievement by itself and in spite of the lethal sanctions that await us if we fail to understand the significance of the supernatural, is undestructible; and that human action, though it be radically insufficient, remains coextensive with God's action."[280]

We have every justification for stressing the ontological scope of this declaration: The supernatural does not suppress nature; it does not absorb it; nature retains its specific and indispensable role.[281] But it is also stated that nature does not suffice, that it is impossible to restrict oneself to it. And this is spelled out clearly a few lines later:

> Philosophy enables us to understand how systematically refusing or abstaining from what it recognizes is implicated by our action constitutes not only a pure privation of a superior and surrogate state but also a positive forfeiture; and how the human order, while it is subsistent and solid enough to serve as a foundation for all the divine constructions, remains indestructible under the burden of its eternal responsibilites. This would seem to throw new light on the question of perdition, which is so painful and scandalous for contemporary minds.[282]

Blondel repeats here the substance of Christian teaching: The refusal of the supernatural, without destroying the human order, constitutes for man a positive defection and leads to his destruction. Duméry, who takes note of this,[283] tries to specify under what rubric philosophy can handle this teaching: "Philosophy, not being able to declare that the ultimate end of man is effectively supernatural, never abandons the hypothesis in favor of the thesis."[284] While the believer admits that the supernatural end is real, the philosopher, as such, can only regard it as "a necessary hypothesis which supposes certain antecedents and implies certain consequences. He examines it from this double point of view without actualizing it."[285] "Thus, he will announce the consequences of the free act—for or against faith—as dependent upon the de facto decision, that is, as hypothetical. He will speak more or less as follows: *If* the supernatural exists and *if* the subject recognizes it, such and such an effect will necessarily follow for him; . . . *if* the supernatural exists and *if* the subject, well aware of the obligation he has of ratifying it, turns away from it, such and such a sanction will ensue for him. Each instance begins with an *if*, that is, is subordinated to a question of existence and to an option about the fact."[286]

Clearly, the supernatural is understood here in the sense defined by Christian dogma (that is why the philosopher can only view it as a hypothesis); and the word "option" designates the act by which one recognizes or rejects the reality of this supernatural. But, in the passage to which Duméry has referred us (and which is limited to a summary of certain decisive developments of the *Letter* and of *L'Action*) the option whose necessity and consequences the philosopher refers to is not the option of explicit faith or declared unbelief when confronted with Christianity; it is, rather, the option of being open or shut to an as yet indeterminate divine action. This is the religious option and not the Christian option. It is not concerned with the question of knowing whether the supernatural defined by Christian dogma exists or not, whether revelation is a fact or a myth; rather, it is concerned with the alternative offered to every man between the solicitations of the hidden God and those of egoism. What the philosopher has in view here is not the Christian supernatural but the thesis concerning the unique necessary. He does not say: *if* the supernatural exists and *if* the subject, knowing that he ought to ratify it, nonetheless turns from it, some particular sanction will follow. He says rather: *Since* there is a unique necessary and *since* every man has at least some obscure knowledge of it, the refusal to open to this unique necessary constitutes for every man a positive defection, an absolute loss.

The purpose of this remark by the philosopher (as we will recall and as Blondel himself reminds us here) is to remove the scandal the unbeliever suffers when confronted by the dogma of eternal damnation incurred by the refusal of a gratuitous divine gift.

In the chapter of *L'Action* that develops this theme, it is easy to grasp what ontological scope the author attributes to the negative option. It does not destroy or invalidate the natural order. It consists precisely in "profiting by the fact that the whole natural order, even when deprived of its achievement, cannot be annihilated," and it is just this that constitutes "the lethal fault."[287] The native field of human activity is simultaneously consistent and insufficient: We destroy ourselves when we want to limit ourselves to this consistency. "Man dies for having pretended to be content with temporal duration and for limiting himself to nature."[288] For then "God no longer is for him." "His being remains without being."[289] To the very roots of his substance, he will perish endlessly because all that he had loved will in some way be devoured and annihilated by the magnitude of his desire."[290]

Let us now read the rest of Duméry's commentary: "Some interpreters believe that the negative option ought to be condemned by the philosopher himself as being in rebellion against real being. That is an improper and dangerous view. For it contradicts the principle of the method of immanence which maintains that philosophy is only critical, that is, incompetent where questions of fact are concerned. The philosopher rejects the negative option because it rips the last link out of the series of ideal and necessary conditions; it constitutes a fault in rigor, a lack of logic. But as regards saying that it is a fault against real being and against the existing supernatural, only the free conscience can make this declaration, along with the theologian, acting as spokesman for its practical obligations."[291]

After the explanation we have given, it can easily be seen how this commentary has to be transposed if it is to express Blondel's thought. The negative option appears to be lacking in logic to the philosopher because he sees in it a fault against real being, or rather, a fault by which we are deprived of real being. But the option whose necessity and consequences the philosopher demonstrates is not directly the option before Christianity; it is, in its initial stage, the option before the unique necessary. Consequently, the philosopher can say that the negative option is a fault against real being without at the same time declaring that it is a fault against the existing supernatural as revealed to the believers by Christianity.

Under the term "ontological plane" or "real plane of action," Duméry constantly mixes two distinct questions: the question of *being* and the question of *fact*. It is true that in certain of Blondel's texts the two coincide. This is especially evident on the last page of *L'Action* where the question, "Is it or is it not?", is susceptible of two different meanings, and where the final reply, "It is," simultaneously affirms the effective existence of the Christian supernatural and the absolute being of all things. But this coincidence occurs only in Christian faith and because Christianity constitutes the insertion of the Absolute into the contingency of history. But when there is no question of faith and when we are not dealing with Christianity, the question of being and the question of fact are distinct, even for Blondel; and the ontological dimension is applicable only in the first case.

If it is true that philosophy is "incompetent on questions of fact," it is nevertheless true that for Blondel himself it does have competence where the ontological question is concerned. It shows that being is necessarily affirmed and it indicates on what conditions it is possessed and on what conditions we are deprived of it. It is in this way that it prepares the "free conscience," the "concrete subject," to recognize the truth of Christianity.

To sum up: The distinction between the "reflexive plane" and the "ontological plane," as conceived for explaining Blondel's thought and rejecting Père de Montcheuil's exegesis, seems to us to harbor two uncertain elements or two ambiguities. It does not allow us to see clearly that the ontological problem concerns the relation between human discourse and the absolute and that the supreme option is concerned primarily with an indeterminate supernatural. On these two points de Montcheuil seems to be more perceptive, though not sufficiently so. The better our grasp of these two points, the more apparent is the vigor and subtlety of Blondel's philosophy, and its agreement with the exigencies of Christian dogma.

# CHAPTER FOUR

# Christian Philosophy

It has often been said that Blondel's work was that of an apologist rather than of a philosopher, or that in various respects it pertained more to theology than to philosophy. Blondel always protested against such an evaluation: He would not accept the label of apologist that was pinned on him; he declared that he had no intention of treading on theological territory; he repeatedly stated that his plan and method were philosophical and that, even when dealing with the religious problem, he only intended to speak as a philosopher. But these often repeated protestations never quite succeeded in laying to rest judgments to the contrary.

Perhaps some of our readers have also been tempted to share these views in spite of the care taken to treat seriously the philosophical intention of the author. Can a thought be regarded as a philosophy in the strict sense of the word when it concludes with the necessity of welcoming the Christian supernatural and attributes to the religious option a necessary role at the heart of the ontological affirmation?

The moment has now come to ask this question. Having gained a sufficient idea of the development and the themes of Blondel's thought, we are now in a position to perceive its form with greater accuracy. In what sense is it a philosophy? What is its method? What are its distinctive characteristics

## HISTORY OF A COMPLEX INTENTION

Blondel himself was perfectly well aware of the fact that it was not easy to construct a "Christian philosophy" that would not be a bogus philosophy; and it was not without some fumbling that he finally managed to provide a definition of its special scheme. The overview of his work that we have given will, hopefully, have provided an intimation of what he was about; but it is worthwhile to bring his plan into sharper focus.

In this task the Blondel Archives at Aix-en-Provence provide us with some precious documents. For one thing, they make it possible for us to follow the elaboration of the first *Action* and grasp how the author progressively gave definition to the philosophical structure of his work.

On November 3, 1882, at the beginning of his second year at the École Normale, Blondel jotted down in his daily memorandum book a commentary on several texts from Aristotle's *Metaphysics* dealing with action, its relation to theory, and the problem of individuation. He ended with these words: "For a thesis on Action."[1]

Learning of his project, some fellow students and then the Secretariat of the Sorbonne reminded him that it was not clear how action could provide material for a philosophical thesis.[2] Lucien Herr, the Librarian of the École, took the matter even more seriously: "My dear Blondel, you won't be able to rely on a single proper name in this thesis of yours, which looks as though it will have to be cut from whole cloth; it's brand new."[3]

In September, 1886, when he had just been accepted for the Agrégation, Blondel wrote to his former professor, Emile Boutroux: "I would like to study action and inquire how it is illumined in thought and how it illumines thought also and guarantees its sincerity, what it takes from it and what it adds to it. . . . Between Aristotelianism which depreciates and subordinates practice to thought and Kantianism which separates the two and exalts practice at the expense of the other, there is something that needs definition; and it is in a very concrete fashion, by the analysis of action, that I would like to determine this."[4]

In this declaration, as well as in the one Blondel will address to the Dean of the Faculté des Lettres on March 2, 1887, petitioning the inscription of his thesis, his preoccupation might seem to be of an ethical rather than a metaphysical nature. But it is clear that the intention is philosophical in the ordinary sense of the word. However, it does assume a special cast, which Blondel indicates in his personal notebook at this period: "I propose to study action because it seems to me that in the Gospel only action is assigned the role of being able to manifest love and win God" (October 10, 1886). "We have scarcely done more than appropriate pagan philosophy to Christianity; as for an authentically Christian philosophy, born of the Gospel itself, there is no such thing" (October 11, 1886). Clearly, then, it is a question of drawing out by the study of action the philosophy immanent in the Gospel.

This enterprise has an apologetic aim. During a retreat[5] in 1887 or 1888, Blondel establishes the objective that he then assigns to the whole of his

future work: "to act by thought," "by the light of Christianity to go beyond
the insight of our modern thinkers," "to rally science and the modern mind
to Christian philosophy and Catholic metaphysics."

In order to elaborate a truly philosophical work along these lines,
where everyone could recognize an autonomous and rational movement,
it was necessary to bring the complex plan into sharper focus and develop
an appropriate method. When a new idea is burgeoning, very often the
inquirer only begins with a very indistinct grasp of it; and if the thrust of
this idea is to link together domains that are separated, its first expression
may seem to confuse everything. Only in the course of epigenesis will it
become apparent that the idea bore within it the power of self-differentia-
tion and organization. It will then profit the historian to look at the first
expression in order to grasp its density and virtual fecundity and from that
point on to follow the process of differentiation.

To the best of our knowledge, the first text in which Blondel succeeded
in expressing the animating idea of his future thesis sharply and forcefully
is found in a letter to Victor Delbos, dated May 6, 1889, that is, at a time
when he had already drawn up several pages of the "first rough draft" (*le
premier brouillon*) of *L'Action.* Having been consulted on a thesis project
that his friend was contemplating at this time entitled, *"Essai sur la dialectique du pantheisme,"* Blondel encouraged him with enthusiasm: "Your
subject seems to me to be contemporary, vital, essential. . . .We are invaded
with pantheism and monism, . . . The old frames of reference of traditional
logic and French understanding have burst asunder. It is good to enlarge
them while restoring them at the same time." Then he remarks that, for
the most part, these questions are the very ones that hold the center of his
own attention, and he takes the occasion to offer a sketch of his own
program. This passage is so significant that we may be excused for citing
it in its entirety in spite of its length.

> What would I hope to end with? Something like this (and may I show
> something of it in my thesis, if the day ever comes when it actually
> exists): The Peripatetic, Scholastic, and French logic of non-contra-
> diction: yes, it is true, this simplistic dialectic, and truer than its
> suspects. Pantheistic logic, contradiction, obscurity, mystery, the un-
> conscious, the unknowable, elevated to the level of a principle of
> explanation and a law of thought; yes, truth is there too. But the logic
> of the Gospel, St. Paul's dialectic, makes room for the other two, and
> in admitting them surpasses both. It claims to illumine and to radiate
> light. It excludes, refutes, condemns and damns, as does the first logic
> which it thus justifies. At the same time, since it is above all a dialectic
> of actions and since action functions in a manner that is quite different

from what takes place in the realm of distinct ideas, it has a breadth that thought cannot measure: It blinds and obscures as much as it had illumined it adduces contrary truths and precepts that are opposed: peace and war, violence and tenderness. After having excluded personality and individuality, is not pantheism led by its very method to admit what it had denied? So, if it is aware of what it is about, willing or not, it ought to be turned toward Christianity. And how urgent it is to show this.

The trinitarian rhythm of Hegel pleases me very much; but regardless of the loftiness of the Thesis and Antithesis, the Christian idea, better understood and developed, always provides a superior Synthesis. They keep trying to invent a better and more beautiful ideal, a broader truth. But to the degree that humanity grows, Christ is enlarged. And the perpetual task of philosophy and of apologetics (for me, are they not basically the same?) is to discover that He is larger, and incomparable.

Where is the solution to the problem of Immanence and Transcendence? It is in the Incarnation and in Communion. The monist confusion between finite and infinite is only an abortive affair, a vague counterfeit of unity. The ideal of unity is to be found in the Eucharistic Host that epitomizes the whole of nature, the fat of the earth, the morning dew, shafts of sunlight, before becoming, by a kind of perfect nutrition, humanity and even divinity, so as to form within us a new being, a reality, dare one say it? more than divine, a truly universal synthesis. It would be strange if anything could be explained outside the One without whom nothing was made or, as I would like to translate it, without whom all that was made became as though it were nothing.

We easily recognize in this text the idea that would animate the future work: a logic of action, drawing its inspiration from the Pauline dialectic and leading, beyond every philosophy closed in upon itself, to the mystery of Christ in whom everything subsists in unity. Yes, the fundamental idea is already present in all its vigor, but in such an undifferentiated manner! Is it philosophy, apologetics, theology? It is difficult to see in this amalgamation how the author would distinguish them.

We experience the same embarrassment in reading the "first rough draft" of *L'Action*,[6] which Blondel had drawn up during this very period (from October, 1888, to January, 1890). Thus he writes: "I am trying to found on action, as on a hypothesis which depends on us for its verification, an experimental metaphysics, a moral initiation to faith. . . . It is a philosophical apology for Christianity that I am attempting in order to show in the passage to conversion where the obstacle lies and to show that the obstacle is of our own making; for if we cannot overcome it alone, we are at least clearly obliged to ask God's help to overcome it."[7] Such was the announced plan. How was it put into execution? In the course of a rather loose-knit development, what we find is a succession or mixture of psychological analyses, moral remarks and exhortations, commentaries on biblical citations, and expositions showing the human significance of the principal Christian dogmas. This early draft, which began with a comparison between the original state of man and the state after the Fall,[8] provides before its conclusion a meditation on the pains of hell, on heavenly beatitude,[9] and on Christ "who contains within him, who bears in His bosom, who builds in His love and redeems in His blood the entire universe."[10]

In short, the author realizes the program he had formulated in certain "seed jottings" (*Notes- semailles*) that date from this period and which he entered on the margin of the "Summary" that accompanied this "first rough draft": "Take the catechism and translate it philosophically." The philosophical intention is incontestably present; for Blondel manifests a concern for disclosing rational necessities, establishing a "scientific connection"[11] between the truths he links together. But he has not yet found his method. When he sets himself the task of "translating Catholic doctrine into philosophical language,"[12] he offers nothing whose nature and rigor exceeds the typical "arguments of convenience" usually proposed by theologians, apologists, or spiritual writers.[13] Very often his design seems more religious than philosophical. Indicating the inspiration of his work in the Introduction, he writes: "I do not hide the fact that it aims to be a work of the heart and of faith rather than of reason and science."[14] It is, for all practical purposes, essentially a moral and spiritual exhortation, developed by a Christian who has reflected on his faith and wishes to communicate it.

In design and method this sketch bears a close resemblance to the work of Ollé-Laprune. This is not surprising, since Blondel had been a student of Ollé-Laprune when the latter was Maître de Conférences at the Ecole Normale. He had also spent a lot of time in his company and had carried on a continuous correspondence with him on the subject of his thesis. So it is natural that the "first rough draft" of *L'Action* would seem to merit the same reservations Blondel would later express about the work of his master. Lest we reprint the celebrated pages of the *Letter* of 1896, let us cite a few lines from a letter to Victor Delbos (1894) dealing with *Le prix de la vie*, which had just been published. "In this new book our beloved master reveals himself more and more. He presents himself as a witness with effusion, as a Christian who develops his interior life and finds in his practical conviction the living grounds for his thought, not as a philosopher who has taken as his starting point the fact of a life contrary to his own.

. . . Isn't there something ill-advised in making believe that this is the authentic apology, the truly philosophical apology?—I am speaking even in the hypothesis that a rational relationship can be established between metaphysics and dogma."[15] It is difficult not to apply this judgment to the first draft of *L'Action*, whose manner so resembles that of Ollé-Laprune.

But, as Blondel wrote in the letter from which we have reproduced a long extract above: "Philosophical thought 'spreads roots' like strawberry plants, and is propagated by layering. We begin by taking root in the mind of another and by being nourished on his substance; then we grow a shoot that goes out and is implanted a bit farther on, and we end by becoming entirely detached from the original stalk."[16]

After the completion of his "first rough draft," Blondel writes at the top of the first page his own judgment on his work. The following remark is of special interest: "At times the transposition from the theological to the philosophical plane is barely outlined: provisional scaffolding." On almost every page of his draft copybook marginal notes indicate corrections to be made, and most of them consist in eliminating professions of faith and purely dogmatic considerations. So Blondel himself was quite aware that his attempt to "translate philosophically" the catechism had not yet resulted in a philosophy, not every in a truly philosophical apologetic.

Could it ever succeed? Would a "transposition" or a philosophical "translation" of the catechism ever provide anything but a catechism expounded in a more learned language? In any case, in *L'Action* of 1893 and in the *Letter* of 1896 Blondel was to state his plan and method with much greater refinement and, all told, in a very different way. The successive drafts of his thesis, preserved at Aix-en-Provence in the Blondel Archives, enable us to follow the progressive evolution of this plan and method.

Between March 12 and April 2, 1890, the author dictated to a fifteen-year-old boy named Charles Despins what he calls in a letter of the period "the edition for children."[17] While we may seriously question whether the secretary understood much of what he was writing, this edition is still compendious, a crude summary. However, in this case Blondel meets the challenge of the great currents of modern thought much more directly, especially "German pantheism." In this way he puts into effect a project he had merely announced in the "first rough draft." He no longer speaks of transposing the catechism, but wants to show that only "Christian metaphysics" or "Catholic philosophy" reconciles without confusing doctrines that otherwise wear an air of exclusiveness and narrowness.[18] He still does not perceive, as he will later on, the ambiguity of this concept of Christian philosophy.

In this draft, as in the preceding one, the plan is simple and the divisions not very numerous. Throughout, the author considers action, first within the ambit of the being who acts, then in the milieu in which it is produced, and finally in relation to the outer world's response to the agent (responsibility and sanction).

A later draft,[19] which Blondel calls "Thesis Project," begun on July 14, 1890, and completed on April 19, 1891, offers a much more structured plan, divided into eight parts. Here the sequence of developments is already very close to what it will be in the definitive text, although the divisions and titles are different. An examination of this chain of developments immediately reveals a much more rigorous movement, a construction that is more rational than in the preceding drafts.

This "Thesis Project," still brief, will be filled out and broken down into divisions later on. The new manuscript, begun November 14, 1891, will be deposited at the Sorbonne in May, 1892, and will receive the *Imprimatur*. Boutroux, who was assigned to examine it, notes in his report to the Dean:[29] "If the conclusion of this work is to lead us to the threshold of religion, its character is, nonetheless, essentially philosophical." But, doubtless, forseeing the objections that other members of the examining board might bring up, he also wrote to the author: "Put the finishing touches on it so as to underline clearly the philosophical significance."[21] (He also pleaded with him above all to make the exposition clearer.)

Blondel then went to work to correct his text from top to bottom and rework whole chapters. In particular, he rewrote almost everything dealing with the idea of the absolute and with transcendence, that is, the chapter on the moral life and nearly the whole of the fourth part.[22] And whereas the affirmation of God made its appearance under the name of "being," it now emerged as the *Unique Necessary*. In place of a summary exposition of the proof for God, he now introduces a renewal of the classical proofs, integrated into the movement of action. Some of the titles, expressed in religious language, are replaced. Thus, the original title of the fourth part, "The Divine Destiny of Man and the Eternity of Action," becomes "The Necessary Being of Action." The title of the fifth part, "The Critique of Supernatural Action," becomes "The Achievement of Action." As for the last chapter of the work, "The Universal and Eternal Consistency of Action," not having time to rework it, Blondel eliminated it. As it was presented in the draft submitted to the Boutroux, he could have been attacked for being more theological than philosophical. For he showed how the human person is the total bond of all things, as long as it is supposed that he has been elevated to the divine life by supernatural grace and participation in the Holy Sacrament. When, after the defense of the thesis, the author reworked the content of this chapter, he presented it in a very much altered form, that is, within a larger development whose aim, as we have seen, is to define a strictly philosophical ontology: "The Bond of Knowledge and Action in Being."

Thus, from the "first rough draft" of *L'Action* to the work published in 1893, Blondel constantly pursued his goal of a "transposition from the theological to the philosophical plane," something he had originally conceived as a philosophical translation of the catechism and which progressively became the elaboration of an autonomous philosophy by retrieving the rational presuppositions of the exigencies of Christianity.

The history we have just outlined in a summary manner documents and illustrates Blondel's later declarations concerning the original problematic of his work. He will often say that he did not propose his problem in function of any existing philosophy but in function of Christianity. "If Catholicism is true, what philosophical attitude is to be expected of the man who wants to establish a balance between his reason and life and his faith?"[23] Or again: "Beginning with the original inspiration for my thesis, I have posed the problem for myself in this way: Granted that Catholicism is true, what is the philosophy that corresponds to it?"[24] Or, finally, there is this statement, which has already been cited: "Let us suppose for a moment, I would say to myself, that the problem has been resolved in the direction of the *Unique Necessary* of human destiny as indicated by Catholicism: What is to be the normal attitude of the philosopher, how can he maintain the autonomy of his research, and how can he explore the entire field open before him in the depths of nature or in the heights of the soul?"[25]

These excerpts do not reflect the progressive maturation of Blondel's program. But they do indicate well the direction it was moving with increasing precision and the form it took in the final text of *L'Action*, which was to erect on the basis of Christianity or, more accurately, in the hypothesis that Christianity is true, an autonomous philosophy that is consonant with it by reason of rational exigencies.

This philosophy aims to lead the unbeliever to the threshold of the faith. It is true that Blondel no longer declares in the 1893 text, as he had written in the first draft: "It is a philosophical apology for Christianity that I am attempting." But we cannot doubt that this is still his intention when we see him throughout the book following the progressive genesis of the idea of the supernatural, showing at the crucial point the necessity of opening to the divine action, defining the hypothetical necessity of dogmas and religious practice, stressing the inescapable role of the supreme option within the compass of the ontological affirmation, and finally inviting the unbeliever to make a trial of the experience of faith. Moreover, in a letter to the Director of *Annales de Philosophie Chrétienne* (September 22, 1895),[26] in which he announces the sharper definition of his thought that will be offered in the *Letter* of 1896, he himself states this objective without beating around the bush. In this work, he says, I will clearly indicate "the exact position I take in the task to which I am committed of providing a philosophical apology for Christianity."

"Philosophical apology for Christianity," "truly philosophical apologetics,"[27] "effort simultaneously philosophical and apologetic":[28] expressions of this kind will continue for many years to come from Blondel's pen when he wants to describe his enterprise. As late as 1924 he was still characterizing the sum total of his work (published and unpublished) as "the apologetic and philosophical effort I have been engaged in for nearly forty years."[29] It is important that the two terms should never be separated. On the one hand, his philosophical work has an apologetic aim; it seeks to shatter complacency and prepare minds for the act of faith. As Blondel puts it in a memo concerning *L'Action* and the *Letter* (May 26, 1899): "Our objective is not so much to bring about an equilibrium of well-coordinated and perfectly coherent thoughts in a state of repose, as to discover means for moving minds and directing consciences by making them emerge from their deceptive repose, by breaking up every artificial equilibrium, by revealing to them the instability of the life within them."

On the other hand, Blondel intends to construct a *philosophical* apologetics, distinct by this very fact from every other apologetics; and he will refuse to accept the classification of "apologist" whenever the label is pinned on him through a misunderstanding of the philosophical nature of his enterprise. It will be recalled that in the *Letter* of 1896 he refused to admit that his dominant idea in *L'Action* had been "to return Christian apologetics to the psychological level."[30] Again, he brushes aside attempts to draw a parallel between his work and that of Ollé-Laprune and Fonsegrive because their method does not seem to him to be essentially philosophical.[31] He says that they start from the fact of a Christian life, whereas one ought to begin with the fact of incredulity in theory and practice. For his own part, he proposes "to say something that will have weight for a mind that is philosophical and unbelieving."[32] It is a question "of getting rid of prejudiced objections, of determining the notion of the supernatural, and of exposing the exigencies and insufficiencies of nature."[33] Only philosophy is capable of this and it will only succeed in the task if it refuses to be changed into an apology,[34] that is, to be corrupted[35] and reduced to the condition of an instrument or means,[36] if it preserves from start to finish its rational autonomy. Blondel insists on this all the more because the rational and philosophical nature of his undertaking had first been challenged from rationalist quarters. That is why it is only with great precaution that he will even allow his work to be called "philosophical apologetics."[37] He will consent to this designation only if it is viewed as "entirely distinct, by the nature of the questions asked and by the scope of the conclusions, from other forms of apologetics."[38]

Thus, he has no intention of working out an "apologetics" in the usual sense of the word. As one careful interpreter felicitously phrases it, "he wants to produce a philosophy which, while faithful to its own principles to the end, will, in addition, constitute an apologetics."[39] As an autonomous development of reason applied to the total field of human action, this philosophy will be simultaneously and in one and the same movement an "integral philosophy" and a "Christian philosophy."[40] Such is the plan of *L'Action* and the program of the *Letter*.

It is true that the controversies stirred up by this latter publication, followed by the Modernist crisis, diverted Blondel for a long time from the task of completing his program for an integral philosophy. Forced to discuss with theologians questions dealing with the nature, presuppositions, and the method of apologetics, with the nature of faith, with the relationship between history and dogma, with miracles, he devoted his philosophical reflection to the service of a task that is traditionally that of the apologist and theologian. In these matters he developed an extraordinary penetration and thus rendered the Christian cause an immense service. But this occasional and sporadic work did not add up to the full program he dreamed of. Nonetheless, Delbos set him on guard against the temptation to divert his activity exclusively in the direction of apologetics and moral and religious questions; he constantly urged him to provide a metaphysical basis for his effort.[41] Blondel then set himself the task of carrying out his program for an integral philosophy that would be a "Catholic philosophy" both by reason of its universal scope and its spontaneous agreement with Catholicism.

In 1932 he would still say that he was pursuing the same enterprise that he had begun in his youth: "to guarantee the formal distinction and real union of the most normally developed Philosophy and of the most authentically defined Catholicism, lived according to its natural exigencies."[42] But he adds: "It is not a question of apologetics; it is a question of pure philosophy."[43] The unequivocal precision of this profession, which seems to be in contradiction with the earlier program for a philosophical apologetics, might lead one to believe that a change in orientation has taken place. Actually, it can be explained by the necessity to react strongly against the interpretation Emile Bréhier had just proposed. In an article that has since become famous and which aimed to show that there never has been a Christian philosophy, Bréhier wrote concerning *L'Action* "The doctrine of M. Blondel is much closer to apologetics than to philosophy."[44] Then, after having summarized the author's proposed solution to the problem of action, he concluded in a still more radical fashion: "It is a question here of apologetics and not of philosophy; it is a question of introducing and defending Christian doctrine, regarded as proved and verified *ex aliunde*, and even of making it something desired."[45] To this judgment, which resurrected the old rationalist complaints, Blondel immediately replied: "My effort I have always believed to be, wanted to be, and called philosophical, nothing more."[46] And he explains how there are in *L'Action* neither foregone conclusions, nor theses admitted *a priori*, nor an irrational apologetics.[47] We see now in what sense he refuses to be called an apologist. Having thrust aside the charge every time it led to a misunderstanding of the philosophical character of his work, he reacted even more vigorously against it to the extent that Bréhier refused to grant any rational value to apologetics. Blondel does not change his orientation: In the depths of his heart he retains the desire to attract minds to Christianity. But, in order to ward off any misunderstanding, he no longer makes a parade of this apologetic aim. Besides, partly blaming himself for the fact that many bypassed the examination of his specifically rational theses, he wants to apply himself to the task of establishing in the most rigorous fashion "the technical proof and the exact determination of the limits, indigence, and demands of reason in the speculative order itself as well as in the practical aspirations of man."[48]

We do not intend to examine the development of the Trilogy or the works dealing with the Christian spirit. We are limiting this study to an analysis of what was originally proposed in *L'Action* of 1893 and defined in the *Letter* of 1896. The statements gathered so far have served to show the complexity of Blondel's intention, which was both philosophical and apologetic. But these statements do not resolve the problem that they delineate: How can a thought developed in the hypothesis of the truth of Christianity and with the aim of leading minds to the threshold of the faith claim to be an autonomous philosophy? We read in the *Letter*: "Things have arrived at a point where, in order to perform the philosophical act without ceasing to be a Christian or to act as a Christian without ceasing to be a philosopher, one no longer has the right to begin secretly with his faith in order to feign arriving there, and one no longer has the power discretely to set a barrier between his beliefs and his own thought."[49] How are these two exigencies compatible? Explaining in retrospect the purpose of *L'Action* and the *Letter*, Blondel speaks of "having attempted, as a believer, a philosopher's effort."[50] This formulation, more radical because of its brevity, brings the problem into sharper focus: How can the effort of a believer be that of a philosopher?

## AN AUTONOMOUS PHILOSOPHY PROMPTED BY THE CHRISTIAN IDEA

***Negation of What Is Supposed.*** We often find the key to a difficulty in a text in which we would never have dreamed of looking for it. At the beginning of his article, "L'illusion idéaliste," Blondel explains that, in order to perceive the strength and weakness of the realist attitude and the idealist attitude, one must have first adverted to another more complex attitude which, taken as a starting point, enables one to come to grips with the implicit dialectic of the illusion. What remains, then, is to make an exhibit of this position in a series of systematically ordered truths. "To verify in this way the validity of one's starting point, by making this point of departure a point of arrival, is also the only way to lead other minds to it, that is, by initially taking a position where they think in order to conduct them, with the chain of intellectual determinism, to where they are."[51]

Although it is propounded here in relation to a simpler problem, this is the method Blondel used in *L'Action* to constitute, on the basis of Christianity, a philosophy conducive to leading others to its door.

For him it was not a question of verifying Christian dogmas, considered in themselves, but of testing the validity of Christianity's global exigency and its claim to be accepted as divine revelation under pain of damnation. To verify any kind of affirmation means, first of all, suspending any affirmation until one has succeeded in establishing the fact of its being well founded. This is to transform the point of departure into the point of arrival with the intention of returning to it only if one is forced to do so by its dialectical reappearance at the term of the negation. Thus, Blondel suspends his affirmation of belief and adopts as his point of departure the negation that various forms of unbelief oppose to it. He begins with what is most radical, the refusal even to admit that there is a problem of destiny and that our actions bear a responsibility within them. But in view of the unavoidable fact of action and after having analyzed what it inevitably implies, he shows step by step that each negation includes precisely what it claims to reject. Since the procedure is a rational one, it is valid in principle for everyone, even the unbeliever. It is the latter who constitutes the philosophy of *L'Action*, which is thus autonomous; it does not set out from faith in order to pretend that it arrives there. Blondel indicates this himself in his reply to Emile Bréhier:

> It has been given out that I secretly set out from previously accepted conclusions, from an irrational faith which must then be introduced, defended, made desirable. But, following the exigencies of the scientific, critical, and philosophical spirit, I have, starting with the Introduction and throughout the course of the work, constantly proceeded by the indirect and negative way, examing all solutions which were only rejected under the twofold constraint of an imperious logic and a vital exigency. I have thus always taken an inflexible stand against the conclusions I was forced to reach.[52]

This was the position he originally took in his thesis defense when confronted by a more subtle objection raised by Emile Boutroux. We cite here only the last lines of this reply, already referred to in the first chapter: "So I examine every variety of attempt that can possibly be made to escape what you call my secret postulate (willing the infinite); I seek with all the energy at my disposal to ignore it, to suppress it; I invent new kinds of ingenuity to escape. . . . But, after all these attempts, there only results a system of linked affirmations which, little by little, leads us to confront reflective thought and the will's option with what was already present at the origin of the movement we use to flee from it."[53]

Thus, far from presupposing the truth of Christianity or even the presence in man of a will for the infinite in his philosophical posture, Blondel makes himself successively the accomplice of all the attitudes and ways of thinking that deny them. And it is only under the pressure of a rational necessity that he goes beyond each one of them and finally brushes aside their common claim to restrict the will of man to the field of his activity.

The affirmation of the truth of Christianity is no more the starting point of the philosophical adventure than its conclusion. From this point of view there is a radical difference between the present question and the problem of idealism mentioned above. As a believer, Blondel knows that the affirmation of the truth of Christianity is not the necessary term of a dialectic but of an act of faith which is itself a gift of God. As a philosopher, he shows that it could not be otherwise if Christianity is divine revelation. The conclusions he feels constrained to end with come to a halt at the threshold of the faith, as he reminds us in his reply to Bréhier: "What do (these conclusions) consist in? Is it a case of proposing any single assertion composing Christian dogma? Not in the least. I do not introduce anything, I nowhere give any evidence of entering into the least content of the Catholic religion. I stop at the threshold; and, as a philosopher, I finally refuse to pronounce the one little word that I would have to utter as a believer."[54]

Thus, while Blondel's philosophy is worked out in view of the hypothesis of the truth of Christianity, it does not begin with this truth as a presupposition, and while it aims to prepare minds for the faith, it never crosses the threshold of the faith. Its intention is to remain from start to finish a purely rational development.

It is possible, of course, that the reader may not be convinced by his argument and may believe he discovers flaws in his logic. The same can be said for all philosophies. But this does not authorize us to question the intellectual autonomy and loyalty of their movement. Thus, it is not without surprise that we read these lines devoted to Blondel: "He thought he left philosophy free because he did not *tell* it that Christianity is true. . . . But he artificially arranged the entire development of philosophy in the direction of a discovery his heart desired. . . . It is possible that there is a free thought in the work of Blondel, but it is not certain that one can ever know where it is to be found."[55] Happily, the author of these remarks adds later on that he is not sure he has succeeded in grasping Blondel's position.[56] Indeed, it does take some application to grasp it; but one who has had the patience to analyze it cannot misunderstand its rational character.

Blondel was so concerned not to introduce any presupposition of faith into the body of his philosophical movement and to avoid every admixture of dogma and free reflection that, except in the first rough outlines of *L'Action*, he always manifested some reserve regarding the idea of "Christian philosophy." In the *Letter* of 1896 he even went so far as to write this statement which anticipated Bréhier's: "According to the sense in which the term is ordinarily understood, 'Christian philosophy' does not exist any more than does Christian physics."[57] It is true that this judgment has to do with the past and does not exclude a future possibility: "Strictly speaking, there has not yet been any Christian philosophy: as for the philosophy that bears this name, it is not entirely satisfactory either from a philosophical or a Christian point of view; if there can be a philosophy that fully merits the name, it has yet to be constituted."[58] Obviously, this is the task that Blondel set before himself. Furthermore, in his reply to Bréhier, he will offer a belated apology for the "juvenile intrepidity" he exhibited in maintaining that Christian philosophy does not exist, and he will withdraw "this all too summary judgment."[59] But he will maintain the concern for philosophical purity that inspired his stand and will continue to warn against the ambiguity of the term. The position he took in the course of the debates with Bréhier and Gilson on Christian philosophy, a position well in keeping with his abiding attitude, has been excellently defined in these lines in which the initial paradox is significant:

> As for Christian philosophy according to M. Blondel, it is *not yet* Christian. For it is philosophy itself which discovers concerning itself, in a final movement which is still only a work of pure rational reflection, that it does not "buckle." It is, then, a philosophy that will be open to Christianity but which in principle does not proceed in any sense from it, since, were it to want so to proceed, it could only do so by removing from Christianity its supernatural character at the very moment it had proclaimed it by its last admission.[60]

**Directive Hypothesis.** Blondel has been so emphatic in insisting on his philosophy's independence of every Christian presupposition that some Catholic thinkers have felt they should reproach him for retaining "a conception of the autonomy of philosophy that is still Cartesian," for conceiving it "as receiving nothing from without, as a deaf philosophy, and for trying to introduce into this deaf philosophy a Christian melody."[61] We have here a complete misunderstanding. If Blondel, as a philosopher, refuses himself the right to borrow directly from revelation and dogma, he is not deaf to the teachings of Christianity. We have seen that his original project was "to take the catechism and to translate it philosophically." Even after he had formulated his plan in a more subtle manner, he never stops repeating that the Christian philosopher "no longer has the power discretely to set a barrier between his beliefs and his own thought,"[62] that "the specifically Catholic idea" ought to give rise to "a philosophy that is better adapted to the extent that it is more autonomous,"[63] "it is a question of taking up again the philosophical problem in function of the idea that Christianity and its *rationabile obsequium* give us of the unique and supreme destiny which is, in fact, ours by obligation,"[64] that the Gospel doctrine must not be regarded as "unfit for penetrating and bringing the philosophical dough to a ferment."[65] Several times he declares that he owed much to the reading of St. Bernard and to the practice of the New Testament, especially of St. Paul.[66] He writes in 1917: "It is from St. Paul that I would willingly borrow the themes that were my inspiration: *Ipsi sibi* *lex . . . Ita ut sint inexcusabiles . . . Deo ignoto . . . Velle adjacet mihi; perficere autem in me non invenio . . . Stipendia peccati mors.* Or think once again of the admirable Psalm 118: *Lex lux."*[67]

We know from other sources that from his youth Blondel assiduously read a number of spiritual writers, ranging from the sixteenth to the nineteenth century. A list of readings he suggested for his cousin around 1887–1888 undoubtedly gives us some idea of what he himself had been reading at the time: St. Teresa, St. Francis de Sales, Guilloré, Rodriquez, Scupoli, Schram, Scaramelli.[68] A memo from the year 1890 supplies us with the information that during this period he had conceived the idea of feeding his philosophical thought. Taking note of the influence of Jacob Boehme and other German mystics on the modern German philosophical movement, he asks himself this question, which evidently manifests a personal project: "Will nothing of a philosophical nature issue from the Catholic saints and from the glorious theological and ascetical renaissance of the seventeenth to the nineteenth centuries?"

The reader of *L'Action* who is the least bit familiar with the writings mentioned by Blondel easily recognizes their influence diffused throughout the work. And in spite of the absence of references, he may even be able to identify the citations, whether explicit or implicit.

Among the authors Blondel borrows the most from, after the New Testament and St. Bernard, is St. Ignatius Loyola. This is explained when it is learned that the young philosopher followed the *Spiritual Exercises*[69] and that in a marginal note on the "first rough draft" of *L'Action* he exhorted himself to make use of them in his own work. There is a clear relationship, which merits analysis, between the "option" that is central in Blondel's thought and the "election" which is the heart of the *Exercises.* In both cases we find a decisive choice on which will depend man's earthly life and his eternal destiny, a choice implying detachment, "indifference" regarding creatures as such,[70] and all leading, through mortification,[71] to a total opening up to the divine action.[72] Citations and reminiscences bear witness to *L'Action's* dependence on the *Exercises.* We cannot refer in detail to everything Blondel borrowed from St. Ignatius,[73] nor can we examine the way he transposed it in order to adapt it to his own needs. But this source should be mentioned.[74]

It will be noted that it is principally in the New Testament and from spiritual writers that the young Blondel drew his knowledge of Christianity. Of course, he had diligently learned his catechism as a child and taken in what the liturgy conveys. But he had studied very little of what is taught under the name of dogmatic theology. He had read a bit of St. Thomas

Aquinas;[75] we find him implicity cited in *L'Action* and the *Letter* eulogizes him.[76] He was familiar with official documents, such as the text of the First Vatican Council.[77] He was in the habit of consulting a Dominican theologian, Père Beaudouin, on difficult points.[78] His knowledge of Christian dogma was solid and sure, but he restricted himself to the essential. He lacked that precision that the study of theology provides.

Later on he was to apply himself more earnestly to this study.[79] Furthermore, he would read St. Augustine, about whom he knew very little at the start; he would study the great Christian mystics, especially St. John of the Cross. His work would bear traces of these new discoveries, but we need not examine them here.

The indications offered above simply aim to demonstrate that Blondel's philosophy, far from wanting to be deaf to Christian teaching, listens to it, on the contrary, with attention. But what is important is to understand how it listens. It does not receive it *directly*, whether as a premise or as a conclusion. Neither at the start nor at the finish of his development as a philosopher did Blondel recognize his right to *affirm the truth* of Christianity. Throughout, he suspends any affirmation of this truth which he holds as a believer and which he feels he can only affirm as such. But also, throughout, he keeps before his eye the Christian *idea* in the form of a *hypothesis*. Not, be it noted, in order to examine it as a simple spectator curious to understand Christianity as he might understand some other religion. He wants to *verify* his hypothesis, at least to the extent that it is capable of being verified, short of the experience of faith.

As we have indicated, the object of the verification is the global experience of Christianity in relation to man, its claim to be accepted as divine revelation under pain of damnation. If this exigency is founded, there ought to be some trace of it in man, purely as man. But the philosopher must be on guard against wanting to find more than man, purely as man, should be able to find. He cannot determine the content of historic revelation nor even the specifically Christian notion of the supernatural. All this is proposed to man from the outside. He can simply show how this exterior datum corresponds to human aspirations. He brings about a confrontation between the Christian mysteries and the enigmas of reflection, but he does not incorporate dogma into philosophy.

Still, we have seen that, before taking up the examination of the Christian supernatural, the philosopher sees emerging out of the determinism of human action the idea of an indeterminate supernatural, that is, of an infinite that each man obscurely wants and to which he should submit himself, even when ignorant of a revelation. In other words, what comes to the fore is the idea of a divine action to which one ought to open up, no matter what it may turn out to be. To define what this opening up should be, Blondel proceeds through a rational analysis of the relation between the human will and the unique necessary. Through this philosophical approach, he makes contact with the most general teachings of Christian spirituality: a disinterested fidelity to duty, detachment and mortification, waiting for God. It is clear that these teachings of spiritual authors guided his development exteriorly, but he makes contact with them again by a rational approach. As distinguished from dogmas, in this case he does incorporate the substance of these spiritual teachings into the content of his philosophy. So instead of a confrontation, he brings about an intussusception. That is why the fourth part of *L'Action* takes on the aspect of a spiritual treatise, while the fifth part refuses to construct a dogmatic treatise.

It is useful to call attention to this difference. But from start to finish, although in different ways, Christianity is always the idea that guides the inquiry insofar as it is a hypothesis that is to be verified. It is the guiding idea from the very first pages of the work where the author raises the problem of human destiny, and throughout the first three parts, which show man's powerlessness in trying to find full satisfaction within the ordinary field of his activity.

We see how the Christian idea prompts or "gives rise to" an autonomous philosophy that is in agreement with the faith. It gives rise to it because what moves the inquiry is the concern to verify this idea, and because the inquiry itself is guided by the idea that helps to uncover the implicit dialectic of the various illusions. But the philosophy thus created is autonomous because it does not accept any idea, any affirmation, except in virtue of a necessity that its negation brings to the surface.

It will be recalled that Blondel speaks of "having attempted, as a believer, a philosopher's effort." This remark, which might have seemed paradoxical, should now be clear. The philosophical effort involved here is that of a believer, in the sense that the author starts with the hypothesis of the truth of Christianity in order to verify it for himself and bring others to it. The development is guided by the Christian idea and it does have an apologetic aim. But what he attempts *as a believer,* he does not bring about *insofar as he is a believer;* for, from start to finish, he suspends his affirmation of faith in order to retrieve progressively the rational presuppositions behind it through an analysis of the logic immanent in every human action.

*Integral Philosophy.* Thus far we have showed how Blondelian thought, although prompted by the Christian idea and aiming to justify it, has the qualities of a truly philosophical development. Is this enough to prove that it is a true philosophy in the classical and plenary sense of the term? To be sure, we no longer have the right to say that it is merely an apologetics in the pejorative sense of an irrational movement, as Bréhier understood the word. But even in the ordinary Christian understanding of the term, apologetics is supposed to be a rational development; and, properly understood, it should develop under the same conditions and satisfy the same exigencies as philosophy does according to Blondel's conception of it. One might be tempted to say, then, that this kind of philosophy corresponds more to what might be called philosophical apologetics than to philosophy. Again, one might want to classify it under the rubric of "Christian philosophy," with the idea that the Christian aim restricts the breadth of the philosophical aim.

A judgment of this kind is directly opposed to what the author expressly says. It is his view that "the only philosophy that suits Catholicism and which it suits" is precisely "Philosophy itself,"[80] and that the problem of constituting "philosophy," pure and simple, is the same as constituting a "Christian philosophy."[81]

This identity, he explains, is the net product of the history of Western philosophy. In a passage of the *Letter* already referred to, he shows that "philosophy itself was gradually transformed and accurately determined under the misunderstood and rejected Christian idea."[82] Hellenic speculation "tended to envelop the entire order of thought and reality in order to make an absolute pronouncement on the truth of objects of every sort, in order to prefer or substitute theory for practice, and in order to find within itself, along with the first and last word on all things, a kind of divine sufficiency. Yes, its tacit postulate was the divinity of Reason, . . . in the sense that our speculative knowledge includes the supreme virtue and by itself consummates the divine work within us."[83] The Middle Ages established a provisional equilibrium between this philosophy and Christianity, but its attempt was shown to be unstable. But "it is just because Scholasticism opened to reason the immensity of the horizons of faith that, left to itself, this human reason could no longer forget the world it had glimpsed nor give up the attempt to find its equivalent. . . . By the very fact that emancipated philosophy still tends, as before, to hold that thought is what is most divine and that it has within it its own sufficiency, it is no longer what it once was. Unknown to itself, it proposes an ideal that does not come from itself alone."[84] It thus proposes a rambling series of proofs and attempts, both useful and deceptive. The author describes them in the course of a brief sketch of the history of modern philosophy.[85] He shows how this philosophy, impregnated with the Christian idea against which it struggles, progressively restricts its own scope and must finally give up the hegemony and autosufficiency claimed by Aristotle's thought or by that of Spinoza.[86] It is brought to recognize that "even an integral knowledge of thought and life fails to supply or suffice for the action of thinking and living,"[87] that philosophy cannot procure being, beatitude, or salvation for man.[88]

An earlier study had already developed the same theme at greater length.[89] Commenting on the book of Victor Delbos, *Le problème moral dans la philosophie de Spinoza et dans l'histoire du Spinozisme*, Blondel discerns in this philosophy "the continuity of the great and vain effort attempted and still pursued by human reason to create for itself, by its own powers, a spiritual home."[90] He shows the transformations that Spinoza's thought had to undergo in the course of its passage through German idealism. Finally, he indicates the transformations it still calls for, and concludes: "The great undertaking of metaphysics to supplant moral and religious practice cannot succeed. It is at this conclusion, one of sovereign importance, that we must arrive. And this whole saga of Spinozan thought will have at least served to emphasize a truth that was implicated in Christianity without a doubt, but which the work of reflection had not yet fully released: It is that knowledge, even adequate knowledge, does not supply for action."[91] "The notion of immanence, which this rationalism that claims to hold a monopoly over 'modern thought' has established as the basis and condition for all philosophy, far from excluding, requires, if it is completely developed, the transcendent truths to which it seemed at first to be so radically hostile."[92] "In discovering, in accordance with the exigencies of the rationalist critique, what is immanent in us, we are necessarily led to recognize the necessity of the transcendent truths that are immanent in it (action)."[93]

We see how Christian philosophy, as Blondel develops it, is in his eyes the normal outcome of the "becoming" of philosophy, and that it can, in this sense, be presented as "philosophy." He says that, "thanks to the secret and gentle action of the Christian spirit, which it seems to combat and which seems to resist it," what triumphs at the term of the secular conflict between rationalism and the Christian spirit is "Philosophy itself, a philosophy which emerges out of the evolution of modern thought, not as a transient accident but as an acquisition justified in itself."[94]

The study on the evolution of Spinozism and various extracts from letters and notes we have had occasion to cite, attest to the fact that

Blondel wanted to do for Catholicism what German idealism did for Protestantism. He explicitly states this in a letter dating from 1894: "In order to extract from Catholicism everything it contains that is rational, I undertook what Germany attempted long ago and continues to try to do for Protestant forms of thought whose philosophy is, admittedly, easier to isolate."[95]

But he does not limit himself to the examination of Christianity. As in the case of German idealism, he integrates this study into the total field of thought and human activity. He aims at "the constitution of integral philosophy within integral Christianity."[96] The Trilogy and the work on the Christian spirit will be offered as the fulfillment of this program. Without claiming to be that complete, *L'Action* of 1893 had already set a very broad perspective before itself. Examining all the doctrines that try to curtail willing to this or that sector of human activity, it runs through the whole field of this activity. Criticizing in progressive order those systems that are like stances of the spirit, it weaves together a rational chain of different postures, which it simultaneously retains and surpasses. It thus realizes for its part some degree of that integrality that is the goal of all philosophy.

Thus, it is not a simple apology for Christianity. Nor is it a simple philosophy of religion. Even when it prefers to take its position in terms of one or the other of these aspects, we must be very careful not to reduce it to any of them.

## THE LOGIC OF ACTION AND THE METHOD OF IMMANENCE

Blondel gave two names to the rational process that warranted his constructing a philosophy that would be autonomous as well as Christian. He called it "logic of action" in *L'Action* and "method of immanence" in the *Letter* of 1896. It was on his own initiative that he created the first term. The second does not appear in *L'Action* and was forced on him by the need to reply to the review of his work that appeared in *Revue de Métaphysique et de Morale* (Léon Brunschvicg was the author) which challenged the rational character of his effort in the name of the "notion of immanence," proposed as the condition for any and every philosophical doctrine.[97] Blondel fought back by insisting that *notion* was exactly the norm of his own approach, adding, however, that, fully developed in the course of a study of action, it did not lead to a *doctrine* of immanence but, rather, demanded those transcendent truths to which it originally seemed hostile. Hence the term: *method of immanence.* Since this term drew opposition from the Catholic side, he quickly abandoned it. For the same reason we have thought it best to limit its use. Except for instances when we were offering a commentary on a text which used the term, we have preferred to advance the term Blondel first chose and never abandoned: logic of action.

"It is the role of the logic of action," wrote Blondel, "to determine the chain of necessities that make up the drama of life and lead inexorably to the denouement."[98] Or, a few pages later, its purpose is "to determine what is inevitable and necessary in the total expansion of human action."[99] This is also the way in which the *Letter* describes the role of the method of immanence: It is a question of analyzing the "determinism of action." If we recall that this term expresses the "dynamism of the spiritual life,"[100] the "logical process of life,"[101] or "the real dialectic of human action,"[102] it can be more easily admitted that "method of immanence" and "logic of action" join forces and that the second term expresses more directly what the issue is.

In presenting *L'Action* and the *Letter,* in describing the genesis of the idea of the supernatural, in explaining the relation between the phenomenological description and the ontological affirmation, we have already given an account of the process referred to. Still, it is not inappropriate to gather together here the scattered raw material and offer some kind of synthesis. We shall do this by first examining Henry Duméry's preferred thesis: The method of immanence is nothing but the reflexive method.

Duméry writes: "Strange as it may seem to some, the fundamental intention of Blondel is to return philosophy to the critical and reflexive attitude."[103] Here the interpreter presents polemically a judgment he will repeat in various commentaries. For the equivocal term, the method of immanence, he substitutes the method of reflexive analysis. Blondel's method, he says, is "to uncover by reflection the conditions of intelligibility and realization for living thought or for effective acting."[104] This method is founded entirely on the distinction between "the formal plane of reflection" and "the real plane of action."[105] Operating on daily human acting, reflection "projects in an ideal order the whole series of notions or norms that form the intelligible structure of action; this ideal order is a determinism, a linking together of determinisms; it 'reflects' all that action is unable not to implicate: the necessary and the universal, which allow it to have a meaning and to realize it." But "this ideal series is only a collection of hypothetical conditions"; their realization depends on freedom. Reflection communicates norms and prescribes that man should decide according to them; it is the option that realizes.[106] Thus, following this distinction, "all notions (ideals or norms) enter into a homogeneous series of intelligible conditions, even though living spirituality and its movements do not enter into the series themselves."[107] So we must say that "the subject, as such, freedom or thought in act (a fortiori, the Absolute) are transcendent in relation to the ideal determinism which, contrariwise, is said to be imma-nent, that is, immanent within the spectrum of reflexive thought. . . . In brief, to practice the method of immanence is, essentially and above all, to induce philosophy to be a reflexive critique and, consequently, to suppose that to advance to the realm of being, to lived values, to God, we must take a step that is not only formal but also reflexive and effective."[108] Blondel's method is related, then, to other forms of reflexive analysis, in particular to Lagneau's method, which, in its turn, reserves for the act of freedom the task of realizing the world for us.[109]

In view of its vivid articulation, its clear distinctions, and its suggestive comparisons, this interpretation is highly illuminating and stimulating. It often helps the reader to find his way in the lush underbrush of Blondel's lavish exposition. Personally, we are indebted to it for a sharper perception of certain relations. But as we compare it step by step with the texts, it seems to simplify and depart from them. So, to speak frankly, with no little esteem for the interpreter and in the course of a friendly dialogue which need not disguise differences, we believe that his description of Blondel's reflexive analysis misses a salient point and that Blondel's philosophical method cannot, in any case, be reduced to reflexive analysis.

***Regressive Analysis.*** It should be noted first that the term "reflexive analysis," so frequently to the fore in Duméry's commentaries, is rare in Blondel's writings. As a matter of fact, we have not succeeded in finding it in *L'Action* nor in the *Letter*. At the end of *L'Action* the author indicates that he has proceeded by "regressive analysis."[110] In later writings he will speak of "analytic reflection" or "retrospection." Perhaps it would be preferable to adhere to this terminology. Still, one cannot condemn the use of a synonym consecrated by long tradition. What is essential is that the process, so designated, be also correctly described.

The regressive analysis begins with an empirical fact and retreats to its conditions of possibility. When the fact in question is action, considered as a dynamism in the process of expansion, the search for conditions of possibility becomes a search for conditions of realization. It is in this sense that Blondel declares that he has carried out a "regressive analysis": he has exposed the series of necessary conditions and means successively required for constituting action little by little.[111] Duméry interprets faithfully, then, when he writes that the reflexive analysis employed by Blondel consists in determining "the series of conditions of realization of action."[112]

But, beyond this general agreement, a specific difference appears. For Blondel, the regressive analysis aims at determining what is "necessary for the will so that action may be set in equation in consciousness."[113] It is a question of discovering "how to equal the term willed and the principle of voluntary aspiration."[114] We successively observe the lack of adequation of each term until the final condition for the equation sought makes its appearance. In a word, the moving element of the analytic regression is the dialectic of the will-as-willed (*volonté voulue*) and the will-as-willing (*volonte voulante*).

But whenever Duméry turns to defining the reflexive method of Blondel, he avoids all mention of this dialectic, not by inadvertence but by set purpose. We have already noted that he judges certain formulas of the *Letter* equivocal, among them the very ones that define the method of immanence, and which define it as a description of this dialectic. In following the movement they suggest, we come to recognize, at the source of voluntary action, a willing of the infinite, a need for the supernatural. But Duméry believes that, according to Blondel, and in conformity with Christian dogma, such a need can only be recognized through a practical verification which is carried out in the act of faith. So, with respect to the formulas in question, it must be admitted that Blondel confuses steps and fails to adhere to the method of immanence, "which ought never to confuse the reflexive and the concrete planes."[115] Consequently, the formula in the *Letter* that seems to Duméry to provide "the most unequivocal definition" is the following: "The method of immanence is limited to determining the dynamism of our representations without our having initially to pronounce on their subjective or objective meaning . . . "[116] Here the distinction between the "reflexive plane" and the "ontological plane" clearly appears. Moreover, once the interpreter has taken care to translate from the start "dynamism of our representations" by "homogeneous series of intelligible conditions,"[117] then the dialectic of the will-as-willed and the will-as-willing, still suggested by Blondel's expression, disappears from the horizon.

This same transposition occurs throughout Duméry's exegesis. When Blondel speaks of the "determinism of action," his interpreter translates determinism by "series of determinations"[118] or "chain of determinations";[119] and he explains that these notions or norms form "the intelligible structure of action."[120] The reflexive analysis consists in releasing this intelligible structure, in projecting this structure in an ideal order which becomes imperative and normative.[121] It is a description of the already lived, from which there emerges a program for action.[122] But we no longer see with sufficient clarity that it is an analysis of the conditions in virtue of which the *volonté voulue* will equal the *volonté voulante.*

We cannot rid ourselves of the idea that this exegesis involves a transmutation or, at least, lets escape what is most characteristic in Blondel's regressive analysis. This characteristic element is to be found precisely in what Duméry regards as equivocal. One would have to recognize this, even if it were to be admitted that Blondel's procedure mixes up levels of action and leads to unacceptable conclusions. In examining the genesis of the idea of the supernatural, we have showed that nothing warrants this harsh judgment. The need for the supernatural that Blondel's dialectic reveals at the heart of willing is not directly the need for the Christian supernatural; and the passage from one notion to the other is brought about in such a way that the exigencies of dogma are respected. On the other hand, the effective willing that the method of immanence uncovers is not the explicit willing that is operative in the realm of faith, but the implicit willing that is at the source of the spontaneous activity of every man, even the unbeliever. Thus, it cannot be said that the respective roles of philosophy and practical decision are mixed up. We have no reason for not accepting in their obvious sense the formulas of the *Letter* that define the method of immanence through a search for the equation between the *volonté voulue* and the *volonté voulante,* or between what is represented and the concrete act of living thought.

In modifying the conception of the regressive analysis, Duméry modifies the Blondelian idea of a philosophy of religion. He makes this philosophy of religion, in great part, a rational critique of positive religion, that is, an "examination of religion itself in its most subtle structure,"[123] an analysis "bearing directly on the structural apparatus of the religious fact,"[124] a movement of philosophy aiming at understanding and judging this fact "as it is distributed along the planes of consciousness of the subject who welcomes it."[125] Confronted with the Christian fact, reserving the question of its effective truth, it is a question of examining the ideal conditions that determine its intelligiblity, and of saying on what conditions it would be reasonable and obligatory to adhere to it. In this view Blondel would be applying to the Christian fact a somewhat revised version of the Kantian method of transcendental analysis.[126]

We have indicated the reservations and qualifications this reduction to the Kantian method seems to require.[127] We may limit ourselves here to recalling what directly concerns the Blondelian method in its examination of positive religion.

The moment the author of *L'Action* begins this examination, he sets out to show that the Christian claim represents what appears to the philosopher as *the necessary condition for the achievement of human action.* Blondel himself indicates that the analytic character of the method lies precisely in this demonstration, which supposes the problem resolved (accepting Christian doctrine and practice as hypotheses), and it verifies the fictitious solution "by way of analysis"[128] (by establishing that the hypothesis is necessary as a condition for the achievement of action). The analysis, then, does not consist in sorting out elements of the Christian claim or in criticizing its structures, but in discovering in the name of the determinism of human action the necessity and coherence of the hypothesis.[129] Dogmas and rites do not constitute for Blondel the idea to be examined but the idea in virtue of which he can determine the ultimate exigencies of willing.

Duméry recognizes that Blondel only partially realized his goal of initiating a direct critique of religious structures; for the most part he limited himself to a confrontation between philosophical problems and theological deliverances.[130] Still his theory of the supernatural was not simply the result of such a confrontation; it was a philosophical critique of a theological notion.[131] Actually, at the beginning of the fifth part of *L'Action*, at the very moment the author takes up the examination of the Christian idea of the supernatural, several pages explicitly bear the running title: "the critique of the notion of the supernatural."[132] But these are the very pages that announce that the method will consist in "confronting" dogmas with the profound exigencies of the will in order eventually to discover there "the image of our real needs."[133] So it is not a question of a critique bearing directly on the structural apparatus of the religious factor or on religious expression. When Blondel initiates the "critique" of the notion of revelation, in no sense does he set about sifting the anthropomorphism of the expression; he simply wants to show that this notion, exteriorly proposed, also wells up from an interior initiative.[134] The term critique here refers to the study of the genesis, as the author explicitly tells us.[135]

It is true that the fourth part of *L'Action* does not include an explicit confrontation between dogmas and philosophical exigencies. It shows how the idea of the indeterminate supernatural rises up in each man. The immanent idea that it throws into relief is the idea through which man will be able to discover a meaning in the specifically Christian idea. This study will then make it possible later on to "deduce" the Christian idea by a confrontation between it and the immanent idea. By the same token it will make it possible to provide a basis for Christian positivity. But Blondel does not require that his study determine what critical coefficient can be drawn out of its various expressions.

We speak here, of course, in the role of a historian. As a philosopher or theologian, we would have to say that it is necessary to set up a critique of religious expression. St. Thomas himself set forth the principle in his doctrine of the analogy of the divine names. This bare outline should be developed, taking into account the acquisitions of modern thought and the science of religions. On this basis, Duméry's enterprise in his personal work as a philosopher is legitimate, and the reservations that some of his conclusions or even some of the principles elicit, should not blind us to this fact.[136] However, Blondel's enterprise was something quite different.

We should remember this when Blondel declares that philosophy is not reduced "to a purely explicative critique without any judicial role," and that "in what is transcendent in immanent thought and action, it discovers an internal principle of absolute judgment."[137] The judicial principle that Blondel draws out of philosophy is not the one Duméry claims for it. It does not consist in "marking each religious structure with a critical index destined to situate it on the scale of levels of consciousness," nor in "differentiating the noetic levels" and "integrating them into the design for a single intentionality."[138] It consists in defining in the name of the determinism of action what our life ought to be. For Blondel, philosophy discovers "that there is in our general and deeper will a *logic* whose actual exigencies we have only to discover as implicated in what we think and as proposed by what we actually do, . . . in order to recognize, under the fragmentary appearances of a life in the process of becoming, what it ought to be, thanks to a clearer understanding of what it is unable not to be."[139] Thus, what philosophy examines and judges are not religious structures but human life. And it judges life in the name of the internal logic of action.

*A Practicing Philosophy.* We have explained the sense in which the method of immanence, which makes explicit this logic of action, is a regressive analysis or an analytic reflection. We must now show that it is also, and necessarily so, a prospection, that is, a direct, practical, and synthetic knowledge.

The distinction and complementarity of these two processes was explained by Blondel in 1906 in an especially precise fashion in the course of a study already mentioned, "Le point de départ de la recherche philosophique."[140]

> There is a first knowledge which, perfect in its genre, is direct, at the service of our real and actual purposes, bound to our total life, turned toward the future which it anticipates as though to gain support from it by foreseeing and evoking it, capable of growing in clarity and precision without losing its unitive and practical character. It is this knowledge that the greater number of men are content with and which, in the business of living, no one can dispense with.[141]

This knowledge suffices for the needs of daily practical action, and it also suffices for resolving the problem of destiny. Viewed precisely as a direct knowledge, it is distinguished from "knowledge turned toward results obtained or procedures used, as analyzed retrospectively by abstraction."[142] So that he may reserve the name "reflection" for this latter type of knowledge, which merits the designation in the strict sense of the word, Blondel proposes to call the first type "prospection," a term which has the advantage of stressing the elements of shrewdness, deliberation, and circumspection.[143]

Referring to this distinction of the two types of knowledge, prospective and retrospective, Duméry declares that philosophy is an example of the second,[144] and this is true. But he does not say that it also employs the first type. Yet in the very study referred to, Blondel explains that philosophy, in its technical construction, ought to unite and coordinate, just as they are in life, practical prospection and reflection.[145]

In somewhat different terms Blondel had already expressed the same idea in a notebook, dated 1900, containing a series of notes for the second edition of *L'Action*.[146] There he distinguishes two aspects of his research: "(1) The progressive and synthetic advance of spontaneous life in the quest for an effective solution. (2) The reflective regression and the technical or intellectual expression which projects the light of the vital term on the origins of the route."[147] On the one hand, he wants "to describe man's groping in search of his destiny," "a work of spontaneous or reflective inquiry that brings into play all our powers of living and thinking," "a work which is life itself" and whose description is "drawn from an inner experience." On the other hand, he wants "to extract from these complex movements of life and from these practical experiences, from these soundings, from these successive and progressive gropings, the theoretical and philosophical meaning they conceal."[148] To avoid misunderstandings, he proposes to distinguish these two aspects of the inquiry more precisely than he did in the first edition. But he does not wish to separate them in two different books because they are vitally united. "The method of dialectical discovery is not legitimately separable from the method of effective progression. . . . Each vital process promotes and permits a process of reflection which, in its turn, sustains and even commands a new movement of life, a new increment of action."[149]

All of this is characteristic of the procedure of the work published in 1893. There the regressive analysis is constantly moved on by a prospection which it commands at each step. But it is not enough to ascertain that such is the case; it cannot even be clearly perceived unless we understand why it must be the case.

In *L'Action* the regressive analysis is not applied as in Kant to a stable given, namely, to science as already constituted or to the moral law as a universal form. It is applied to human action seen as a dynamism in the process of expansion. This action, which is a fact, is still not exactly a "given"; rather, it "gives" itself out in the course of the movement by which it expands. That is the reason why the intellectual movement that reflects it ought to be prospective as well as regressive. It is a question of determining "what is inevitable and necessary in the total expansion of human action."[150] The disclosure of the necessary is surely a regressive analysis. But the necessities interior to action "are only revealed in and through the development of its inner history. So it is necessary to take one's position, as it were, within it and take part in this dialectic of real life."[151] If the will, says Blondel,

> . . . has a rule to observe, an operation to produce, moral and social relations to institute, it is through this expansion that it will discover them, thanks to a method of incomparable originality. For it is the *a priori* initiative of this free activity which, in its expansion, ought to reconstitute the necessity to which it is subject, so to speak, *a posteriori*; thus, the heteronomy of the law will correspond to its interior autonomy. . . . Here lies the unique character of practical experimentation: Voluntary action in some way provokes the response and the teachings of what is outside; and these lessons imposed on the will are, nonetheless, enveloped in this will itself. All that follows will justify this view.[152]

Blondel will often make the same point in various forms adapted to each step.[153] Each time the same circumincession of the *a priori* and the *a posteriori* makes its appearance. The initial *élan* of the will is measured only in the context of the successive experiences it assumes. The description of its expansion is inseparably both analytic reflection and synthetic prospection.

That is why we cannot admit that the "fundamental intention of Maurice Blondel" was to "lead philosophy to the reflexive and critical attitude."[154] Certainly, Duméry does not intend to deny the prospective character of Blondel's thought. But he rarely mentions it. He even seems to look on it as an imperfection.[155] For him, what constitutes philosophy is the reflexive analysis. But Blondel consciously wanted to go beyond this conception, which seemed incomplete to him. Thus, he wrote: "It seems to be a foregone conclusion that philosophy is nothing but a retrospection on realities and initiatives that precede its intervention and are independent of it. Speculation is given the task of releasing and determining the theoretical principles that rule the natural order and practical applications. But one does not ordinarily suppose that actual practice is, in its turn, an original source of knowledge and of lessons."[156] "Not only should philosophy live and grow in a man, but his human life ought to enter as an integrating element in his philosophy, as a living wellspring, as a new force of intellectual speculation."[157] It is this that characterizes the philosophy of action; it is a "practicing philosophy."[158] It is in this way that Blondel expresses his thought in 1937 when he was reworking the *Action* of 1893 to integrate it into the speculative philosophy of the Trilogy. At the start of his career he was even more radical: "Philosophy," he said, "only begins when, not content with drawing upon the idea of action as its proper object, it subordinates itself to effective action and becomes 'practicing.' Action done is an integrating condition for philosophical knowledge."[159] In this perspective "philosophy no longer appears as a simple extract of life, as a representation, as a spectacle; it is life itself in the process of assuming consciousness and direction of itself."[160] Let us say that the philosophy of action is less a reflection *on* action than a reflection *of* action on itself.

So it is developed in a way that is quite different from that of a simple transcendental analysis. If the development of Blondel's thought bears some resemblance to the thought of Kant or Hegel, it is more reminiscent of the Hegel of the *Phenomenology of the Spirit*. No doubt, whether it is a question of the method or of conclusions, the difference between the two works is profound. But one thing is of interest here, and it is that, in spite of everything, we find in both cases a "scientific knowledge" which gives itself over, without reservation, to life and the dialectic movement of human reality, and which thus assists in its own genesis and evolution.

Duméry recognizes that Blondelian philosophy maintains the "solidarity" of the two "planes," the reflexive and the concrete.[161] But this is not saying enough; there is circumincession. To speak of "planes," even when they are solidary, even when linked together, does not indicate sufficiently that reflection emerges from life and leads back to it, that "the idea is living and full to the degree that it aims at action itself and is nourished by it."[162] It is surely a laudable task to want to clear this position of the charge of anti-intellectualism. But, while it is true that Blondelian philosophy does not denigrate intelligence, it is also hard to characterize it as an "integral intellectualism."[163] To reach this conclusion, one would have to relax considerably the tight intercommunication Blondel established between reflection and practice.

That he clearly distinguished them within this communication is incontestable. We have seen how much care he gave to this concern, and Duméry was right to insist on it. But we ought also to recall that, in a "study of action by action,"[164] this distinction comes out as purely formal because the form released by reflection is identical with the form of action and cannot be released except by following the movement of action. The intelligible structure of human action is identical with the real dialectic of human action.

This identity is veiled in Duméry's definition of the word *immanence*. He says that for Blondel the word refers to "the plane of analytic reflection (where the philosopher acts professionally)," whereas transcendence refers to "the plane of concrete acting, where the freedom of man, the divine presence and action are situated."[165] Note, first, that it would be hard to force into this scheme Blondel's different uses of the two terms. It is true that he writes that the reflective or philosophical view is transcendent with respect to the action it represents; and when he declares that action is transcendent with respect to the reflective view, he understands that this action itself is immanent to us. This association of the relations is occasionally brought out in a single sentence: "On the one hand, what is immanent to us, as action and living thought, remains transcendent to the reflective or philosophical view that we have of it, and, on the other hand, this philosophical knowledge constitutes a phenomenon that is subsequent to and transcendent to what it represents."[166] So we cannot say purely and simply that immanence refers to the plane of analytic reflection, whereas transcendence refers to the plane of concrete acting.[167] Actually, immanence always refers to what is immanent in us, "what is truly in consciousness,"[168] "what we truly and invincibly think,"[169] "the integral series of our inevitable ideas and our solidary conceptions";[170] in a word, to the determinism of action. Depending on whether this determinism is seen as implicitly lived or explicitly known, the same term, immanence, covers both action or spontaneous thought and reflection. So it is not wedded solely to the plane of reflection. Consequently, from the point of view of terminology, "method of immanence" is not synonymous with "reflexive method." The term signifies, rather, that reflection releases the exigencies that are immanent to action or to spontaneous thought. Thus, it refers both to the identity as well as to the distinction of the intelligible structure and the real dialectic of action. "For we do not seek anything within ourselves that is not there already seminally, and we find nothing there that is not made evident and valid by the work of reflection."[171]

It is undeniable that Blondel regarded this affirmation as of paramount importance, that no one seriously denies this, but that philosophers, in his estimation, have generally neglected it: "Life and the knowledge of life are distinct"; "action and the idea of action are heterogeneous and irreducible."[172] The question then arises as to how Duméry, whose exegesis gives a central place to the distinction Blondel made central in his thought, manages to arrive at an interpretation of this thought that is sometimes incomplete and sometimes inexact. The reason seems to be that he has not paid sufficient attention to the typical Blondelian sense of this distinction and, moreover, wanted to find in it the soul of the method of immanence, whereas it simply defines the limit this method imposes.

Every reflexive philosophy (and, in fact, every philosophy conscious of itself) sets up at the start the distinction between the lived concrete and the formal conditions for intelligibility. But this is not *all* that Blondel means when he declares that action and the idea of action are heterogeneous and irreducible. Beyond this and above all he affirms the insufficiency of philosophy's power to put us in possession of being, that is, of the absolute, and the necessity for a generous action, if it is to be attained. Such is the obvious sense of the explanations that follow the statement: "Every system stubbornly bent on situating being at the term of speculative inquiry will finally fail in its affirmations. For the plenitude of being lies precisely in what separates the abstract idea from the act which is its origin, from the act to which it directs us as its unique mission."[173] "It is not just by viewing alone but by life that we advance into being, by making a kind of leap of generosity beyond the range of intellectual justifications. To possess is more than to affirm, but we only affirm better to the degree that we possess more: we cannot have being more in the mind without having it more in our acts."[174] "Once it closes in on itself, pretending to suffice unto itself and for life, philosophy is against nature."[175]

These citations indicate clearly the sense in which Blondel proposes his distinction between life and the knowledge of life. The reader will recognize here the thesis we explained at length when studying the role of the religious option in the ontological affirmation and the relation between the knowledge of phenomena and the plenary knowledge of being. We have already indicated at the end of the chapter in question that the distinction between the "reflexive plane" and the "ontological plane," as understood by Duméry, does not show clearly that for Blondel the ontological problem is the problem of the relation between human discourse and the absolute. And we gave the reasons: Under the name of "ontological plane," the interpreter constantly mixes two very distinct questions: the question of *being* and the question of *fact*.[176] By the question of fact or of existence or of reality, he means particularly the question of knowing whether there is a divine revelation and whether Christianity is, in fact, this revelation. But this is something quite different from the question of knowing how each man, even when ignorant of Christianity, can affirm and possess being, that is, enter into communion with the absolute. In treating the "ontological plane," on the one hand, as synonymous with the "concrete plane" or the "real plane of action," on the other hand, one all but obliterates what is most characteristic in Blondel's thought. The pregnant distinction, by which he signifies the insufficiency of reflection and the necessity of sacrifice in order to communicate with the absolute, is reduced to a simple and banal distinction between the ideal and the real, between what is reflected upon and lived.

When Blondel says that theory does not supply for practice, it is translated: "The idea must always lead back to the real, knowledge must always be directed to willing and doing."[177] The translation is exact enough but insufficient. As we have seen, what Blondel wants to say is that philosophy is unable "to furnish the being whose notion it studies, to contain the life whose exigencies it analyzes, to suffice unto that whose sufficient conditions it stipulates, even to realize that concerning which it must say that it necessarily conceives it as real."[178] This surely goes far beyond the simple prescription to return to the real and to act in conformity with the norms discerned by reflection.

Moreover, it is important to understand the sense in which Blondelian philosophy "prescribes."[179] We are told that after having manifested to the understanding "the ideal order that action implies," "reflection imposes on freedom the necessity of pronouncing, of *opting*, that is, of choosing for or against the order."[180] Actually, it is not simply a question of choosing for or against the order but, more profoundly, as the same interpreter indicates elsewhere,[181] of choosing for or against opening to the absolute, to the unique necessary. But what we wish to stress above all is that, strictly speaking, the philosophy of action *does not prescribe opting*, but shows that every man *opts necessarily*. Then it establishes that only the positive option puts him in possession of being; and it is in this very precise sense that it prescribes opting, not for or against, but *for* openness to the unique necessary. This remark is not just cavilling with words. It sets in relief that by means of which Blondel wants to guarantee the unity of theory and practice or "the bond of knowledge and action in being." The bond lies precisely in the fact that the necessary affirmation of being *inevitably* moves through an option which renders it privative or possessive of being.

Thus, when Blondel distinguishes theory and practice and declares that the former does not supply for the latter, his aim goes far beyond the implications of the explanations offered us on the distinction between the reflective plane and the concrete plane. And the relationship he establishes between them is not simply one of solidarity but a dialectical relation implying a return from division to unity.

Finally, let it be noted that this distinction is not the soul of the method of immanence, but simply indicates its limit. It is this limit that is specified by the formula purported to contain "the most unequivocal definition" of the Blondelian method: "The method of immanence is limited to determining the dynamism of our representations, without our having initially to pronounce on their subjective or objective sense. . . ."[182] The rest of the sentence moves in the same direction: " . . . it is a question simply of analyzing this inevitable idea of a relation of dependence between reason and the human will and all the consequences it implies." Blondel than repeats this notion even more pointedly: Philosophy "restricts the formal signification of its conclusions within the limits of its method of immanence," in the sense that it does not claim "to supply for the effective solution which it cannot furnish."[183] But before indicating the limits of the method, he defined its movement which, as we have seen, consists in the quest for the equation between the *volonté voulue* and the *volonté voulante,* or between representation and the concrete act of living thought. It is here that we must find the soul of the method of immanence.

Let us call a halt at this point to the discussion of this method. We began with an interpretation proposed in these terms: "Curious as it may seem to some, the fundamental intention of Blondel is to bring philosophy· back to the reflexive and critical attitude."[184] We believe we have showed how this judgment is "curious," what reservations it evokes, what kind of reduction was back of it, and how the truth it contains should be preserved.

***Agnition.*** Among the characteristics of Blondel's "practicing philosophy," there is one we have not as yet directly treated: The philosophy of action cannot be constituted nor win acceptance unless there is free consent. It is true that throughout *L'Action* passage from one step to another is only brought about in terms of a rational necessity. However, Blondel himself says that this necessity is not something that is simply recorded; it has to be freely recognized. This is a constant element in Blondelian thought. It is proper to make a special point of this and show how it does not contradict the rationality that his thought lays claim to.

We read in the 1937 edition of *L'Action*: "At each stage the temptation to halt arises, to become complacent, to bank on our acquired positions. At each stage we are not so much constrained as sincerely obliged to pass beyond."[185]

This declaration does not appear in the text of 1893. In fact, we find in the earlier edition some formulas that seem to attribute a constraining value to the dialectic. In a passage found in the Conclusion, inserted at the last moment as a response to the objection of Boutroux to which reference has been made above, Blondel wrote: "If this need (of the infinite) is in us, how can we pretend that it is not, how escape from the necessity of recognizing it?" Out of the many attempts to discover an escapeway, "all that results is a system of linked affirmations which, little by little, *constrain* us to set before reflective thought the term that was already present at the origin of the movement used to flee from it."[186]

As Cartier has remarked in his unusually penetrating analysis, "here Blondel's expressions go beyond the depth of his thought."[187] Carried away by his desire to justify the rationality of the movement, the young philosopher would seem to imply that the necessary truth of action must be imposed on all minds without their having freely to recognize it. But it must also be noted that the expressions whose obvious sense would seem to favor this interpretation (they have already been indicated above), are completely absent from the account of the thesis defense published by the Abbé Wehrlé fourteen years later and sanctioned by Blondel (see above).[188]

Above all, it must be noted that in *L'Action* itself Blondel was emphatic in noting that the internal exigencies of the *volonté voulante*, in spite of their inexorable character, can only be freely recognized. One passage in the last chapter is particularly precise in this respect since it links the two complementary aspects in a single sentence. Of "all the conditions of human life, sensible, scientific, intellectual, moral, and religious," Blondel maintains that "although they are spontaneously implied in us, we have to recognize them by a free effort; ... although we can revolt against them, they do not cease to be realized in us."[189]

It might be said that this is a global affirmation, that it simply refers to the resumption of the total determinism of action in the context of the religious option, that it in no way signifies the freedom of the process by which we advance step by step along the line of the determinism itself. We think that such an interpretation unduly limits the scope of the affirmation. No doubt, in his eagerness to convince and carry the reader along, Blondel insists throughout his work on the rational necessity of going beyond each step when one might be tempted to stop. Even when he develops the dialectic of freedom, he writes: "This rigorous chain of conditions involves a scientific determinism: there is a necessary logic of freedom."[190] But he does not forget that this necessary logic is a logic of freedom that, consequently, it cannot be recorded without being recognized. For example, when the critique of pessimism leads him to propose the vague affirmation: "there is something," he calls this proposition "a sincere admission of the will,"[191] a "datum that is consented to."[192] He even insists: "There is something. This datum that even they concede who concede the least, this avowal of naïve experience, is not imposed on me in spite of myself: I have willed that there be something."[193] Must we say that the author is speaking here of the *volonté voulante?* Yes, but he also indicates that it has also been ratified at this point by the *volonté voulue:* "We have opted for this *something* that is immediately sensed, known, desired by all; . . . we have done this in a spirit of defiance against the other alternative that has been brought forth and whose unknown character has appeared to be large with disturbing superstitions. I will remain faithful to this design . . . ."[194]

In Cartier's judgment, Blondel did not stress sufficiently "that the universal and necessary science (of action) can only be constituted by a free and personal 'engagement,' something that his readers have to assume, if they are to follow him."[195] The example we have cited and the more general declarations we have adduced just prior to it show that he was consciously aware of the role of freedom. When the author fails to repeat this point, or when certain forced expressions might lead one to believe that he forgets it, it is up to the reader to supply for the omission.

We would hesitate, then, to say that Blondel, unfaithful to his principle, sometimes separates thought and action, union and affirmation.[196] If he seems to do this in the letter he wrote in 1894 to the *Revue de Méta-physique et de Morale* and in the *Letter on apologetics* (1896), this was because his immediate objective led him to view philosophy as a whole in order to show that the Christian option does not intervene in its rational development. But in *L'Action* this whole or block is differentiated; the philosophical development proceeds step by step. There the development advanced from one step to another through the consent of the *volonté voulue* to the *volonté voulante* (a consent which is not to be identified with the religious option, although it sets the stage for it and can, under certain conditions, substitute for it). "Thus, freedom becomes interior to the very task of thought."[197] It is in full accord with Blondel's explicit declarations that we can give allegiance to this excellent formula.

On the other hand, one might risk confusing the reader by adding that the Blondelian dialectic is "an advance of thought from free option to free option."[198] For the author of *L'Action* and his interpreters, the word "option" signifies for the most part the supreme option before the unique necessary. Even in *La Pensée*, where the idea of an "option of thought" is introduced, distinct from the practical option, it is still a question of an attitude before the infinite.[199] In any case, Blondel soon got rid of the term "intellectual option," both because readers confused it with the practical option and because the word seemed to him to be ill suited to the role of indicating the initiative by which intelligence, throughout the course of its advance, actively recognizes truth.[200] To designate this initiative, he invented the term "agnition." "Agnition," he says, "is the recognition that, along the route of its mental growth, the human spirit will have to make of all the truths that are light the nourishment and end of intelligence."[201] Elsewhere he defines it as a "spiritual assent" and a "personal consent."[202] These various terms: recognition, agnition, assent, consent, seem to be more appropriate than the term "option" for indicating what is in question here.

In a similar vein, we would avoid saying that, to perceive rational necessities and establish relationships, thought should be involved or take a stand (*"s'engager"*).[203] For, while this word is appropriate enough in itself, in recent years it has taken on a meaning that does not fit here. Nor would we say that the Blondelian dialectic presupposes as its moving force "the good will."[204] This term seems to be both too vague and too moralizing. Blondel speaks rather of "fidelity of conscience to its interior norm."[205]

But these are questions of nuances or quibbles about words. The interpreter in question characterizes Blondel's development in other instances most accurately: "Regarding the necessary truth of action, there is never only a passive recording but always a free recognition."[206] Blondel ascertains what is "because he consents to what it should be."[207] "His dialectic is a work of reason, but of reason on the march."[208] Might it not be added that he discovers the truth "because he verifies it in living it," through the metaphysical experiences of abnegation, suffering, and charity"?[209] Yes, of course; but on condition that we specify, as Blondel did explicitly in the Trilogy, that a certain recognition of the truth can precede its practical verification in the individual subject. If this distinction is granted, we have no problem about admitting that the dialectic of *L'Action* is "a concrete, existential dialectic."[210]

We would make the same observation concerning a paragraph in which Père Cartier explains how the affirmation of God is an act that is both most rational and most free.[211] The author would appear to omit, as far as language is concerned, the important distinction that is quite clear in *L'Action* between "the necessary avowal" of the existence of God and "the option" that this avowal, once consented to, imposes on man (the option of opening or closing to the divine action). If one were to substitute in the commentary in question terms like avowal, recognition, or consent in place of the word option, we would have an excellent reply to those who judge that Blondel's position is anti-intellectual. Because "every thought is both act and knowledge,"[212] says Cartier quite accurately, there is "a reciprocal envelopment of reason and freedom,"[213] which accompanies the concrete dialectic that binds together the necessary relations. It is in virtue of this reciprocal immanence that the free passage of one attitude to another carries its own justification within it.[214] And, with Blondel, we would add that it carries it so well that what a man refuses does not cease to be realized in him, in spite of him, against him. If there are necessary truths that are not necessitating for our intelligence, they are, nevertheless, necessary in themselves and in us.[215]

To those who might be tempted to believe that the intervention of free recognition in the course of a dialectic prevents it from being rational, we would note that this same intervention is introduced by a philosopher hardly suspect of irrationalism and far removed from Blondel's thought. In his *Logique de la philosophie*, in linking together pure attitudes defined by their categories, Eric Weil remarks that "the passage from one category to the following one is free" and even that it is, in a sense, "incomprehensible."[216] What this means is that we cannot force a man to go beyond a position he has taken. But we can show that he has already gone beyond it without noticing it.[217] And it is in this way that we set forth the "logic of philosophy."

In an analogous way, though from a very different point of view, Blondel sets forth the "logic of action." There is no more irrationalism in one case than in the other, but simply a real apperception of what human thought is.

**Dialectic of Conversion.** In Blondel the reciprocal dialectic of reason and freedom reaches its culminating point when the critique of life makes it clear that man must open himself to the divine action by sacrifice. The author indicates this in moving terms, which reveal the experience of an interior struggle: "When, in order to justify (our intellectual, moral, and religious obligations) we make use of an indirect and constraining method which manifests their burdensome necessity; when we acknowledge that the natural order is not sufficient for our nature which, nevertheless, recoils before the supernatural . . . ; when we seek out every avenue of escape only to show that in the end we cannot withdraw from what weighs on us all the more, fine! But let's not pretend that we are saying all this for the pleasure of imposing on others burdens whose weight we do not carry, . . . that it doesn't cost us something in the first place, that this history of a soul in flight and in search of itself is nothing but pretense, that we have not struggled against our reason and our heart to avoid what we are blamed for having given out as inevitable, . . . that we have succeeded in embracing the faith without finding the crown of thorns, and that, finally, we have no comprehension of the extent to which a truly philosophical apologetics is the visible work, the permanent and personal work of interior conversion. In a word, just as we had to condemn that false separatism that isolated the religious from the philosophical problem, we must also condemn the false separatism that isolates the speculative work of thought from ascetical efforts and the toilsome instruction of life."[218]

It is clear that here Blondel does not abandon the road of rational discourse to slip onto the road of exhortation or of edifying confidentiality. He always aims at manifesting a necessity, if only by an analysis of the vanity of the arguments we invent to excape from it. But because it is a question of an "onerous necessity," it cannot be seriously recognized unless we accept the burden it imposes. The moment the science of action makes the obligation of opening to an exacting supernatural apparent, the recognition of the truth of rational discourse becomes a consent to sacrifice. The logic of action thus becomes a dialectic of conversion.

On the last page of *L'Action* the author invites the reader to undergo the Christian experience, and he assures him, on the basis of his own experience, that he will only find there reasons for affirming the reality of the supernatural proclaimed by Christianity. As a final testimony, Blondel himself pronounces that word which "surpasses the competence of philosophy," "the only word, in view of Christianity, capable of expressing that portion, and the best portion, of the certitude that cannot be communicated because it only arises out of the intimacy of an entirely personal action," the word which is itself an action: "It is." Let us suppose that the reader does not undertake the experience recommended and is not induced to pronounce this word: Unless he is willing to be inconsistent, he will have to backtrack and challenge the rational argumentation that established the necessity of taking Christianity seriously. Perhaps he will only challenge the correspondence between Christian dogma and human aspirations. Perhaps he will also challenge the necessity of a religious attitude. Perhaps he will reject the very idea of God. Perhaps, returning his challenge to the starting point, he will try to show that the problem of human destiny is a false problem. In any case he will always have to find a flaw somewhere in the chain of necessary relationships established by the philosophy of action. Blondel is well aware that such a challenge is always possible; he experienced it himself. But he also knows that, if the truth cannot be "cognized" without being recognized, it will, nevertheless, judge those who misunderstand it. The necessity of a consent to the dialectic of real life does not suppress the necessity immanent in this dialectric.

## PHILOSOPHY AND THEOLOGY

***Distinction and Relation.*** We some hope that we have showed that the "philosophy of action" is a philosophy in the strict sense of the word, that its movement is autonomous and rational, even when it recognizes the necessity of welcoming the supernatural, even when it discovers in Christian dogma an appropriate response to the expectancy of the human act of willing. Still, it is evident that such a philosophy impinges upon the object of theology. So, we are justified in asking what relationship it entertains with theology, all the more so since theology itself has some claim to being scientific and rational.

Blondel has always declared that his philosophical reflection did not tread on theological ground and, in fact, could not do so. He indicated this briefly in *L'Action*[219] and more at length in the *Letter*. In the *Letter*[220] he wrote: "Philosophy only considers the supernatural to the extent that its notion is immanent in us." Earlier he had said that philosophy comes to grips with this notion "under its natural aspect."[221] It shows that "it remains conformed to the idea we conceive of it only to the extent that it remains in our estimate beyond our human grasp."[222] Thus, it denies to itself the power of attaining its reality; it establishes that only faith in revelation can bring us to a knowledge of the existence and essence of the supernatural order proclaimed by Christian teaching. Therefore, it preserves, outside itself, the irreplaceable role of faith. It preserves it even when it determines the genesis of the idea of revelation and indicates the necessity of revealed dogmas and precepts. For in this case, as already noted, it does nothing but "trace out empty frames within which nothing that is ours can fix the reality or fill out the abstract design."²²³ What faith "imposes on us as real," philosophy "conceives as necessary and also impracticable for us." The two "coincide, then, in that they do not overlap, and in that the one is empty while the other is full. Even when their affirmations seem to cover the same ground, at least in part and *sub specie materiae seu objecti*, they remain entirely heterogeneous *vi formae*."²²⁴ As science of faith, theology remains entirely distinct from philosophy.

Blondel never tires of grounding and emphasizing this distinction: "Since even in its proper domain philosophy cannot lay claim to substitute for the real, the field remains free for a dogma which, with quite different claims, governs thought and life and speaks in the absolute. In this sense, theological doctrines, even when they touch upon the natural order, have a range and significance entirely different from philosophical theses over which they seem to be exactly superimposed."²²⁵ *Duplex cognitionis ordo, non solum principio, sed objecto.*²²⁶

There can be no doubt, says Blondel, that theology aspires to be a science; it does employ reason. But, lest we end in total confusion, we must "distinguish what is theologically rational from what is philosophically rational (just as we must distinguish it from what is scientifically rational, which is of a completely different order)."²²⁷ Reason develops positive science by applying itself to sense data. It constitutes sacred science by working "on revealed dogmas and deliverances, which are like a kind of experience of the divine and a supernatural empiricism, *argumentum non apparentium.*"²²⁸ "Theology supposes just this rational organization of elements that are no longer due to reason; and in this sense it applies a form, philosophical if you wish, to elements that are foreign to philosophy."²²⁹ Philosophy, for its part, free from all alloy, consists "no longer in the heteronomous application of reason to a subject matter or an object, whether derived from the senses or from revelation, but in the autonomous application of reason to itself."²³⁰ That is why its results do not compromise the teachings of theology. That is also the reason why they are not so fixed and suppose a greater freedom. "The use of reason in the area of dogma and under the discipline of faith consists in penetrating endlessly the infinite depths of a fixed truth which reason does not seek to renovate but to understand."²³¹ For its part, philosophy does not seek "anywhere but in itself the principle and guarantee for always controlling its own conclusions."²³²

We observe here the motive that leads the author to insist so much on the distinction between the theological and philosophical employment of reason. It is a question of vindicating for philosophy this autonomy, this freedom without which there could be no philosophy. It is only when it is applied to understanding the meaning of dogma that reason is *ancilla theologiae*.[233] When it is applied to itself, it depends only on itself. "Theologians do not allow philosophers to tread on their territory; they are right . . . : Very well (it follows logically and should be recognized), philosophers, if they truly remain where they belong, should not and cannot permit theologians to penetrate into their domain. The advantages of the distinction are reciprocal and the domain of each science remains inviolable."[234] Philosophy "is not fertile, nor does it completely fulfill its role as precursor (with respect to faith) unless it is impartial and free. It represents all that is human and nothing but the human; but this portion is essential."[235] If it is true that it cannot develop its complete autonomy without becoming involved in the whole religious problem, it can only touch it profitably by maintaining an intransigent and jealous discretion, which is expressed in the acknowledgment of its own incompetence and is the safeguard of its own dignity. *"Non libera nisi adjutrix, non adjutrix nisi libera philosophia."*[236]

Concerned above all to vindicate the necessary freedom of his philosophical work by showing that the results of this free exercise are in accord with the exigencies of dogma and that they do not threaten its stability, Blondel did not delve into the concept of theology as he had done in the case of philosophy. He limited himself to accepting a summary version of the common teaching. Duméry has observed very justly that, as far as the relationship between philosophy and theology is concerned, Blondel's opinion is "rather classical, almost academic, aside from the originality of the method of immanence."[237] The reservation that concludes this observation indicates that the classic element of the relation lies in the very concept of theology. And this is quite true. When Blondel urges theologians to remain "theologians to the fullest degree," to speak to us "concerning what they alone can give us," he reminds us that their mission is to develop for us "the rational system of faith," that is, to show "that the order of dogma, considered as dogma, forms an organic synthesis, and that sacred science is a science."[238] Even when they assume the apologist's role, their first task in this age of religious ignorance is "to expose in its defined unity and rich simplicity, the logical synthesis of Catholic dogma."[239] He extols the "theological rationalism" of St. Thomas.[240] Surely, it might be questioned whether he understood very well at this period the characteristic movement of Thomistic thought. Later on he will admit that he had an

inadequate idea of it. Above all, it could be questioned whether his conception of theology is complete. And we shall question this presently. But it
cannot be denied that it reflects faithfully the classic notion and indicates
what ought to be the primary object of the theologian's teaching.

From this point of view Blondel is right: The philosophy he develops,
even when it takes up the religious problem and considers Christian
dogma, remains radically distinct from theology. For it does not aim to
expound "what is of faith or consequent upon faith setting out from faith,"
but to unfold "what is of reason, whether antecedent to or in agreement
with faith, setting out from reason."[241] It is not *fides quaerens intellectum*
but *intellectus quaerens fidem.*[242]

While he strives more than others to define the radical distinction
between the philosophical and theological points of view, the author, as
already noted, seeks to establish a "connection closer than ever" between
the philosophical problem and the religious problem, or better still, their
"unity." Thus, he condemns what he calls "a false separatism."[243] "Instead
of turning away from the religious problem, our whole effort is aimed at
proving that it cannot be eliminated, that philosophy is not free, not complete, not itself, if it does not focus on the problem in its most acute
aspect."[244] And this "is in harmony with theology which neither allows one
to touch it in its depths nor to detach or exempt oneself from it; for if there
is 'the supernatural' that is humanly inaccessible, there is also 'the unique
necessary,' with the consequence that . . . we can neither de jure nor de
facto be disinterested in it."[245] In following the determinism of action, and
thanks to the reservations that the method of immanence imposes,
"philosophy becomes capable of approaching all the most exact questions
of Christian consciousness without altering its own nature or their
nature."[246]

Beyond the enlarging of philosophical perspectives, what follows from
this is "a human progress of the religious consciousness or of the very
understanding of Christianity."[247] Blondel shows this by various examples
that need only be recalled briefly since we have already met with them. The
philosophy of action helps us understand that salvation is accessible to all,
even in ignorance of Christianity, but that it is not for us to say what form
it must take *in concreto.* The beauty of the method of immanence is that
it manages "to place in each one what judges each one."[248] The same
philosophy casts light on the question of damnation, the doctrine of
"vicarious satisfaction."[249] Beyond that, it seems that "in seeking out, in
order to conceive the effective realization of the integral order of things,
an element distinct both from nature and from God its author (philosophy)

sheds light on and justifies from its own point of view what is perhaps an implicit dogma, the Emmanuel, the final cause of the creative design."[250] Recall also that the author of *L'Action* and the *Letter* was eventually led to illumine, in the name of his own principles, the nature of faith, the method of apologetics, the relation between history and dogma, the theological notion of tradition, and so on.

In his own thought this entire effort aiming at a better "understanding of Christianity" remains specifically philosophical. We have showed that this is actually the case[251] and how it is so. We have no intention, then, of retracting or weakening what was said earlier. But we do wonder whether this philosophical understanding of Christianity is not *at the same time* also theological understanding. In other words, without challenging Blondel's idea of the competence of philosophy, we wonder whether he did not restrict that of theology.

*Understanding of Faith.* Before demonstrating this by an examination of the concept itself, we would like to suggest it by the use of a comparison. We have just seen that Blondel shows that philosophy, normally developed, contributes to "the very understanding of Christianity."[252] This term, which is his own, inevitably evokes the term "understanding of faith," so frequent in the writings of the Fathers of the Church and medieval theologians. Grammatically it is synonymous whenever the second word in the expression *"intellectus fidei"* is an objective genitive, referring to the content of the Christian faith (and not to the act of faith). Moreover, what the ancients practiced under the name of understanding of the faith implied (beyond the almost constant return to salvation history, which is the source of dogma) a reflection whose aim was to show that Christianity reveals man to himself. Blondelian thought is not without analogy to this reflection. However, the differences are so great and the procedure of the ancients is so different from author to author that it would be difficult and vain to insist on determining, without possible equivocation, the real resemblances. But there is one case where the comparison is easiest and the analogy more striking: that of St. Anselm.

Taking up St. Augustine's program of *fides quaerens intellectum*, Anselm wants to understand what he believes, to explore the *ratio fidei*. The readers he addresses himself to are Christians, more exactly, monks, his Benedictine brethren. His work, then, is the meditation of a believer, written for believers. In this respect, it would appear to be totally different from the Blondelian work, which is addressed to unbelievers and takes its position from the point of view of the unbeliever.

Nevertheless, at the request of the monks themselves, Anselm under-takes the task of proving what he believes without recourse to the authority of Scripture, by the necessity of reason alone.[253] He wants to show how a man who has not heard the divine Word or who does not believe it could be persuaded, by reason alone, to accept the truths that are the object of faith.[254] In other words, he intends to prove these truths by necessary reason, valid for every mind, even for the unbeliever. By this means, he hopes to show every man that they must be believed.[255] Reasoning from the point of view of the hypothetical unbeliever, the *fides quaerens intellec-tum* becomes *intellectus quaerens fidem.*[256]

It is here that the analogy between the thought of Anselm and Blondel appears. They are both believers who, without putting their personal faith in doubt, want to understand its rationality and make it understood in such a way that the unbeliever himself may be led to believe.[257] Both accept at the outset of their intellectual investigation the unbeliever's questioning of their faith; they suspend their affirmation as believers and take their posi-tion at the point of view of the one who denies. And it is with this starting point that they develop a rational argument which, while not implying any premise of faith, should be valid in principle for every mind.[258]

This global analogy extends rather far into the detail of the demonstra-tion, although the arguments proposed are not the same. Both believe that they can not only prove the existence of God but even provide valid and more or less necessary reasons in favor of dogmas that are specifically Christian: Trinity, Incarnation, Redemption. In his *Monologion*, St. An-selm offers a kind of rational deduction of the Trinity: *"Ecce patet omni homini expedire ut credat in quamdam ineffabilem trinam unitatem et unam trinitatem."*[259] He introduces more precautions here than is gener-ally believed. Paul Vignaux shows this well: In composing a *De Trinitate* in dialectical form, he "simply supposes that, abstracting from the value they have by divine authority, the trinitarian terms can be to some extent valid insofar as they are expressions of the movement of human thought toward an *optimum et maximum* proposed as the Absolute."[260] Now, Blondel, inquiring about the possibility of an "absolutely subsistent Thought" which would found our own in the absolute, shows, for his part, that such a Thought is only conceivable as trinitarian.[261] On the other hand, in the *Cur Deus Homo*, St. Anselm wants to establish by necessary reasons, abstracting from what the believer knows of Christ, that man cannot be saved and attain immortal beatitude save by a God-man.[262] Like him, although the argumentation is different, Blondel shows why it was necessary that a God-man suffer and die.[263]

With the two thinkers the *ratio* that is thus separated off remains *ratio fidei*, in the sense that it requires the confirmation of a superior authority and does not dispense one from believing. "When a line of reasoning makes his conclusion seem necessary to the author of the *Monologion, quasi necessarium*, this necessity must be considered, not as absolute, *omnino necessarium*, but only as provisional, *interim necessarium*, so long as this same conclusion has not been confirmed by a *major auctoritas*. This superior authority is found, of course, in Scripture and Tradition."[264] This is precisely what describes Blondel's design in the fifth part of *L'Action*. And we can also apply to him what follows in the same commentary on Anselm's thought: "If, after the dialectic is complete, faith appears to correspond to a rational exigency, this exigency is not placed higher than faith, as a principle founding it; on the contrary, it is developed on an explicitly lower plane, referring to faith, as it were, from below: . . . in the last chapters (of the *Monologion*) this exigency (is expressed) in a necessity to believe, which is in the order of obligation, of the *debere*, of a supreme interest and radical need of the created spirit. . . . St. Anselm, by his method does not hope 'to communicate his faith'; if some incredulous person follows his line of reasoning to the end, the rational persuasion that he will acquire will remain on this side of, below if you wish, the state of the believer."[265]

As a matter of fact, this rational persuasion will remain purely formal, in some way empty, as long as it shall not have been filled out by the experience of faith. *"Quantum enim rei auditum superat experientia, tantum vincit audientis cognitionem experientis scientia."*[266] Anselm claims that his treatment has a logical structure, valid for every mind, including the unbeliever. But he also knows that this treatment does not suffice to communicate a filled-out knowledge of divine realities. Only the experience of faith actualizes understanding of the faith. It is in this sense that one must believe in order to understand. Now, as we have seen, Blondel also teaches the necessity of the Christian experience, if we are to succeed in affirming the reality whose necessity is showed by the rational dialectic.

This long series of analogies between Anselmian and Blondelian thought should not disguise their evident diversity. What constitutes the originality of Blondel's thought, insofar as it is a logic of action, is foreign to the Anselmian meditation. Moreover, Blondel profited by many of the clarifications theology achieved after the time of Anselm; in particular, he distinguishes more clearly, as did St. Thomas, absolute necessities and the necessities interior to contingent events (those which form the basis for accommodated arguments or "arguments de convenance"). Clearly we must be on our guard not to misunderstand these differences. But the analogy that remains in spite of them helps us to understand how Blon-delian thought, without ceasing for an instant to be philosophical, has, nonetheless, a theological quality, just as Anselmian thought, without ceasing to be theological, also has a philosophical character.

It is true that there has been much discussion on the question of whether Anselmian meditation should be classed under the rubric of theology or under that of philosophy, or in some intermediate category.[267] Since the author himself failed to apply either of these labels to his own thought, the interpreter qualifies it on his own responsibility by the use of terms Anselm did not use and whose signification is much more circumscribed today than it was in his day. Thus, if we understand by theology a science which argues exclusively on the basis of the authority of Scripture, Tradition, and the Magisterium, and which links together dogmas thus established, it must be admitted that the principal works of Anselm do not belong to theology. But perhaps this notion is incomplete. Where else can we situate, unless in theology, the rational meditation of a believer on what constitutes the object of his faith, a meditation offered to monks to sustain their contemplative prayer?

Still, this meditation provides within it the outline of an autonomous philosophy. By the very fact that it introduces at the start the hypothetical unbeliever and sets out to satisfy his requirements, it aims to develop a system of universally valid reasons. After having discovered the proof for God that is presented in the *Proslogion*, Anselm cries out: "Thanks, O Lord; for what I at first believed through Thy gift, I have now understood through Thy light, in such a way that, were I to will not to believe that Thou dost exist, I would not be able not to understand it."[268] Thus, he indicates that the proof, discovered and understood in faith and prayer, has, independent of them, a meaning and a rigor. It can, therefore, be maintained that Anselm is "for the historian of philosophy, the first scholastic who truly insinuated the existence of an autonomous philosophy, that is, independent of theology."[269] We can say this on condition that we add that, for the historian of theology, this autonomous philosophy remains interior to a theology, which does not wish to argue in any other way than by this rational approach to which we here give the name philosophy.

Anselm proposes the same arguments to those who are within and to those who are without. "If there is an *insipiens*," writes the interpreter already cited, "the *Proslogion* can be in two in two ways: it can be presented within to believers and without to the unbeliever."[270] This remark is fully justified, but we do not think that the statement that follows is quite compatible with it: "The confessional character of the work is immediately neutralized: it no longer belongs to the domain of spirituality nor of theology but, obliquely at least, to a reason which only refers to its own norms and exigencies."[271] This judgment would seem to betray the thought of the commentator. For a work does not cease to be confessional simply because it justifies rationally the credibility of what it confesses; and if it is admitted that the work of Anslem no longer belongs to the field of spirituality or of theology the moment it invokes universally valid rational necessities, it must be excluded from the field of theology; for the *Monologion,* the *Proslogion,* the *Cur Deus Homo,* etc., bring in nothing but necessities of this kind.

If it is true that the "understanding of faith" in St. Anselm is a theological meditation which generates within it the outline of an autonomous philosophy, it should also be admitted that the "understanding of Christianity" pursued by Blondelian philosophy constitutes the outline of a speculative theology. The work of Blondel, to be sure, is essentially philosophical because it is addressed to unbelievers, to those on the outside; and the work of Anselm is essentially theological because it is addressed to believers, to those on the inside. But, just as Anselm presents to those of the interior a rationality that is valid for those of the exterior, similarly, Blondel exposes to those of the exterior "the rational element" contained in what those of the interior profess. The procedure, while directed to a different end, is, as we have seen, nonetheless, analogous. We cannot challenge its philosophical character; but neither can we misunderstand its theological character, once we recognize this quality in the procedure of St. Anselm.[272]

We have chosen the comparison with St. Anselm because it is particularly appropriate. But many other comparisons could be made. Among the great theologians of the Middle Ages, there are many who developed within theology itself a philosophy that claimed both to refer only to the norms of reason and to express the rational implications of the Christian faith. Gilson has showed with increasing precision that, even in St. Thomas, who insisted more than others on the autonomy of reason in the philosophical process, the latter always remains interior to theology. Now this is a fact that Blondel did not grasp, even after he had acquired a deeper knowledge of Thomism than he had when he wrote the *Letter.* On the authority of a few interpreters, he admitted that the demonstration of the natural desire to see God, expounded in the third book of the *Contra Gentiles,* has a purely philosophical character. No doubt, St. Thomas intended it to be rational and philosophical; but he also regarded it as theological. The *Contra Gentiles* was actually presented from the start as a work of theology: "Propositum nostrae intentionis est veritatem *quam fides catholica profitetur* pro nostro modulo manifestare."[273] And when the author introduces the part specially devoted to the Christian truths that reason can attain by itself, he writes: "primum nitemur ad manifestationem illius veritatis quam *fides profitetur et ratio investigat.*"[274] Could one say more clearly that the manifestation of the truth will be simultaneously a theology and a philosophy, the second interior to the first?

This example, among many others that might be adduced, shows that the medieval notion of theology was notably more expansive than might be supposed from the scholastic façade of the manuals whose definitions caught Blondel's eye. It will be said, perhaps, that this medieval notion was as yet poorly differentiated. One of Blondel's observations could be interpreted in this sense: "Perhaps," he wrote, "we must suppose that even the rational truths that revelation ratifies or consecrates have, under their theological aspect, a scope that is completely other than when they are seen under their philosophical aspect because, after all, we cannot realize absolutely the integral order, even of natural things, without passing, at least implicitly, through Him of whom St. Paul teaches that He is the *primogenitus omnis creaturae in quo constant omnia,* and of whom it is said that without Him all that had been made by him would return to nothingness."[275] Let it first be noted that the theologians of the Middle Ages knew this, and that Duns Scotus was particularly insistent upon it. On the other hand, the same Blondel shows a few pages farther on (as already noted) that, to conceive the integral order of things, philosophy requires, perhaps, the Emmanuel, the final cause of the creative design.[276] He thus opts, *as a philosopher,* for a "theological opinion" illumined by the name of Duns Scotus. Here, as was often the case among theologians of the Middle Ages, one and the same *ratio* is both philosophical and theological.[277]

*Fundamental Theology.* All this notwithstanding, the comparisons we have outlined are not sufficient to establish fully what they suggest. For the concept of theology has evolved since the Middle Ages, as also that of philosophy, although to a lesser degree. So we must set out from the notion that has become more commonly accepted, in the form accepted by Blondel, and see what it implies.

With Blondel, we have recognized that we ought "to make a distinction between what is of the faith or consequent upon faith, setting out from faith, and what is of reason, whether antecedent to or in agreement with faith, setting out from reason."[278] The first element constitutes the object of what we call today dogmatic theology, and it is regarded as the essential part of theology. Let us assume that this is the case.

The question now is to determine whether this dogmatic theology does not suppose, in the very act by which it takes its origin and develops, a fundamental theology whose proper object would be to unfold what is "antecedent to or in agreement with faith, setting out from reason." While dogmatic theology, setting out from faith, shows, following a hypothetico-deductive method, that "the order of dogma, considered as dogma, forms an organic synthesis,"[279] the second approach, following a regressive method, seeks the *transcendental* condition and the *historic* condition of faith. This fundamental theology would not be simply a treatise preceding dogmatics and which the latter might, thereafter, neglect. It would express the fundamental position to which dogmatic theology would always have to return because this is where dogma begins to take on meaning. Viewed as a quest for the transcendental conditions of faith, that is, of the rational *intrastructure* implied in the act of faith, fundamental theology corresponds to the procedure of philosophy when the latter is applied to an analysis of the genesis of the idea of the supernatural and to the task of extricating from Christianity "the entire rational element it contains."[280] Thus, Blondelian philosophy, without ceasing to be a philosophy, would be in a position to accomplish a theological task.

In order to demonstrate that dogmatic theology presupposes a fundamental theology and that Blondelian philosophy includes, at the very least, an outline of this theology, it is enough if we retrace certain lines of a development in the course of which Henry Duméry explains how Blondel, even while treating the Christian supernatural, is a "philosopher and nothing but a philosopher." "Unless we are willing to suppose that the faith is absurd, bereft of all signification and foundation, there must be somehow, underneath the states of pure reason and the states of faith, a single framework, a single intelligible texture, in virtue of which what we believe remains coherent and compatible with what we know."[281] "The order of notions underlying the act of faith is in no way different from the necessary rational foundation that the religious departure requires, lest it be arbitrary; without this 'order' it would, in addition, be evanescent: neither structured nor structurable."[282] "Were one to suppose this order absent, the theologian would no longer be able to think or express his faith, for he draws from this faith all its rational substructures, that is, all that constitutes its very conditions of possibility. Thus, the ideal order, in its formal rigor, . . . is that in virtue of which faith has succeeded in providing itself with a human intelligibility, that is, in developing into theological reason. It is the order without which faith could not have acquired any hold on the human spirit, no foundation in reason."[283]

After this analysis, which expresses in terms that are at times debatable a basically correct idea, Duméry continues: "Now the examination of the conditions of possibility of an object is always pertinent to philosophy, no matter what the object in question may be. In declaring that the order of immanent notions belongs to philosophical critique, Blondel does nothing more than render to philosophy what is proper to it."[284] This premise with its conclusion seems to be incontestable. What seems to us to be unacceptable is the implied exclusion. It is our opinion that the rational examination of the conditions of possibility *of faith* belong *also* and *properly* to theology, and that this examination unfolds by means of a philosophical critique.[285] If this is denied, then one would have to admit that theology is a *blind* science, which proceeds without knowing what it is doing. It would be necessary to agree that it is ignorant of "that in virtue of which faith has succeeded in providing itself with a human intelligibility, that is, in developing into theological reason," of that "without which faith could not have acquired any hold on the human spirit, no foundation in reason," of that without which the religious departure would be "arbitrary" and "evanescent: neither structured nor structurable." Duméry's formulas, which express so well the conditions for a reasonable and structured faith, indicate by the same token the function of theology insofar as it enjoys a reflex consciousness of its object, insofar as it thinks its own thought, that is, insofar as it is fundamental and speculative theology.

We find the same thing implied in every analogous formula of the same interpreter: "No doubt, in the consciousness of the believer we ought to hold that the ideal order is equivalent to what is theologically rational; for it serves to mediate an experience of faith. But this does not exclude, it actually requires that the notional series be, from another point of view, equivalent to what is philosophically logico-rational. In other words, even before the theologian intervenes, and in order that he may intervene, we must suppose an intelligible structure which, were it lacking, would result in the complete dissociation of religious experience from reason."[286] This is correct; but it also means that, unless he is blind to what he presupposes, the theologian must make fundamental theology prior to dogmatic theology and have the latter accompanied by speculative theology. Duméry continues: "If it is proved . . . that the ideal order, whose crux is the hypothesis of the supernatural, is found to be both the logic inherent in Christian practice and the very fabric of the notional determinism that presides over the dialectic of action, then philosophy will have to assimilate and retrieve this hypothesis under penalty of making concrete action an inexact description."[287] We agree with this analysis and recognize that Blondel, in assuming his task, worked as a philosopher. But we hasten to add that, *at the same time and by this very fact,* he also performed the work of the theologian—not a work of dogmatic theology, we repeat, but a work of fundamental theology—since the philosophy of action, when it describes the genesis of the idea of the supernatural, reveals *at the same time* both the conditions for the achievement of action *and* the immanent logic of faith.

If Blondel was so insistent on the distinction of areas, let us not forget that it was to legitimate the autonomy of his inquiry in the eyes of theologians and to vindicate it in the eyes of philosophers. The requirements of his defense made it hard for him to declare openly the theological character of his work. Beyond this, the school theology of the nineteenth century offered him scant means for describing it in exact terms. What we call fundamental theology today hardly existed in those days. When the word was used it referred to something quite different. Theology for Blondel only meant "the logical synthesis of dogma" as presented in the schools.

As a matter of fact, he was on the verge of beginning to see that this notion was incomplete. In the *Letter,* immediately after having reminded theologians that their mission is to expound the logical synthesis of dogma with the authority that becomes them, and that they gain nothing "by humanizing their teaching" in subjecting everything to philosophical arguments, he adds these remarkable lines: "With a more and more intelligent respect for the sensitivities of conscience, it is necessary that the believer, the apologist, the theologian in whom the whole man ought to subsist with his human exigencies and aspirations, should take pains, as others do and for others, so as to speak only as an expert regarding the problems of science, only as a historian regarding the problems of the past, only as a philosopher regarding the anxieties of thought, only as one alive regarding the things of life. Let him not suppress what is natural in the supernatural itself. While it is necessary to avoid confusing roles and disciplines, it is equally urgent to break down supposed airtight divisions that falsely separate the Christian from the man and the citizen, and the man of God from the progress of the world."[288] This would mean, if taken seriously, that the human should enter in some way into the very fabric of the work of theology, that science, history, philosophy, and the experience of life have a role to play within it; and, in particular, that the theologian ought to make his own the human exigencies revealed by the philosophy of action. Thus, Blondel is on the verge of seeing that the very movement of his philosophy obliges him to go beyond the conception of theology he entertained, a conception he drew from the manuals of his day.

If he himself did not succeed in going beyond the common notion, he did lead theologians to do so. It was partly through his influence that fundamental theology, as we understand it today, began gradually to take shape after the turn of the century. Here we see verified an observation of Heidegger: "That a thought should remain behind what it thinks indicates its creative character."[289]

If we have succeeded in showing the theological quality of Blondelian thought, even using the arguments Duméry advances to deny it, it is evident that what separates us on this point lies much less in the interpretation of this thought than in the conception of theology. According to Duméry, "the theologian, as distinct from the philosopher, imposes a limit on his inquiry from the start. He does not undertake a radical reexamination of the foundations of his subject matter. By the act of faith he makes a decision on the global meaning of the data he receives; then he mines this given, seeking in it the significance of the detail in strict conformity with the general sense."[290] "The philosopher is the only one to know the underside of the cards."[291] If it is true that the theologian imposes a limit on his inquiry so that he does not undertake a radical reexamination of his foundations, we would have to agree with Duméry that Blondelian philosophy, in undertaking precisely this examination, takes its position by this very fact outside the whole theological sphere. But we refuse to accept this conception of theology and regard as essential to the work of the theologian at least a portion of what Duméry would reserve to the "philosopher of religion."

Of course, it would be possible to list a considerable number of theological writings in which the idea of an examination of the foundations is totally absent. The merit of a work like Duméry's lies precisely in the fact that it reminds theologians of an obligation to reflect, from which they too often dispense themselves. But no serious theologian will admit in principle that his role is simply to mine the given of faith without ever taking into careful account the human conditioning of this given, without ever returning to the historical and rational presuppositions of the faith. The theologian who would refuse "to know the underside of the cards" would do little more than expound in more or less learned prattle the "faith of the coalvendor." More recently, Duméry has specified that, in dispensing the theologian from having to undertake rational critique, he did not deny him all reflexive activity.[292] This was clear to the attentive reader even in the earlier work. But what we challenge is exactly what the second essay maintains, namely, that the philosophical critique of the conditions of possibility of faith is a task the theologian could be dispensed from.[293] It is not enough to concede that "a theologian could on occasion do this."[294] He *ought* to do it, or run the risk of not understanding the exact import of what he says and of not being able to locate it as a judgment of truth.

One vindicates this critical task for the philosopher in the name of the principle that Lachelier formulated: "It is the office of the philosopher to understand everything, even religion."[295] We have no intention of challenging this right of the philosopher. But we also note that understanding religion pertains to the office of reflective and speculative theology. The question, then, is to know what relation there is between the two understandings. When the believer can recognize in some "philosophy of religion" an exact understanding of the rational presuppositions of his faith, this philosophy accomplishes, in part at least, the very task of fundamental theology. Philosophy and theology, though they be distinct, meet in such a case at the precise point where they discern by a like reflection the same foundations of religion. We know, however, that many a philosophy of religion has resulted in reducing or naturalizing Christianity, or they have claimed to have gone beyond it.[296] One wonders whether this kind of result could be avoided by any other method than the one defined by Blondel, which was to set out from Christianity (or more exactly from Catholicism), supposed to be true from another source, and to verify rationally the hypothesis of this truth in every way that it allows of being verified. But this represents the initial procedure of a well-understood fundamental theology. Thus, it would appear that a philosophy of religion will not be surely in accord with the Christian faith unless it is conceived at the outset as fundamental theology in the sense we have defined.

***Reply to Certain Criticisms.*** It was largely because of an excessively narrow conception of theology that the meaning of my first study of Blondel was at times misunderstood. I said then that Blondelian thought is neither pure philosophy nor theology in the strict sense of the word, that it revived a type of reflection analogous to what the ancients called the "understanding of faith."[297] Duméry took this to mean that I intended to define for Blondel and assign to him a road midway between philosophy and theology,[298] that I was thereby challenging the specifically philosophical character of his study of the religious problem and attributing to him a "philosophico-theological concordism," which he formally excluded.[299] I recognize that my development (it could not have been expanded in the course of a simple article) was a bit rapid and that it did not contain all the explanations that would have been helpful so that it might have been easily understood by readers unfamiliar with the practice of theology. Still, since I have repeated many times that the work of Blondel was properly philosophical, one might have been cautious about accepting an interpretation that made me say the opposite. When I wrote that this work was not pure philosophy, I specified by adding, "if by this one means a separated philosophy."[300] I thus used Blondelian language[301] to describe a Blondelian intention, the intention of developing an autonomous philosophy *in the hypothesis of the truth of Christianity.* I said exactly what Duméry himself later formulated when he wrote: Blondel "knew pertinently that he was setting out from Christianity, supposed true from another source . . .";[302] he "attempts a transposition" from the theological to the philosophical and "seeks to constitute an autonomous philosophy, setting out from Christianity."[303] When I wrote that he was not doing theology in the narrow sense this word often receives in ordinary language, I meant that he did not assume the role of treating "the positive knowledge of revealed truths in the light of Christian sources."[304] In other words, he was not dealing with dogmatic theology. Finally, when I said that he seeks the "understanding of faith," that he analyzes the *ratio fidei*, I qualified this by saying that it must be understood in the Anselmian rather than in the Augustinian sense.[305] Having said this, I explicitly affirmed what I am reproached for having misunderstood, namely, that Blondel "sought to forge a method that would be valid for the unbeliever as well as for the believer."[306] I thus indicated that his thought, while authentically philosophical, also has *at the same time and by the same movement* a theological character, which is something quite different from assigning him a *road midway* between philosophy and theology. "I do not grant myself the right," says Duméry, "not to take seriously the will of Blondel, expressed many times in the *Letter,* to elaborate a philosophy that would be a universal and apodictic science."[307] But where have I claimed this right? If anyone thought that I did not take Blondel's intention seriously, it is because there was a failure to grasp what I meant by "understanding of faith." Where has anyone read that it consisted "in manufacturing reason from the real content of faith?"[308] What relation is there between this strange idea and the procedure of St. Anselm?

Carried away by the concern, very legitimate in itself, to scout every interpretation that might tend to rob Blondel of his title as a philosopher, Duméry manages to conjure up a phantom in order to exorcize it. In the course of a note in which he discusses our study, he adds: "In a particularly

penetrating article, Père de Lubac had already spoken of his embarrassment in having to choose between the terms philosophy and theology when
applied to Christian philosophy according to Blondel."[309] Now it is precisely in this article that we find the crisp declaration we have cited earlier:
"As for Christian philosophy according to M. Blondel, it is *not yet* Christian. For it is philosophy itself discovering concerning itself, in a final
movement which is still only a work of pure rational reflection, that it does
not 'buckle.' It is, then, a philosophy that will be open to Christianity but
which in principle does not proceed in any sense from it. . . ."[310] Can
anyone see here the least occasion for embarrassment in recognizing the
specifically philosophical intention of Blondel? It is true that a little farther
on, on the page indicated by Duméry's reference, Père de Lubac admits
that one might hesitate over the choice of the word: philosophy or theology.[311] But, a word of caution: It is no longer a question of Blondel but of
another conception of Christian philosophy, the one familiar to the Fathers
of the Church; the author even indicates explicitly how this conception is
distinguished from the Blondelian idea.[312]

It is not to be wondered at, then, that Blondel himself should have
warmly praised this article, and without any reservations. "There it is
powerfully demonstrated," he writes, "that in its most rational autonomy
philosophy covers the total field of human experience and of universal life.
Many occasions for confusion and timidity are eliminated by this vigorous
and learned study."[313] Thus, Blondel recognizes his own thought where
Duméry does not believe it is accurately interpreted.

Duméry refers again to another article in which Père de Lubac would
seem to have expressed the "same hesitation" with respect to Blondel.[314]
Was it opportune, immediately after having declared that consideration
would be limited to Blondelian thought as presented in the *Letter*,[315] to
introduce an article dealing with *L'Etre et les êtres*, a work that appeared
forty years later and one dealing with an entirely different problem? Be that
as it may, we fail to find in this article any trace of the hesitation referred
to. The principal objective is to answer a complaint formulated by a critic
on the subject of *L'Etre et les etres*. Blondel, in his theory about the motive
for creation, is alleged to have combined two incompatible conceptions,
one Greek and the other evangelical. In the place in the text referred to
by Duméry, Père de Lubac writes: "We are not examining here, we repeat,
whether M. Blondel's effort of understanding on this precise point is
strictly philosophical, nor whether the result he seeks is fully realized: we
maintain that it is in principle integrally Christian."[316] Note first that
reserving a question does not mean that the response would turn out to be

negative or hesitant. But even in the supposition that it did, it would only concern here a narrowly circumscribed point (the motive for creation), and not the whole of Blondel's thought. Finally, since the author cited says that he is repeating something he had already said, let us go back to the first statement. The tenor is precisely the reverse of what Duméry thought it to be. Pointing out that in the eyes of certain critics *L'Etre et les êtres* is not a philosophical work because it attempts an apparently rational organization of data received from faith and thus supposes, from the start, the conclusions it seems to move toward, Père de Lubac declares that he will not examine this charge.[317] But he immediately refers to a study by Jeanne Mercier which, he says, "implicitly provides the refutation by reason of the long analysis it makes of the work, . . . by explaining the internal principle of the movement without having to bring in any of the theological accommodations that fill so many pages." And he adds this remark: "The success, truly unforeseen in its triumphal quality, that M. Blondel enjoyed at the Congress of Philosophy in Paris, would be hard to explain if philosophers were of the impression that the one they were acclaiming had betrayed in oblique ways what they value the most amidst their differences: the autonomy of rational inquiry."[318] Could anything be more to the point?

Now we come to a judgment on the idea we are both supposed to have regarding philosophy, a judgment based on hasty reading: "If Fathers de Lubac and Bouillard believe that the enlarging of philosophy by Blondel introduces into it a patron of a rationality that is different from that of pure or separated philosophy, this is because, to my way of thinking, they imply that philosophy left to itself is in its own way a particular dogmatism, not an analytic reflection whose sphere of application is life in all its forms."[319] Bad luck again. In the last article mentioned by Duméry, Père de Lubac writes: "The true philosopher . . . knows that philosophy consists less in a system of defined knowledge, in the enunciation of theses, than in the very mode of their systemization. . . ."[320] This comes down to saying that philosophy is not a dogmatism, whether particular or general. In this I share my friend's opinion. We read the Dialogues of Plato and the *Critique of Pure Reason* early enough to know that philosophy, even when it is set forth in a system, is not a dogmatism. At the end of my article on Blondel, in order to locate precisely the philosophical character of his thought at the moment of encounter with the Christian faith, I insisted on the *negative* aspect of his method,[321] thereby stressing that philosophy is something quite different from a dogmatism. As for determining whether Blondelian philosophy is a reflexive analysis in Duméry's sense, I have made myself sufficiently clear in the course of the present study.

We come finally to the conclusion of the same note: "When theologians write that Blondel is not a philosopher in the same way that others are, this only serves to strengthen on the rebound the old rationalist complaint that we seek to demolish."[322] To the extent that this remark is based on the conviction that I would assign to Blondel "a road midway between philosophy and theology,"[323] it is incorrect. The fact remains, however, that I have recognized and still do recognize a theological quality in his thought. But in view of the way I have specified this qualification it refers here to nothing other than the intention expressed so many times by Blondel: to reconsider the whole philosophical problem in function of the idea of human destiny provided by Christianity, not to separate one's beliefs from one's thought but consider that the evangelical doctrine ought to penetrate and make the philosophical dough ferment; finally, to expect from this effort a better understanding of Christianity. We have indicated how this effort remained fully rational and specifically philosophical.

Because Blondelian thought was developed with reference to Christianity, it has evidently to be distinguished from philosophies that have ignored Christianity or put it aside. But it bears an affinity to all the philosophies that have adopted the same reference in one way or another. Recall that the great medieval philosophies were developed not only in function of the Christian idea but in the bosom of a theology. It is true that since that time philosophy has striven to be more independent. But there are innumerable philosophers one could also call theologians without challenging in the least the rational autonomy of their procedure. Take Malebranche, for example. In the remarkable study devoted to him, M. Gueroult finds that according to Malebranche "metaphysics, if properly rational, cannot dispense with the data of faith, be content, like mathematics and physics, with reason and experience. Thus, the dogmas of Original Sin and the Incarnation will prove to be absolutely indispensable in enabling reason to resolve the 'contradictions' that experience causes it to discover in the universe."[324] Malebranche could thus make his own not only the *fides quaerens intellectum* of St. Anselm but the *crede ut intelligas* of St. Augustine.[325] These simple observations are enough to indicate that in Malebranche the data of faith are integrated more profoundly into philosophy than in Blondel's case, something Blondel himself was aware of.[326] But this does not prevent M. Gueroult from hailing Malebranche as "one of the greatest philosophers of all time."[327] When another historian, M. Gouhier, writes that this philosophy is a "theologian's philosophy,"[328] he in no way intends to signify that it is not an authentic philosophy.

Another example. It has often been said of Hegel that he was in some respects a theologian. All the Protestant histories of theology grant him a place, whether because of the influence he exercised on theological thought or precisely as a theologian. In his many-volume *History of Modern Evangelical Theology*, Emmanuel Hirsch devotes an attentive study to Hegel and declares explicitly that "he is in his place," more than many others, "in a history of theology."[329] We find here no hint of wanting to take from him his title of philosopher.

These examples, and many others could be cited, are sufficient to show that we do not rob Blondel of this title in pointing out the theological character of his thought. Under pretext of not wanting "to strengthen on the rebound the old rationalist complaint," let us not ascribe to the author of *L'Action* the rationalism that he justly sought to go beyond. Let us not believe that we risk discrediting as a philosopher one who has won his spurs as a Christian thinker. This is the place to recall a delicious observation by Gilson: "The principal reason that prevents so many historians, philosophers, and theologians from giving the name theology to what they prefer to call philosophy is that, in their mind, the notion of theology excludes that of philosophy."[330]

In his fine work on Hegel and Blondel,[331] Peter Henrici has showed very well that the Blondelian dialectic is "purely philosophical" in the sense that it never relies on theological presuppositions, that it does not introduce into its foundations any premise borrowed from the data of faith.[332] But he, too, thought that I should be interpreted as having challenged this when I wrote in my article on Blondel that his thought is not "pure philosophy," that it takes its place in the tradition of the *fides quaerens intellectum*.[333] I have sufficiently explained that I gave another sense at that time to the term "pure philosophy," and that I understood by analysis of the *ratio fidei* a prodecure without presupposition since its point of departure is a radical questioning of the affirmations of faith. I wrote in that article: "The evangelical conception of human destiny is not, to be sure, the postulate but the directive and organizing idea of (Blondel's) philosophical inquiry."[334] Citing this passage,[335] Henrici inadvertently omitted the words: "not, to be sure, the postulate." As a result the reader can no longer see the limits of the statement. As much as anyone, I have rejected the idea that the evangelical conception could be the premise or the presupposition upon which the Blondelian dialectic is based.

From another point of view, it does not seem that Henrici has given enough attention to the fact that, following the declarations of Blondel himself, the evangelical conception is the directive hypothesis of the inquiry. This omission is explained well enough because of the angle of vision. Henrici believes that "the advance of Blondel's dialectic comes to an end" with the completion of the fourth part.[336] The reflections that go to make up the fifth part on the idea of revelation and religious practice and on the being of phenomena are, for him, supplementary materials that lead us beyond the dialectic.[337] But if, prior to this last part, it had been possible to abstract from the fact that Blondel allows himself to be guided by the Christian conception in his philosophical analysis, once he introduces the idea of positive revelation this becomes impossible. Henrici himself brings out the fact that Blondel at this point takes Christian dogma as guide (*Richtweiser*) for his transcendental analysis.[338] And when the last chapter of *L'Action* introduces (with greater precautions than he allows) the idea of the Incarnation, he sees in this a conclusion that goes beyond the scope of the Blondelian method and constitutes a reflection of theological knowledge.[339] Thus, he would recognize the role of Christianity as directive idea, if he did not place the fifth part of *L'Action* beyond the term of Blondel's dialectic. Now, in the course of our study of the genesis of the idea of the supernatural, we have seen that this part, while less fundamental than what precedes, is an essential element in the dialectic of *L'Action*.

To the degree that he neglects the directive function of the Christian idea in Blondel's development, Henrici is led to a paradoxical conclusion in his final parallel between *L'Action* and the *Phenomenology of the Spirit*. He gives us to understand that, because it is purely philosophical, the Blondelian dialectic cannot be situated in the tradition of the *fides quaerens intellectum*;[340] whereas the Hegelian dialectic, while it too is purely philosophical,[341] can be located in this same tradition.[342] He explains that the reason for this is that Hegel's dialectic returns to a theological vision.[343] Whereupon we would like to observe that it does not return to it without "dialecticizing" it, and that Blondel, by another route, does the same thing. The real difference appears to be elsewhere: whereas Hegel practices "the understanding of faith" in such a way that the "understanding," that is, philosophy, goes beyond "faith," Blondel practices it in such a way that "faith," as a supernatural adherence, always goes beyond philosophy. As a consequence, Hegel's philosophy absorbs dogmatic theology by suppressing it in its dogmatic aspect. But Blondel's philosophy stops at the threshold of dogmatic theology; it only absorbs (and then only in part) fundamental theology, while proposing it as fundamental. The first philosophy is a rationalized theology; the second is a rational apologetics.[344]

***Sanctity of Reason.*** At the beginning of this chapter we asked whether Blondelian thought was a philosophy, an apologetics, or a theology. We are now in possession of the various elements of a reply which remains overwhelmingly complex. To the degree that this thought brings about an understanding of faith, it has a theological character. To the extent that it aims to lead minds to the threshold of the faith, it has an apologetic character. By this double title, it is a *Christian* philosophy. But nothing in all this should lead us to forget that it is, above all, *philosophy* in the strict sense of the word, that is, a rational and autonomous process. So we can say with Duméry that it is "a Christian philosophy obtained in an autonomous manner through a return to the exigencies of faith."[345] If we would stress what *L'Action* contributes to modern philosophy that is most original and most precious in the eyes of the believer, we might call attention to the definition Blondel himself supplied: "philosophical apology for Christianity." Or we might have recourse to the elegant formula proposed by Père Auguste Valensin in describing the book: "philosophical commentary on the Gospel."[346] But we must not forget that the term "philosophical," far from referring to an accessory and to some degree accidental specification, describes the very structure of the thought.

If we are now asked how Blondelian thought, being essentially philosophical, can also have, and by the very fact that it is philosophical, an apologetic aim and a theological scope, we shall reply: It is because it is a philosophy of action. As we have seen, the author was aware of this from the time he decided on the subject of his thesis; it is the study of action that allows us to link philosophy to the Gospel. He took his position, as it were, in the action that is common to every man, with the goal of witnessing the dialectic of real life. To him this dialectic seemed to lead inevitably to an option on the basis of which man would be lost or saved. For the achievement of action it was necessary that the option before the unique necessary be positive, that is, that it welcome an Absolute that goes beyond what philosophy can attain. To the degree that it is a reflection of action on itself, philosophy remains itself at the very moment it perceives the necessity of surpassing itself through a religious option. In his own terminology, Henrici has expressed this very well. After having shown that the philosophical dialectic of Blondel is "an intermediate phase in the existential accomplishment of the total being of man," he says: "It is a purely philosophical dialectic which does not rest on any theological presupposition, any prior theological decision; but it cannot be this save to the extent that, as a simple element in the total accomplishment of existence, it has already gone beyond the sphere of 'pure' philosophy."[347]

Only such a philosophy of action can, without contradiction, affirm the insufficiency of philosophy. For what is declared in this way is not an insufficiency that is peculiar to philosophy, but the insufficiency of all human action, including the *exercise* of philosophy. When philosophy limits itself to being a pure analysis of the form of meaning, that is, of the formal meaning that is at the basis of all concrete meanings, it must be said that it suffices fully unto itself. It completes its circle without a break. (Or if it believes that it has finally come to a standstill and pronounces on its own precariousness, because all senses seem to be haunted by nonsense, this admission, in itself, does not lead, any more than in the case of a successful unfolding of the formal meaning, to a negative or positive religious option.) The analysis of the form of meaning seems to be the essential task of philosophy. Blondel may not have fully realized this goal, even in the Trilogy where he tried even harder to do so. (That is why this work does not seem to be as adequate in terms of its object as *L'Action* with reference to its object.) But the task he assigned himself, which was that of determining the specific role of philosophy within the context of *human* activity, is also necessary and properly philosophical. For it is still up to the philosopher to indicate the formal relation between the formal and the concrete; and it is important to show how and why the concrete acting subject, man in other words, is not exhausted in the formal subject who takes the form of meaning proposed as object. It is here that the philosophy of action assumes its role and is able to pronounce on the insufficiency of philosophy without challenging either its coherence or necessity.

It is only from the point of view of a philosophy of action that Blondel could have written this paradox: "It is not only the man living in each philosophy, it is philosophy itself that is naturally and will always be normally a figure in prayer."[348] Or take this other declaration, so dear to him: "Sacrifice is the solution to the metaphysical problem through the experimental method. And if action, throughout the course of its development, has seemed to be a new source of illumination, it is also necessary that in the end the knowledge that follows the perfect act of abnegation should contain a fuller knowledge of being. It no longer views it from the outside; it grasps it, it possesses it, it finds it within itself: *Authentic philosophy is the sanctity of reason.*"[349]

# Conclusion

We have studied in Blondel, and especially in his early writings, the genesis of the idea of the supernatural, the role of the religious option in the ontological affirmation, the specific characteristics of a Christian philosophy. These are three aspects of a single relation: philosophy's openness to Christianity.

Our work has been to analyze more than to produce a synthesis. To proceed in this way at the start was indispensable. Although Blondel's thought always unites prospection and retrospection, it spontaneously favors the former. It does not always define its concepts and movement with perfect clarity. And this explains differences of interpretation. So it was necessary, in dealing with an especially delicate matter, to analyze carefully the meaning of terms, the succession of geneses, the nature of logical connections, the exact scope of affirmations. This was the only way to rally together faithfully the aspects of a thought which is more clearly defined and faithful to its distinctions than certain of its expressions would at first lead one to believe.

Because of its necessarily analytic character, our work does not call for a conclusion. Any conclusion would have to take the form either of a resumé or a critique of the whole, unless it were to attempt to present both in succession. But a resumé would make all that was demonstrative or useful in the analysis disappear; and the reader who would be satisfied with it would only retain affirmations divorced from the original context and foundation. On the other hand, a critique of the whole would also be quite inappropriate. In the course of this study we have indicated certain obscure points, certain elements that could seem problematic, or the possibility of different angles of vision. Gathering all this together in a systematic fashion might well lead us to provide the outline of another philosophy. That, however, is not our purpose here.

But if our study does not call for a conclusion, it does require a complement. Having taken the works apart to examine them one by one, they must be put back together again so that we may see them in operation. Having analyzed Blondel's procedure, it is only proper to restore its movement. The exposition offered is like those filmstrips that show sports in slow motion, such as diving, track, or horseracing. Slowing movement down allows one to grasp the arc of forms in motion in finest detail. But, taken by itself, this would only provide an inexact view since it deprives the mobile figure of the *élan* that propels it. So the film has to be speeded up to restore the portrayal of real motion. For the same reason, the reader might expect a sequel to the present work which would communicate a sense of the raw movement we have broken down into parts.

But why offer such a sequel to one who already stands at the gate of the stadium? If you want not only to contemplate the thrust of Blondel's thought but also to experience its power, all you have to do is to read *L'Action*.

# SOME DATES IN THE LIFE
# OF MAURICE BLONDEL

Born in Dijon, France: November 2, 1861.

Pupil in primary school: 1867–1870.

Studied at the Lycée de Dijon: October, 1870–July, 1879.

Licencié ès Lettres (philosophy): July 14, 1880.

Bachelier ès Science: July 28, 1880.

Bachelier en droit: November, 1883.

Studied at the Ecole Normale Supérieure: August, 1881–November, 1884.

Taught as a substitute at the Lycée de Chaumont (beginning September 14, 1885) and at the Lycée de Montauban (beginning April 15, 1886).

Agrégé de l'Université (philosophy): 1886.

Professor at the Lycée de Montauban (beginning October 1, 1886).

Professor at the Lycée d'Aix-en-Provence: October 21, 1886–July 14, 1889.

Request for the inscription of his thesis topics at the Sorbonne: March 22, 1887.

Obtained a leave of absence for the writing of his thesis: October 2, 1889.

Taught as a substitute at the Collège Stanislas, then Collège d'État: December, 1891–April, 1892.

Defended his doctoral thesis at the Sorbonne: June 7, 1893.

*L'Action* reached the book shops: November, 1893.

Married: December 12, 1894, to Mlle. Rose Royer. (She died March 7, 1919, having borne three children.)

Named Maître de Conférences (philosophy) on the Faculté des Lettres at Lille: April 30, 1895. Reappointed on July 27 for the scholastic year 1895–1896.

Chargé de Cours on the Faculté des Lettres at Aix-Marseille: December 29, 1896. Adjunct-Professor by decree of December 4, 1897. Titulary Professor: January 8, 1899–1927.

*Letter on Apologetics*; violent attack of Père Schwalm and Abbé Gayraud: 1896, beginning of controversies.

Beginning of friendship with Laberthonnière: 1897.

Correspondence with Loisy, Hügel, Batiffol, and others concerning Loisy's theses: 1902–1905.

Directed, with Laberthonnière, the *Annales de Philosophie Chrétienne*, 1905–1913.

Elected corresponding member of the Académie des Sciences Morales et Politiques: July 4, 1914.

Stopped teaching, 1927. Losing his eyesight, he began his retirement on June 18, at his own request. Devoted the remainder of his years to drafting his "philosophical testament."

Took part in the dispute on "Christian philosophy": 1931–1934.

Denounced the Nazi peril in *Lutte pour la civilisation et philosophie de la paix*: 1939.

Died: June 14, 1949, at the age of eighty-eight, in his home at Aix-en-Provence, his mind still filled with projects to be completed.

# LIST OF ABBREVIATIONS USED IN THE NOTES

| | |
|---|---|
| APC | *Annales de Philosophie Chrétienne* |
| Correspondance | Correspondance: Maurice Blondel–Auguste Valensin |
| Et. blond. | *Etudes blondéliennes* |
| L'itinéraire | *L'itinéraire philosophique de Maurice Blondel: Propos recueillis par Frédéric Lefèvre* |
| Lettre | "Lettre sur les exigences de la pensée contemporaine en matière d'apologétique et sur la méthode de la philosophie dans l'étude du problème religieux" |
| NRT | *Nouvelle Revue Théologique* |
| L'oeuvre phil. | P. Archambault, *Vers un réalisme integral: L'oeuvre philosophique de Maurice Blondel* |
| Les premiers écrits | *Les premiers écrits de Maurice Blondel* |
| Le problème de la phil. cath. | *Le problème de la philosophie catholique* |
| Le procès | *Le procès de l'intelligence* |
| Rev. des Sc. Ph. et Th. | *Revue des Sciences Philosophiques et Théologiques* |
| Rev. du Cl. Fr. | *Revue du Clergé Français* |
| Rev. Néoscol. | *Revue Néoscolastique de Philosophie* |
| RMM | *Revue de Métaphysique et de Morale* |
| La tentation | H. Duméry, *La tentation de faire du bien* |

# NOTES TO CHAPTER ONE

1. M. Blondel, *Une énigme historique. Le "Vinculum Substantiale" d'après Leibniz et l'ébauche d'un réalisme supérieur* (Paris: Beauchesne, 1930), p. 116.
2. Letter of Blondel to Jean Lacroix, cited in *Esprit* (January, 1937), 636.
3. The present chapter reproduces, with some rather extensive modifications, part of a study published in 1949: "L'intention 36 (1949), de Maurice Blondel et la théologie," *Recherche de Science Religieuse* 36 (1949), 321–402.
4. *L'itinéraire philosophique de Maurice Blondel. Propos recueillis par Frédéric Lefèvre* (Paris: Spes, 1928), pp. 66–67. Cf. *Une énigme historique,* p. 131ff. The latter work is not a translation, but an adaptation of the Latin thesis.
5. To our knowledge, the best of the early accounts of *L'Action* is that of Victor Delbos; cf. *Revue Philosophique* (December, 1894), 634–641. A résumé of the book also appears in Paul Archambault, *Vers un réalisme intégral: l'oeuvre philosophique de M. Blondel* (Paris: Bloud et Gay, 1928), pp. 13–32. An excellent more recent analysis is that of Auguste Valensin, "Maurice Blondel et la dialectique de l'action," *Etudes* 263 (November, 1949), 145–163.
6. *L'Action,* pp. vii–viii.
7. *Ibid.,* pp. xx–xxi.
8. *Ibid.,* p. 319.
9. *Ibid.,* p. 41.
10. *Ibid.,* p. 487.
11. "Determinism of action": This term recurs frequently in the early writings of Blondel. Here determinism includes the idea both of necessary linking and development or expansion. The determinism of action is "the logical process of life" (*Les premiers écrits,* II:141), the "dynamism of the spiritual life" (p. 98), the "real dialectic II: 141), human actions" (p. 125), all of which link our acts and thoughts together according to the inexorable logic of life. Keeping in mind that Blondel often uses the term "dialectic"

as synonymous with "determinism," we can translate "determinism of action" by "dialectic of action."

12. *L'Action*, p. 475.

13. *Ibid.*, p. 473.

14. Following the account of J. Wehrlé, "Une soutenance de thèse,"*APC* 154 (April–September, 1907), 118–119. The text is reprinted in *Et. blond.*, I:82–83.

15. *L'itinéraire*. We have it on good authority that these "propos" or remarks were drawn up in their entirety (questions and answers) by Blondel himself, except the pages dealing with the theories of Père Jousse. They constitute a most agreeable introduction to the reading of Blondel's work.

16. *L'itinéraire*, p. 66.

17. *Ibid.*, p. 76; cf. pp. 77–78.

18. *Ibid.*, p. 79. ". . . the concrete which, as the word itself indicates, signifies both an expressive and distinct unity and an effective and synthetic multiplicity."

19. *Ibid.*, pp. 66–67; cf. p. 79.

20. *L'Action*, p. 435.

21. "Une soutenance de thèse," APC 154 (May, 1907), 124–125; *Et. blond.* I:87.

22. *L'Action*, p. 440.

23. *Ibid.*, p. 463.

24. Gabriel Marcel, *Etre et avoir* (Paris, 1935), p. 123.

25. Preface to the book by T. Cremer, *Le problème religieux dans la philosophie de l'action* (Paris, 1912), p. vii. The same text was also printed in *APC* 163 (November, 1911), 113–118. The lines cited are on p. 114. Blondel was fond of this passage.

26. *L'itinéraire*, p. 41.

27. "Une soutenance de thèse," p. 139; *Et. blond.*, I:96.

28. *L'Action*, pp. 385–388.

29. *Ibid.*, p. vii.

30. *Ibid.*, p. 15.

31. The most complete accounts of the history of the controversies will be found in: Maurice Blondel, *Le problème de la phil. cath.*, first part; P. Archambault, *L'oeuvre phil.*; Lecanuet, *La vie de l'Eglise sous Léon XIII* (Paris, 1930), phil.; XI; Roger Aubert, *Le problème de l'acte de foi* (Louvain, 1945), part two, chapter II.

32. The author of this anonymous review was Léon Brunschvicg.

33. *RMM*, Supplément for January, 1894, p. 7.

34. Some criticisms were expressed with moderation, courtesy, and lively praise by Dom. L. Delatte in *Le Mois Bibliographique*, a Catholic bulletin

of works and reviews (August 1, 1894), pp. 328–334. Blondel thanked the author for this review and replied to his objections in a letter (August 31, 1894); cf. *Lettres philosophiques* (Paris: Aubier, 1961).

35. To abbreviate this exceedingly long title for purposes of citation, it has been customary to write: *Lettre sur l'apologétique*. Recently, some interpreters have complained that this abbreviation gives an inexact idea of its contents. While this is to some extent true, it is worth noting that Blondel himself frequently used it in his own correspondence. Often he wrote: *Lettre aux Annales*. The *Letter* has been translated into English: Alexander Dru and Illtyd Trethowan, *Maurice Blondel: "The Letter on Apologetics" and "History and Dogma"* (New York: Holt, Rinehart & Winston, 1964). This fine version has not been used by the translator because Père Bouillard often centers an important argument around a point of textual exegesis that would be obscured were the elegant literary translation used. This is by no means an adverse reflection on the Trethowan version, which, for almost any other purpose, could hardly be improved on.

36. *Lettre*, p. 34. All references are to *Les premiers écrits*, II, which contains the full text of the *Lettre*.

37. *Ibid.*, p. 37.

38. *Ibid.*, p. 39.

39. *Ibid.*, p. 40.

40. *Ibid.*, p. 43.

41. *Ibid.*, p. 51.

42. Brunschvicg judged it "extremely remarkable," and from this time forward testified to his esteem for Blondel. Cf. *RMM* 4 (1896), 383–384.

43. M.-B. Schwalm, "Les illusions de l'idéalisme et leurs dangers pour la foi," *Revue Thomiste* 4 (September, 1896), 440. It is worth noting that the author of this article later on, after an extended exchange with Blondel, apologized to him for his harsh judgment. Cf. *L'itinéraire*, p. 104.

44. Schwalm, "Les illusions de l'idéalisme," *Revue Thomiste* 4 (1896), 413.

45. *L'Action*, pp. 27–28, 451–454, 457, 460.

46. *Ibid.*, p. 28.

47. *Lettre*, p. 65.

48. Letter of Blondel to Lalande (1902), reproduced in *Vocabulaire de la Société Française de Philosophie* (6th ed., 1951), p. 1230.

49. *Ibid.*, p. 1231.

50. *L'Action*, p. 341.

51. J. de Tonquédec, *Immanence. Essai critique sur la doctrine de M. Maurice Blondel* (Paris: Beauchesne, 1913), pp. 95–96.

52. *L'Action*, p. 350.

53. *Ibid.*, p. 457.

54. *Ibid.*, p. 437.

55. *Ibid.*, p. 438.

56. *Ibid.*, p. 436.

57. *Lettre*, p. 43.

58. H. Gayraud, "Une nouvelle apologétique chrétienne," *APC* 132 (December, 1896), 268. Cf. p. 271: ". . . not, without doubt, the naturalism that positively excludes every supernatural, but that subtle form of naturalism which, supposing nature to be insufficient, claims that the supernatural, whose name is carefully preserved, is absolutely necessary for him: in this way the supernatural order is in some way circumscribed within the purely rational order."

59. This is what Blondel explained in a letter to Laberthonnière, cited by the latter in *Essais de philosophie religieuse* (Paris: Lethielleux, 1903), p. 317. He protested against those who accused him of naturalism, "as though I had said that the supernatural is *exacted* by us and *necessitated* by our nature, whereas, on the contrary, I say that it is *necessitating* for our nature and *exigent* in us!" But, he adds, we should not forget that, according to revelation, the supernatural is necessary for man, indispensable.—Several critics have thought that Blondel, in denying that he had "said that the supernatural is exacted by nature," was contradicting and disavowing the thesis in *L'Action*, announced, for example, on page 462: "It is impossible that the supernatural order . . . not be, because the whole natural order guarantees it by exacting it." Actually, there is no contradiction. Later in the same book (p. 464), the author qualifies this: "What we require to act is, first of all, exacted of us."

60. L. Laberthonnière, "Le problème religieux," *APC* 132 (February and March, 1897), 497–511, 615–632. Reproduced in *Essais de philosophie religieuse*, pp. 151–190.

61. *Essais*, pp. 171–172.

62. *APC* 151 (1905–06), 68–91, 449–471, 625–645; 153 (1906–07), 562–591.

63. *APC* 151 (1905–06), 180–186; 153 (1906–07), 47–59.

64. *APC* 154 (1907), 337–361.

65. *APC* 165 (1912–13), 27–53, 137–184, 359–397; 166 (1913), 5–45, 150–190.

66. "Quelle est la valeur de l'apologétique interne?", *Rev. des Sc. Ph. et Th.* I (1907), 449–473; *L'objet intégral de l'apologétique* (Paris, 1912).

67. Cf. examples and testimonials cited by Albert Milet, *Rev. Néoscol.* 43, (1940–45), 250–251, note 65.

68. On this subject cf. Albert Milet, "Les 'Cahiers' du P. Maréchal," *Rev. Néoscol.* 43 (1940–45), 241–247. The correspondence exchanged between Blondel and Maréchal has been published in *Mélanges Maréchal* (Bruxelles–Paris: 1950), I:338–352. In 1957, Père André Hayen published in *Convivium* (Estudios Filosóficos) a text by Maréchal on the Philosophy of Action.

69. *Lettre*, 28.

70. The densest treatment is in a letter by Blondel to the Société de Philosophie, printed in the *Bulletin*, meeting of December 28, 1911.

71. The already classic treatments of the subject by J. Werhlé, L. de Grandmaison, P. Tiberghien, J. Mouroux, etc., depend on Blondel.

72. In his book, *Le problème de l'acte de foi*, Roger Aubert analyzes and judges fairly the controversies that centered around the method of immanence. He does justice to Blondel's work. From another point of view, one may refer to Père de Montcheuil's Introduction to *Pages religieuses de Maurice Blondel*, pp. 14–33.

73. "A propos de la certitude religieuse" (reply to Abbé E. Pêchegut), *Revue du Clergé Francais* (February, 1902), 643–659.

74. In *La Quinzaine* 56 (January and February, 1904), 145–167, 349–373, 433–458. Add another related article: "De la valeur historique du dogme," *Bulletin de Littérature Ecclésiastique de Toulouse* 7 (February, 1905), 61–77. Both essays are reprinted in *Les premiers écrits, II*.

75. *Les premiers écrits*, II:204.

76. *Ibid.*, 228.

77. *Ibid.*, 204–205.

78. *Ibid.*, 210.

79. The role Blondel played in the crisis occasioned by Loisy's Little Red Books appears even more important now that the letters Blondel exchanged with Wehrlé, Mourret, Loisy, von Hügel, etc., have been published. Cf. *Au coeur de la crise moderniste. Le dossier inédit d'une controverse*, Letters presented by René Marlé (Paris: Aubier, 1960). The correspondence reveals the clarity with which Blondel saw from the outset the philosophical and theological deficiencies of Loisy's theory.

80. *La "Semaine Sociale" de Bordeaux*, a series of articles that appeared in *APC* between October, 1909, and May, 1910, followed by replies to critics (December, 1910). Also reprinted separately as *La Semaine Sociale de Bordeaux et le Monophorisme* (Paris: 1910). Blondel criticized, under the name of Monophorism, the theory according to which Christianity was viewed as coming entirely from the outside without corresponding to any interior aspiration, and as being imposed uniquely by an authoritarian decree.

81. In *RMM* 6 (1898), 726–745.

82. *APC* 151 (1905–06), 337–360; 152 (1906), 225–249.

83. *APC* 151 (1905–06), 342.

84. *APC* 152 (1906), 234–235. This is the source of the three lines for which Blondel was often so bitterly reproached: "For the abstract and chimerical *adaequatio speculativa rei et intellectus*, there is substituted the methodical search for the *adaequatio realis mentis et vitae*" (p. 235). This paradoxical sentence, equivocal if read in isolation, should not be detached from its

context. It does not mean that truth is perpetually changing, or that it is measured on the basis of practical utility, or that it is not a correpondence of knowledge with its object. Blondel explains on what condition truth spontaneously known is reflexively justified in the eyes of the philosopher. It is on condition that it is referred to a universal and incontrovertible judicial principle, to the spiritual dynamism that directs and judges all thought and human activity. And this dynamism has an ontological scope, since its total expansion leads necessarily to the affirmation of the being that is its source.

85. In *Bibliothèque du Congrès International de Philosophie de 1900*, volume II: *Morale Générale.*

86. This is an appropriate place to state categorically, against persistent rumors, that no work by Blondel was ever placed on the Index, that he was never the object of any ecclesiastical censure, and that, on the contrary, he was encouraged by the highest Church authorities. Cf. *L'itinéraire*, pp. 99–100; also the letter of the Vatican Secretary of State, the present Pope Paul VI, dated December 2, 1944, cited in *Documentation Catholique*, July 8, 1945; the eulogy pronounced by His Excellency, Monsignor de Provenchères, at Blondel's funeral, an address from which several typical lines are cited in *La Vie Intellectuelle* (July, 1949), p. 53.

87. *APC* 166 (1913), 1.

88. One can easily satisfy oneself on this point today by reading the notes for a new edition of *L'Action* drawn up between 1895 and 1900. They were published posthumously in *Et. blond.*, II (1952), 7–46. See also in *Et. blond.*, I (1951), 7–58, the projects and outlines from the years 1927–29.

89. *Rev. du Cl. Fr.* (July 15, 1913), 246–247. The letter, dated June 20, 1913, was written a month after the *Annales de Philosophie Chrétienne* had been put on the Index.

90. *Rev. du Cl. Fr.* (September 1, 1919), 383–387.

91. *Ibid.*(February 15, 1902), p. 652 (letter to Abbé Pêchegut).

92. *Histoire et dogme* (*Les premiers écrits*, II:210, etc.) See also the articles, signed by Abbé Mallet, on the work of Cardinal Dechamps. When Blondel reproduced them again in 1932 in *Le problème de la phil. cath.*, he eliminated all the passages praising the merits of "the philosophy of action."

93. Cited by Archambault in *L'oeuvre phil.*, p. 5, note 3.

94. *APC* 152 (1906), 235.

95. Letter to Archambault, cited in *L'oeuvre philosophique*, p. 6, note.

96. Originally published as a series of articles in *La Nouvelle Journée* in 1921. Reprinted in 1922 in the volume bearing the same title: *Le procès de l'intelligence* (Paris: Bloud et Gay, 1922). References are to the latter publication.

97. *Le procès*, pp. 236–237, 264–266.

98. "Le problème de la mystique," *Qu'est-ce que la mystique?* Cahiers de La Nouvelle Journée, 3 (Paris: Bloud et Gay, 1925).

99. *Ibid.*, 49–50. Blondel wrote to Paul Archambault along the same lines in 1918: "Metaphysics is only a schema, a *mimicking* of the real; similarly and *a fortiori*, a study of the religious life, no matter how intense, is like a shell . . ." (Cited by Archambault, *L'oeuvre phil.*, p. 73, note.)

100. *La Pensée*, II:25.

101. *L'itinéraire*, p. 169.

102. Cited by Archambault, *L'oeuvre phil.*, p. 74, note.

103. This change was noted by B. Romeyer, *La philosophie religeiuse de Maurice Blondel* (Paris: Aubier, 1943), pp. 173–178.

104. "Le problème de la phil. cath.," pp. 25–26.

105. *Ibid.*, p. 171, note 1.

106. *Ibid.*, p. 25.

107. In *Recherches de Science Religieuse* (1924), 193–246.

108. "Le problème de la phil. cath.," 26, 165.

109. *Ibid.*, pp. 166–173.

110. *Ibid.*, p. 167, note 1.

111. *Ibid.*, p. 175, note 1.

112. *La Pensée*, II:21.

113. *Ibid.*, II:41.

114. *Ibid.*, I:169–204, 390–400, 401–411; II:89–109, 279–306.

115. "Fidélité conservée par la croissance même de la tradition," *Revue Thomiste* 40 (1936), 611–626. (Irenic reply to the criticism of P. Garrigou-Lagrange.) Cf. *L'Action* (1936), I:305–307.

116. *L'Action* (1936), I:353–354; see Excursus 12, 15, and 16 of this volume. On "agnition," see J. Paliard, "A propos de l'idée d'agnition dans la philosophie de Maurice Blondel," *Revue Philosophique* 125 (January–June, 1938), 96–109. The idea of agnition is equally fruitful in the theology of faith.

117. *L'Action* (1937), II:14.

118. For a discussion of *La Pensée* and *L'Etre et les êtres*, see Jeanne Mercier, "La philosophie de Maurice Blondel," *RMM* 44 (1937), 623–658; also P. Vignaux, "Sur quelques tendances de la philosophie de Maurice Blondel," *Recherche Philosophique* 6 (1936–37), 363–372.

119. "Le point de départ de la recherche philosophique," *APC* 152 (1906), 235.

120. On this subject see Pierre Lachièze-Rey, "Reflexions sur la portée ontologique de la méthode blondélienne," *Hommages à Maurice Blondel* (Paris: Bloud et Gay, 1946), pp. 115–156.

121. It is curious to observe that Blondel here no longer seems to understand the methodological reserve of the phenomenological epoche prac-

ticed in the first *L'Action*. In *La Pensée*, II:501–502, in order to show that
he never contested the objective value of our knowledge and the reality of
the physical, psychological, and metaphysical order, he writes as though
it were a misinterpretation when his critics attributed to him the "indefen-
sible" and "chimerical" thesis referred to: "To believe that we can attain
being and legitimately affirm any reality whatsoever without having
reached the very term of the series that leads from the first sense intuition
to the necessity of God and religious practice, is to court illusion . . ." Yet
these lines are to be found textually in the first *L'Action* (p. 428). They
summarize one of the essential theses of the last chapter. Subsequently,
Blondel would read them in the light of the controversies they would
generate. He was right to criticize them in the sense often given to them.
But this was not their true meaning, as we shall have occasion to show.

122. *La philosophie et l'esprit chrétien*, I:211–212.

123. *La Pensée*, II:336.

124. *Ibid.*, II:337.

125. *Ibid.*, II:332–333.

126. *Ibid.*, II:302–303. Cf. *L'Action*, II:367.

127. *La Pensée*, II:338.

128. *Ibid.*, II:327–328.

129. Expression used by H. Duméry in an article on "La philosophie de
l'action," in *La tentation de faire du bien* (Paris: Editions du Seuil, 1956),
pp. 182–183.

130. *Ibid.*, p. 183.

131. *Ibid.*, p. 168.

132. H. Duméry, *Blondel et la religion, essai critique sur la "Lettre" de 1896*
(Paris: P.U.F., 1954), pp. 5–7; *La tentation*, p. 183.

# NOTES TO CHAPTER TWO

1. H. Duméry, *Blondel et la religion, essai critique sur la "Lettre" de 1896,* (Paris: P.U.F., 1954), pp. 2, 82. We find the same concern in several pages of *Critique et religion* (Paris: Sedes, 1957), pp. 99–112. The earlier work of the same interpreter, *La philosophie de l'action* (Paris: Aubier, 1948), had a different design, which was to study *L'Action* of 1893 "as the mother-cell of the entirety" of the Blondelian work (p. 16).

2. *Blondel et la religion,* pp. *41–42;* cf. also by the same author, *Critique et religion,* pp. 103–107.

3. *Blondel et la religion,* p. 94.

4. *Ibid.,* pp. 52, 84–85, 92–93.

5. *Ibid.,* p. 94.

6. *Ibid.,* p. 80.

7. *Ibid.,* p. 9. "The joy of the historian lies in critical detachment. How great it is, then, when he discovers that some incriminated text means something quite different from what it was supposed to mean. The *Letter* held this kind of surprise for us. Without further ado we must let the reader in on the matter."

8. *Ibid.,* p. 103. He seems to regard the "eulogists" as responsible for the blame inflicted by the "detractors." This is the more surprising since the only eulogist mentioned in this place published more than forty years after the first detractors.

9. *Ibid.,* p. 102, note 2.

10. Cf. Yves de Montcheuil's Introduction to his *Pages religieuses:* "We would be even farther removed [from the true thought of Blondel] were we to suppose it possible by this way to succeed not only in showing that the supernatural is necessary for us but that it effectively exists. It would then be necessary to admit as a postulate from the start that the aspirations of the will ought to be satisfied and that all that the will requires is really given. Now, no such postulate lies at the basis of the philosophy of action." *Maurice Blondel: pages religieuses* (Paris, 1942), p. 24.

11. *Blondel et la religion*, p. 77.

12. *Ibid.*, pp. 77–79.

13. *Lettre* (1896), p. 45 (p. 39 in the reprint cited by Duméry).

14. *Ibid.*, p. 45 (39).

15. *Blondel et la religion*, pp. 77–79.

16. *Ibid.*, p. 79.

17. *Ibid.*, p. 79, note 5.

18. Objection proposed by a fellow student; cf. *Le problème de la philosophie catholique*, p. ii, note.

19. Letter to Maurice Léna, March 23, 1890.

20. We shall return in the last chapter to the attention Blondel gave to Spinozism and what he called in those days "German pantheism."

21. We found these phrases in notes dating from 1894 used in preparing the article to be cited farther on, dealing with "the evolution of Spinozism" (in connection of the work of Delbos).

22. *Lettre*, p. 34.

23. Perhaps it is an exaggeration to say that "people are in general content to illustrate the method of immanence" by this text (Duméry, *Blondel et la religion*, p. 38, note 1). We do not know of any example of this among serious interpreters. Only polemicists, like Abbé Gayraud, confused the whole issue. (Cf. "Une nouvelle apologétique chrétienne," *APC* 132 (1896), 267–268.)

24. In seeming to confront the supernatural with the notion of immanence, Blondel is not teaching here that the supernatural can enter man only if it comes out of him. We should not confuse the objection and the reply.

25. In the November, 1893, Supplément of *RMM*; reprinted in *Et. blond.*, I:99.

26. Under the pseudonym Bernard Aimant, "Une des sources de la pensée moderne: l'évolution du Spinozisme," *APC* 128 (1894), 262.

27. *Lettre, p. 36.*

28. *Ibid.*, pp. 35–36.

29. *Ibid.*, p. 37. Duméry wrote that Blondel, in the last proposition cited here, "seems to mean that nature has an exigency for the supernatural," thus apparently contradicting other declarations (*Blondel et la religion*, p. 78, note 3). In reality, the word "exigency" in this proposition clearly has the same signification as the word "exigencies" in the preceding sentence. So it is not a question of an exigency of nature with regard to the supernatural, but of the exigency of revelation with respect to man.

30. Was Blondel thinking of pure nature when he wrote another passage of the *Lettre*? He says that in showing the necessity of the supernatural he does not intend "to deny that a neutral state is conceivable for one not called to use reason or receive by pure grace a communication regarding

the mediating power" (p. 44). Duméry is of the opinion that "by this formula Blondel intends to make a bow in the direction of the hypothesis of pure nature" (*Blondel et la religion*, p. 34, note 1). We do not think so. As a matter of fact, Blondel is not thinking here of the idea of a state that could have been that of humanity in general, but of the idea of a state that could be, even in the present economy, that of some men, of those who have not had the use of reason and to whom, in the hypothesis, God would not communicate the mediating power although dispensing them from all cooperation. In the *Lettre* and in *L'Action* Blondel does not deny the possibility of a state of pure nature; he simply does not speak about it.

31. *Lettre*, p. 21.

32. *Ibid.* p. 45.

33. Do not forget that, whereas *L'Action* is addressed to the unbelieving philosopher, the *Lettre* is addressed directly to believers, apologists, or theologians in order to explain to them the legitimate exigencies of philosophy and thus to show indirectly those philosophers who will read it the rational character of the Blondelian enterprise.

34. *Lettre*, p. 30.

35. *Ibid.*, p. 15.

36. *Ibid.*, p. 28.

37. *Ibid.*, p. 13.

38. *Ibid.*, p. 28.

39. *Ibid.*, p. 13–14. When Blondel declares that "man cannot with impunity pass up" the supernatural life, he implies, says Duméry, "in the case that it really exists" (*Blondel et la religion*, p. 57, note 1). We do not think that this conditional is warranted here; for in this passage Blondel is addressing himself to believers who admit, as he does, the reality of the supernatural. (We shall see later on the sense in which he views the supernatural as a hypothesis when addressing the unbelieving philosopher.) Again, the formula, "this necessary and impracticable life," does not contain any ambiguity. It simply repeats the Gospel teaching: Faith is necessary for salvation, although no human means can give rise to it because it is a gratuitous gift.

40. *Lettre*, p. 14.

41. *Ibid.*, p. 38.

42. *Ibid.*, p. 39. Cf. p. 85: "Philosophy, using a complex and compelling method which permits it to cross and draw into the current of the same determinism all the forms of thought and life, has for its role to show what we inevitable are and what we necessarily lack, so that we may be able to reintegrate into our willed action all that is proposed and postulated by our spontaneous action."

43. *Blondel et la religion*, p. 79.

44. *Ibid.*, pp. 47–49.
45. In his *Pages religieuses*, Introduction, p. 13.
46. *Existence et vérité* (Paris: P.U.F., 1955), pp. 60–64. These pages offer most illuminating explanations. However, since they deal with the Blondelian critique of dilettantism, they contain some expressions which are not entirely suitable for the following steps of *L'Action*.
47. *L'Action* (1937), II:354.
48. *L'Action* (1893), p. 323.
49. Cf. Duméry, *Blondel et la religion*, pp. 47, 49.
50. *Ibid.*, p. 49.
51. This is what Duméry seems to be saying, *ibid.*, pp. 47 and 54, note 1. Compare the two passages.
52. *Lettre*, p. 44.
53. Duméry, *Blondel et la religion*, p. 78, note 3.
54. The word Duméry prefers.
55. *Lettre*, p. 21.
56. In a letter *RMM* (1894); reprinted in *Et. blond.*, I:102.
57. *Ibid.*, p. 103.
58. *Ibid.*, p. 103.
59. *L'Action*, pp. 406–407.
60. *Blondel et la religion*, p. 75.
61. *L'Action*, p. 394; cf. *Lettre*, p. 41.
62. *L'Action*, p. 394.
63. *Ibid.*, p. 397.
64. *L'Action*, p. 41.
65. Note, drawn up by Blondel, to be inserted in the volumes of the second *L'Action*; reprinted in *Et. blond.*, I:78.
66. *L'Action*, p. 44.
67. *Ibid.*, p. 44.
68. *Ibid.*, pp. 279–290.
69. *Ibid.*, pp. 290–297.
70. *Ibid.*, p. 296.
71. *Ibid.*, pp. 297–303.
72. *Ibid.*, p. 303.
73. *Ibid.*, p. 304.
74. *Ibid.*, p. 314.
75. *Ibid.*, p. 319.
76. No doubt, the absolute or the divine from which specifically moral action is suspended, is none other, in itself, than God himself. But this has not yet been made manifest. As for the claim of the metaphysician who

believes he can manipulate transcendent Being by his method and by his natural religion, we have seen that Blondel regards it as subtle idolatry.

77. *L'Action*, p. 322.

78. *Ibid.*, pp. 323–338.

79. *Ibid.*, p. 339.

80. *Ibid.*, p. 338; see also pp. 351–354.

81. *Ibid.*, pp. 354–355.

82. *Ibid.*, p. 372.

83. *Ibid.*, p. 374.

84. *Ibid.*, p. 375.

85. *L'Action*, p. 385. This sentence, as will be seen below, is the transposition of an idea of St. Ignatius Loyola.

86. *L'Action*, p. 387.

87. *Ibid.*, p. 388.

88. *Ibid.*

89. In his often remarkable study, *Hegel und Blondel*, Peter Henrici has developed a subtle and ingenious way of weakening the sense of the word "necessary." Cf. Excursus III, pp. 199–202. His demonstration does not seem convincing. What should have been toned down was the sense of the word "supernatural."

90. *L'Action*, pp. 386–387.

91. *Ibid.*, p. 388. In an earlier draft of *L'Action*, Blondel said that it was to this "truly divine life that Aristotle, the Platonists, the Alexandrines, Spinoza, Maine de Biran aspired." He noted in the margin that they aspired to it "theoretically, rather than practically, *in objecto, non in intimo affectu cordis.*" Known as "Thesis Project," drawn up between June 14, 1890, and April 19, 1891, the manuscript is preserved at the Blondel Archives, Aix-en-Provence (p. 182 of the MS). In the *Lettre*, Blondel, referring to the same text of Aristotle, will write that "far from seeing here a kind of stepping-stone for the supernatural," it must be recognized "as pure philosophy's permanent candidacy for the supreme rank, higher than we do put it" (pp. 56–57). Thus, he takes his position from a different angle of vision. Both are legitimate, as we shall indicate at the end of this chapter.

92. *L'Action*, p. 388.

93. *Ibid.*, p. 388.

94. St. Thomas Aquinas used to say that creation requires a "supernatural" principle or agent. (See Bouillard, *Conversion et grâce chez saint Thomas d'Aquin* [Paris, 1944], p. 203). Today we would say "transcendent," because this usage has been progressively introduced by theologians in order to reserve the term "supernatural" for the divine life communicated in Jesus Christ.

95. *L'Action*, p. 40 (supernatural) and p. 42 (transcendent). Compare the

two passages. Cf. the *Lettre*, pp. 40–41. Elsewhere in the *Lettre* (p. 34) Blondel distinguishes the "supernatural" from the "transcendent in the simple metaphysical sense of the word"; but in that place it is a question of the specifically Christian sense of the supernatural.

96. *L'Action* (1937), II:521.

97. *L'Action* (1937), II:521, note.

98. *L'Action* (1893), p. 390.

99. *L'Action*, p. 391.

100. *Ibid.*, p. 391.

101. *Ibid.*, p. 391.

102. In the manuscript Blondel turned in at the Sorbonne in May, 1892, to secure permission to have the thesis printed, this was indicated by the very title of this fifth part, "The Critique of Supernatural Action. The Philosophy of Catholicism" (p. 355 of the MS in the Blondel Archives). The positive determination of this title is at odds with the general nature of the title given to the fourth part: "The Divine Destiny of Man and the Eternity of Action." We shall see later on how the author changed these titles in order to make the philosophical character of his work more evident.

103. *L'Action*, p. 390.

104. *Ibid.*, p. 390.

105. *Ibid*, p. 356.

106. *Ibid.*, p. 393.

107. *Ibid.*, p. 391.

108. *Ibid.*, pp. 406–407.

109. *Ibid.*, p. 407, note 1.

110. *Ibid.*, p. 407, note 1.

111. *Ibid.*, p. 391.

112. *Ibid.*, p. 491.

113. *Ibid*, pp. 491–492.

114. *Ibid.*, p. 406.

115. *Ibid.*, p. 406.

116. *L'Action*, p. 153. Note here that Blondel anticipates the idea of the "corps propre" that will be the object of Merleau-Ponty's analyses in *Phénoménologie de la perception*.

117. *L'Action*, pp. 153–154.

118. *Ibid.*, p. 156.

119. *Ibid.*, p. 397.

120. *Ibid.*, pp. 394–399.

121. *Ibid.*, pp. 400–404, 405–422.

122. *Ibid.*, pp. 400–401, 403.

123. *Ibid.*, p. 418.

124. *Ibid.*, pp. 398–399.

125. Cf. the *Lettre*, pp. 90–91.

126. We borrow this formula from an excellent observation by Jean Trouillard concerning the Blondelian dialectic in general. He says that the necessity that links together the multiple conditions of our own equation "is not an *analytic* necessity or one of inclusion, because the principal movement in Blondel is ascending, and a lower step does not contain one that lies beyond it and follows it. . . . The necessity that makes us move from condition to condition is *synthetic.* This means that it rigorously imposes the passage upward, not because the lower includes the higher, but because the lesser here requires the greater to sustain a non-being which, far from being nothingness, is a concrete lack. There is, then, real progress from the same to the other by the other of the same, according to the model given by Plato in the Sophist." Cf. "La structure de la recherche métaphysique selon Maurice Blondel," *Les Etudes Philosophiques* (1952), pp. 370–371.

127. *L'Action,* p. 426.

128. *L'Action,* fifth part, chapters I and II.

129. *L'Action,* fourth part. In the manuscript deposited at the Sorbonne to secure permission to print his thesis, Blondel had written "Decisive Part" in place of "Fourth part."

130. *L'Action,* p. 487.

131. *Ibid.,* p. 462.

132. Duméry, *La philosophie de l'action,* p. 149.

133. *L'Action,* p. 343.

134. *Ibid.,* p. 344.

135. *Ibid.,* p. 487.

136. *Blondel et la religion,* pp. 47, note 1; 52; 58–76.

137. *La philosophie de l'action,* pp. 143–147.

138. *L'Action,* pp. 374–388.

139. *La philosophie de l'action,* p. 146.

140. *Ibid.,* p. 145.

141. *Ibid.,* p. 148.

142. *L'Action,* p. 388.

143. *La philosophie de l'action,* p. 148.

144. *L'Action,* p. 388.

145. *Ibid.,* p. 388.

146. *Blondel et la religion,* pp. 58–62.

147. *Ibid.,* pp. 58–60.

148. *Ibid.,* pp. 60–62.

149. However, we would avoid saying that for philosophy the supernatural is a "necessary possible" (*Blondel et la religion,* pp. 33–34). This unaccus-

tomed expression does not appear anywhere in Blondel. It has the disadvantage of associating two terms which he explicitly sets in opposition one to the other: "It is neither to a reality, nor to a possibility, but to a necessity that the complete study of the determinism of action leads" (*L'Action*, p. 406). Duméry does not seem to contradict this declaration by Blondel, because he gives another meaning to the word "possible." However, it would be better to avoid such an equivocal expression.

150. *L'Action*, p. 458.

151. *Lettre*, p. 46.

152. *Ibid.*, pp. 45–46.

153. *L'Action*, p. 463.

154. *Ibid.*, p. 426.

155. *Ibid.*, p. 433; cf. p. 453.

156. In the course of this commentary, he distinguishes two planes: a *natural* plane and *essential necessities*, a *transnatural* plane and *hypothetical necessities* (*La philosophie de l'action*, p. 159). But, as pointed out above, the necessity of the supernatural is situated entirely on the second plane, without any reference to the distinction of the two final stages indicated by Blondel.

157. Blondel tells us this himself in a letter to Abbé Bricout (April 4, 1897): "In my *Lettre* to the *Annales*, I simply touched, and from a restricted angle, a question of 'method': I had no need then to indicate the material content of philosophical doctrines that I do believe are conformed to the common exigencies of reason and faith. It is in my study of *Action* that I have indicated more precisely the sequence of philosophical ideas."

158. *Lettre*, p. 43.

159. *Ibid.*, p. 43.

160. *Lettre*, p. 44.

161. *Blondel et la religion*, pp. 51, 63.

162. *Ibid.*, p. 92.

163. See especially the end, pp. 353–356.

164. *Lettre*, pp. 44–45.

165. *L'Action*, p. 388.

166. *Lettre*, pp. 44–45.

167. *L'Action*, p. 388.

168. *Ibid.*, p. 388.

169. *Lettre*, p. 44.

170. *Ibid.*, p. 45.

171. *Blondel et la religion*, p. 92.

172. *Lettre*, p. 45.

173. *Ibid.*, p. 44.

174. *Ibid.*, p. 45.
175. *Ibid.*, p. 45.
176. *Ibid.*, p. 45.
177. *Lettre*, p. 44.
178. Contrary to Duméry's opinion (*Blondel et la religion*, pp. 85–86).
179. *Lettre*, p. 45.
180. *Ibid.*, pp. 44, 67–68.
181. *Ibid.*, p. 68.
182. *Ibid.*, p. 37.
183. *Ibid.*, pp. 87–88; cf. *L'Action*, p. 399.
184. *Lettre*, p. 90; cf. *L'Action*, pp. 460–461, 463–464.
185. *Lettre*, p. 41.
186. *Ibid.*, p. 47.
187. Cf. *Lettre*, pp. 12–26.
188. *Ibid.*, p. 47.
189. *Ibid.*, pp. 86–87.
190. *Ibid.*, pp. 88–89.
191. *Ibid.*, p. 43.
192. *Ibid.*, p. 46.
193. *Ibid.*, p. 40.
194. *Ibid.*, p. 45.
195. *Ibid.*, p. 41.
196. "I have never dreamed of indicating a real continuity between the world of reason and that of faith, or of making the supernatural order enter into the determinism of action; I have stated on various occasions . . . that we can neither conceive by the effort of thought nor attain by the development of action the supernatural order which elevates man above every created or conceivable being. I have simply sought to show that the determinism of our own will constrains us to acknowledge its insufficiency, leads us to the felt need for an increase which cannot come from ourselves, gives us the aptitude, not to produce it or define it, but to recognize and receive it, opens to us, in a word, this baptism of desire which remains, nonetheless, everywhere accessible, even to one who has no notion of revelation."
197. This letter, written in Italian, is preserved in the Blondel Archives. It is cited on the basis of a translation that the archivist, Mlle. Panis, had made for our purpose.
198. We see that Semeria understands by "pure nature" human nature insofar as it is not vitiated in itself by original sin. This conforms with the usage of the period. After some thirty years, the custom has been progressively established of designating by the term "pure nature" human nature insofar as it could be conceived as not having a supernatural destiny.

199. It seems that this sentence could be taken as the definition of the term "subjective faith" used above. The following sentence gives explicitly the definition of the term "objective faith," with an indication of its relation to subjective faith. This provides us the wherewithal to clarify the meaning of a sufficiently obscure statement in the *Lettre* (p. 40): "Formally identical with objective faith, subjective faith is entirely given over to rational criticism, without the first faith being able to be touched in its depths." This formal identity is not an identity of content: By itself subjective faith has only a very indeterminate content.

200. Reprinted in *Essais de philosophie religieuse* (Paris: Lethielleux, 1903).

201. *Essais*, p. 1.

202. *Ibid.*, pp. 171–173.

203. In a letter (May 9, 1897) to Père Beaudouin, O.P., he himself took up the defense of Laberthonnière.

204. *Histoire et dogme*, in *Les Premiers écrits*, II:224.

205. *Ibid.*, p. 224, note.

206. *APC* 159 (1909), 268; page 61 of the brochure that gathers together the series of articles, *La Semaine Sociale de Bordeaux et le Monophorisme*. See in A. Lalande's *Vocabulaire de la philosophie*, Blondel's contribution under the word *Transnaturel* (introduced at his request). Cf. also the clarifications given to Père Auguste Valensin in a letter, dated January 21, 1912, as well as the references indicated in a note by the editor of the correspondence (*Correspondance*, II:264–265).

207. *La Semaine Sociale de Bordeaux*, *APC* 159 (December, 1909), 268–269; pages 62–63 in the brochure.

208. Cf. "L'oeuvre du Cardinal Dechamps et la Méthode de l'apologétique," *APC* 151 (1905), 68–91.

209. *APC* 153 (1907), 582.

210. *Ibid.*, p. 564.

211. *Ibid.*, p. 564.

212. *Ibid.*, p. 585.

213. *Oeuvres complètes du Cardinal Dechamps* (Malines: Dessain), XVI; 406.

214. More accurately, he no longer mentions it in his published writings of this period. But he does preserve it in an important document that I discovered among his unpublished papers after the French edition of my work had appeared. This text, dated September 5, 1904, is entitled: *Ébauche d'un plan pour "l'Esprit Chrétien"* (*Outline of a Plan for "The Christian Spirit"*). After a first step, which ought to manifest in man a positive "void," Blondel envisions a second step in which will appear "the idea of an indeterminate supernatural" (*"l'idée d'un surnaturel indéterminé"*—the expression is his). In a third step he foresees the "meeting with the specifi-

cally Christian data." I have presented and commented on this text in my article, "Philosophie de l'action et logique de la foi," *Archives de Philosophie* 27 (January–March, 1964, 123–127).

215. *APC* 153 (March, 1907), 569.

216. *Ibid.*, pp. 564–565. Blondel tells us here (p. 564) that it was from Dechamps that he borrowed the word "void." Subsequently, he will use it often (and not always with happy results). In particular, he will use it to define Christian philosophy as he understands it (*Bulletin de la Société Française de Philosophie*, meeting for March 21, 1931, p. 88). It is not without value to refer here to lines from the later (1935) *L'Etre et les êtres* (p. 454): "In some respects philosophical assertions create a void where religious deliverances bring a fullness, but without the union or compenetration ever becoming either the ascertainment of a psychological fact or the conclusion of a discursive and strictly demonstrative proof."

217. *Le problème de la phil. cath.*, p. 106, note.

218. *Ibid.*, p. 104, note; cf. p. 113, note.

219. Ibid., p. 63, note.

220. *Ibid.*, p. 25.

221. *Ibid.*, pp. 25–27.

222. *Ibid.*, p. 25.

223. *Ibid.*, pp. 25–26.

224. *Ibid.*, p. 165, note.

225. *L'Action* (1937), II:401.

226. *La philosophie et l'esprit chrétien.* I:211.

227. *Exigences philosophiques du Christianisme*, p. 298: "Just as the mathematician who can legitimately suppose a problem solved so as to then analyze and rigorously justify the data and deductions which prove what was at first only a hypothesis, so also do we find in positive religion a conclusion to be verified, and this quite independent of our knowing whether this hypothesis is in itself founded." Cf. *L'Action* (1893), p. 391.

228. We shall see an example below.

229. *L'Action* (1937), II:87; cf. *L'Action* (1893), p. 42. The text is the same in both cases, except that "immanent" has replaced "natural."

230. *L'Action* (1937), II:93; cf. *L'Action* (1893), p. 44: "Is the declared will to limit and content man within the natural order of facts, whatever they be, in accord with the deeper will . . .?"

231. *L'Action* (1937), II:338; cf. *L'Action* (1893), p. 319. Same idea in different terms. Once again "natural order" is replaced by "immanent order."

232. *L'Action* (1937), II:34–64.

233. *L'Action* (1893), p. 388.

234. *L'Action* (1937), II:364.

235. *L'Action* (1893), p. 388.

236. *L'Action* (1937), II:364.

237. *Ibid.*, II:365.

238. *Ibid.*, II:375.

239. *Ibid.*, II:375.

240. *Ibid.*, II:371.

241. *Ibid.*, II:513.

242. *L'Etre et les êtres*, p. 491. In *La Pensée* Blondel had already unambiguously declared that a state of pure nature was conceivable and realizable (II:336); but he insisted more on the obligation to go beyond this view and on the failure of human nature to reach its full "achievement." He refused to divide God "into two pieces, with one portion presumed to be humanly available, and the other inaccessible and thought to be the refuge of every living mystery" (II:312; cf. p. 507). The objections of certain theologians induced him to lay greater stress on the idea of pure nature.

243. *L'Etre et les êtres*, p. 292.

244. *Ibid.*, p. 293.

245. *L'Action* (1937), II:365. As opposed to what he did in the first *L'Action*, we see Blondel including here, under the term "natural order," the idea of the relation between creature and Creator. He uses the word in the theological sense of a state of pure nature, and no longer in the philosophical sense of the world of phenomena.

246. *L'Action* (1937), II:367, 371–374.

247. *Ibid.*, pp. 372, 385.

248. *Ibid.*, pp. 375–376.

249. *Ibid.*, pp. 377–378.

250. *Ibid.*, pp. 377, 402.

251. *Ibid.*, p. 386.

252. *L'Action* (1893), p. 491; cf. p. 402.

253. *La philosophie et l'esprit chrétien*, I:289, note.

254. *L'Etre et les êtres*, pp. 307–308.

255. *L'Action* (1937), II:379.

256. *Ibid.*, II:379.

257. *L'Action* (1937), II:381; cf. *L'Action* (1893), pp. 371–372, 375, 386–387.

258. *L'Etre et les êtres*, p. 455.

259. *L'Action* (1893), pp. 371–372.

260. *Ibid.*, p. 384.

261. *Ibid.*, p. 374.

262. *Ibid.*, p. 383.

263. *Ibid.*, p. 423.

264. *Ibid.*, p. 464.

265. *Lettre*, p. 83.

# NOTES TO CHAPTER THREE

1. *L'Action* (1893), p. 424.
2. *Ibid.*, p. 425.
3. Letter from Blondel to Valensin, May 16, 1912 (*Correspondance*, II:320–322). See also letter to M. Castelli cited by B. Romeyer, *La philosophie religieuse de Maurice Blondel* (Paris, 1943), p. 305, note 61.
4. Letter from Delbos to Blondel, May 14, 1893.
5. Letter from Delbos to Blondel, May 30, 1893.
6. *L'Action* (1893), p. 464.
7. *Ibid.*, p. 464.
8. Especially the manuscript filed at the Sorbonne in May, 1892, and the corrections on the page proofs for the printed edition. These documents were published in the Blondel Centenary issue of *Archives de Philosophie* 24 (1961), 29–113.
9. *L'Action*, p. 425.
10. Letter from Delbos to Blondel, September 26, 1893.
11. Letter from Blondel to Delbos, September 25, 1894.
12. In *RMM* 6 (1898), 727–746; reprinted in *Les premiers écrits*, II (Paris: P.U.F., 1956). References are to the 1956 edition.
13. "*L'illusion idéaliste,*" pp. 108–109.
14. *Ibid.*, p. 116.
15. *L'Action*, p. 427.
16. *Ibid.*, p. 428.
17. *Ibid.*, p. 481.
18. *Ibid.*, pp. 483–486.
19. *Ibid.*, pp. 481–486.
20. *Ibid.*, pp. 435, 447–450, 452–453.
21. *Ibid.*, p. 427.
22. *Ibid.*, p. 472.

23. *Ibid.*, pp. 424, 426–427.

24. *Ibid.*, p. 425.

25. *Ibid.*, pp. 427–428.

26. *Ibid.*, p. 428.

27. *Ibid.*, p. 428. The chapter we are analyzing is developed in three points: (1) How the affirmation of being arises necessarily (section I); (2) How it subsists, with a privative character, in the one who is closed to "the unique necessary" (section II); (3) How it becomes a possession of being when one opens to the divine action (sections III, IV, V). Here we are considering the first two sections, along with the beginning of the third. This constitutes a whole; it is the block that was not drafted until after the thesis defense. Since it is not our purpose to offer a literal commentary, we do not follow the text step by step. It seemed more useful to select and explain the essential theses. In the next division of this chapter, we shall analyze the object of the third part of the chapter (sections III, IV, V).

28. *L'Action*, p. 431.

29. *Ibid.*, p. 431.

30. *Ibid.*, p. 431.

31. *Ibid.*, p. 431.

32. *L'Action*, p. 432.

33. *Ibid.*, p. 433.

34. *Ibid.*, p. 435.

35. *Ibid.*, p. 435.

36. *Ibid.*, p. 429.

37. *Ibid.*, pp. 435–436.

38. *Ibid.*, p. 436.

39. *Ibid.*, p. 437.

40. *Ibid.*, p. 439.

41. *Ibid.*, p. 437.

42. *Ibid.*, p. 439.

43. *La philosophie de l'action*, p. 113.

44. *Ibid.*, p. 113.

45. *Ibid.*, pp. 111–112.

46. *Ibid.*, p. 114.

47. *Ibid.*, p. 116.

48. *Ibid.*, p. 114, note.

49. Duméry will proceed in another way in his subsequent studies (*Blondel et la religion* and *Critique et religion*). The realizing option will then appear as a second stage which will succeed the stage of analytic reflection (*Blondel et la religion*, pp. 81, 85). The earlier stage, says the author, *prepares* the option; it calls on living freedom to opt in conformity with the

meanings it has uncovered (*Critique et religion*, pp. 131–132; *La tentation*, pp. 186–187). But under the name option, he will have in mind principally and in a privileged fashion the option before the Christian supernatural, the act of faith; and this is the case throughout *Blondel et la religion*. (See also *La tentation*, p. 179.) From this point of view, the knowledge provided by the option will be different from the knowledge that preceded it in time. We shall examine below the difficulties presented by this new interpretation.

50. A. Cartier, *Existence et vérité* (Paris: 1955), p. 185.

51. *Ibid.*, p. 186.

52. This does not mean that the option intervenes at every instance and in the case of each singular reality. The author of *L'Action* does say, it is true, that "every particular object can become for the will matter for an option and lead us to resolve the alternative that decides life" (*L'Action*, pp. 433–434; cited by Duméry in *La philosophie de l'action*, p. 113). But what he affirms is not a possibility, not a necessity, not even a constant reality.

53. Letter from Blondel to Dom Bède Lebbe, April 3, 1903.

54. *Ibid.*

55. *Ibid.*

56. Duméry, *La philosophie de l'action*, p. 114, note.

57. Cartier, *Existence et vérité*, p. 185.

58. *L'Action*, p. 438.

59. *Ibid.*, p. 438.

60. *Ibid.*, p. 438.

61. *Ibid.*, p. 439.

62. *Ibid.*, p. 486.

63. *Ibid.*, p. 438.

64. *Ibid.*, p. 440.

65. *Ibid.*, p. 436.

66. *Ibid.*, p. 428.

67. *Ibid.*, p. 427.

68. *Ibid.*, p. 428.

69. *Ibid.*, p. 428.

70. *Ibid.*, pp. 439, 440.

71. *Ibid.*, p. 438.

72. *Ibid.*, p. 438.

73. *Ibid.*, p. 439.

74. *Ibid.*, p. 486.

75. On p. 450 Blondel says that this knowledge too is "subjective" to the degree that it is "voluntary." He then explains, as we shall see, that what is specifically real and objective in our knowledge is what distinguishes and

unites voluntary knowledge and necessary knowledge.

76. *L'Action*, p. 440.

77. *Ibid.*, p. 438.

78. *Ibid.*, p. 438.

79. *Ibid.*, p. 438.

80. *Ibid.*, p. 437.

81. Letter from Blondel to Dom Bède Lebbe, April 3, 1903. See also "Plan pour une refonte de *L'Action"* (Oct. 14, 1900), published in *Et. blond*, II:24. The distinction between speculative knowledge and effective knowledge will later become the distinction between notional knowledge and real knowledge. But as we said in the first chapter, the meaning is not quite the same; and later the distinction between noetic thought and pneumatic thought will answer a still more complex problem.

82. And also in the Introduction.

83. *L'Action*, pp. 470–474.

84. *Ibid.*, pp. 474–480.

85. Letter from Blondel to Abbé J.-M. Bernard, May 31, 1897.

86. *L'Action*, p. 488.

87. *Lettre*, p. 66.

88. *Lettre*, p. 56.

89. *Ibid.*, p. 55.

90. *Ibid.*, p. 56.

91. *Ibid.*, p. 61.

92. *Ibid.*, pp. 60–64.

93. *Ibid.*, p. 66.

94. *Ibid.*, p. 76.

95. *Ibid.*, p. 62.

96. Letter of May 8, 1912 (*Correspondance*, II: 309–310). See also the letter of May 16, p. 322: To know being in the full and total sense is "to know, not as Mr. X knows Mrs. Z, but, if I dare say it, in the biblical sense in which Jacob intimately knew Leah and Rachel."

97. Letter to the *RMM* 2 (January, 1894), Supplément; reprinted in *Et. blond.*, I:102.

98. *L'Action*, p. 437.

99. *Ibid.*, p. 437.

100. *Ibid.*, p. 440.

101. *Ibid.*, p. 440.

102. *Ibid.*, p. 440.

103. *Ibid.*, p. 440.

104. *Ibid.*, p. 441.

105. *Ibid.*, p. 438.

106. *Ibid.*, p. 438.
107. *Ibid.*, p. 438.
108. *Ibid.*, p. 439.
109. *Ibid.*, p. 436.
110. Beginning exactly with the last two lines of page 441.
111. At the end of the introduction to the chapter (p. 429), the author announces a division into three sections. Actually, there are five, and it is the third that was divided into three sections on the galley sheets.
112. *L'Action*, p. 440.
113. *Ibid.*, p. 441.
114. *Ibid.*, pp. 339–357, 357–388.
115. *Ibid.*, pp. 441–443.
116. *Ibid.*, pp. 443–446.
117. *Ibid.*, p. 446.
118. *Ibid.*, p. 446.
119. *Ibid.*, p. 447.
120. *Ibid.*, p. 447.
121. *Ibid.*, pp. 447–448.
122. *-bid.*, p. 449.
123. *-bid.*, p. 451.
124. *Ibid.*, p. 453.
125. *Ibid.*, pp. 453–454.
126. *Ibid.*, pp. 454–456.
127. *Ibid.*, p. 457.
128. *Ibid.*, p. 457.
129. *Ibid.*, p. 458.
130. See *Correspondance*, I:43–48 (the second long note is superbly documented).
131. *Ibid.*, pp. 44–46.
132. St. Bernard, *De gradibus humilitatis et superbiae*, chapter III: "Quod natura sciebat ab aeterno, temporali didicit experimento" (No. 6). "Non debet absurdum videri, si dicitur Christum . . . scire tamen alio modo misericordiam ab aeterno per divinitatem, et aliter in tempore didicisse per carnem" (No. 10).
133. Text cited in *L'Action*, p. 460. Neither the author nor the work is indicated, but the reference is given in the notes used in preparing *L'Action:* S. Bernard, *De gradibus humilitatis*, III:6. There is a still freer version cited in *La philosophie et l'esprit chrétien*, I:90.
134. It is in the parallel passage of *La philosophie et l'esprit chrétien*, I:90.
135. *L'Action*, p. 459.
136. *Ibid.*, p. 461.

137. *Ibid.*, p. 461. The double possibility that Blondel leaves open here is also mentioned in the *Lettre*, p. 90, note 1.

138. Letter of December 19, 1901 (*Correspondance*, I:43).

139. Letter of March 2, 1902, to Auguste Valensin (*Correspondance*, I:53–54).

140. See *La philosophie et l'esprit chrétien*, I:83–103 (fourth part), and Excursus II, pp. 268–275.

141. Letter to Abbé J.-M. Bernard, May 31, 1897.

142. *Lettre*, p. 89.

143. He uses the word several times. See the long note already referred to in *Correspondance*, I:44.

144. *L'Action*, pp. 398–399.

145. *Lettre*, pp. 89–91. The Modernist crisis will furnish Blondel the occasion to develop his Christology in its own right. Instead of simply introducing it as an eventual solution to a philosophical problem, he will bring it to bear against the Christologies of Loisy and Hegel in order to safeguard what he regards as essential to the Christian faith. In this way he will propose certain valuable and solid views (mixed, perhaps, with some questionable elements). The documents are gathered together in *Au coeur de la crise moderniste* (Paris: Aubier, 1960).

146. *L'Action*, p. 461.

147. *Ibid.*, p. 461.

148. *Ibid.*, p. 462.

149. *Ibid.*, p. 462.

150. *Ibid.*, p. 463.

151. *Ibid.*, p. 463.

152. *Ibid.*, p. 463.

153. *Ibid.*, pp. 463–464.

154. Letter to Abbé J.-M. Bernard, March 31, 1897.

155. *L'Action*, p. 464.

156. *Ibid.*, p. 464.

157. *Ibid.*, p. 465.

158. *Ibid.*, p. 464.

159. *Ibid.*, pp. 464–465.

160. Letter from Blondel to Valensin, December 7, 1910 (*Correspondance*, II:191).

161. "L'illusion idéaliste" in *Les premiers écrits*, II:114–115.

162. *L'Action*, p. 428.

163. *Ibid.*, pp. 481–482.

164. *Ibid.*, pp. 482–483, 486.

165. Here the word "phenomenism" refers to a doctrine Blondel rejects.

166. Cf. *Et. blond.*, I:86.
167. Cf. *Et. Blond.*, I:103.
168. *Lettre*, p. 89.
169. Letter to Dom Bède Lebbe, April 3, 1903.
170. Letter to Amédée de Margerie, September 4, 1896.
171. *L'Action*, p. 452.
172. *Ibid.*, p. 458.
173. *Ibid.*, p. 458.
174. Letter from Blondel to Amédée de Margerie, September 4, 1896.
175. *Ibid.*
176. According to a letter from Blondel to Laberthonnière, February 26, 1921.
177. *L'Action* (1937), II:407.
178. *Ibid.*, II:409.
179. *Le problème de la phil. cath.*, p. 175, note 1.
180. *L'Action* (1937), II:409.
181. *Ibid.*, pp. 407–416.
182. *Ibid.*, p. 12.
183. In a letter to Paul Archambault (April 24, 1918) Blondel will write: "Metaphysics is only a schema, a *mimicking* of the real." This unfortunate formula goes beyond what the author said in *L'Action* and the *Lettre*. In any case, he will retract it in a letter to the same correspondent, dated February 23, 1928. Both letters are to be found in Archambault's *L'oeuvre phil.*, p. 73 and p. 74, note.
184. *L'Action*, p. 488.
185. *Ibid.*, p. 429.
186. *Ibid.*, p. 426.
187. P. Lachièze-Rey, "Réflections sur la portée ontologique de la méthode blondélienne," *Hommage à Maurice Blondel*, pp. 149–150.
188. *L'Action*, p. 339.
189. *Ibid.*, p. 340.
190. *Ibid.*, p. 341.
191. *Ibid.*, pp. 341–350.
192. *Ibid.*, p. 343.
193. *Ibid.*, p. 348.
194. *Ibid.*
195. Blondel said this explicitly in a letter to Abbé Bricout, April 4, 1897: "You ask me whether I affirm 'the reality of God,' and whether one can 'rationally demonstrate' it. I reply absolutely *yes*; and this is the sense of the chapter in *L'Action* entitled: 'The Unique Necessary' [pp. 338–357]. I show there how all the determinism of our knowledge and action leads us

to this term. . . . We necessarily conceive God; by the effort of reflection we justify this spontaneous and necessary conception, by demonstrating rationally that God is affirmed as real and as efficacious in us."

196. *L'Action*, pp. 354–355.

197. *Ibid.*, p. 426.

198. *Ibid.*, p. 441.

199. *Ibid.*, p. 351.

200. *Ibid.*, p. 351.

201. *Ibid.*, p. 352.

202. *Ibid.*, p. 354.

203. *Ibid.*, p. 354.

204. *Ibid.*, pp. 354–355.

205. *Ibid.*, p. 441.

206, *Ibid.*, pp. 441–442.

207. *Ibid.*, p. 426.

208. *Ibid.*, p. 426.

209. *Ibid.*, p. 426.

210. *Ibid.*, p. 351.

211. *Ibid.*, p. 35.

212. See his letter to Archambault, February 15, 1917; cited in *L'oeuvre phil.*, p. 51, note.

213. Romans 1:20–21.

214. See commentary on the text of the Epistle to the Romans in my *Karl Barth*, III:119–124.

215. *L'Action*, p. 95, note. See also p. 42 and p. 65, note 2: "The words *being, reality*, used here, have no metaphysical value; up to the present they refer only to a system of given phenomena."

216. *Ibid.*, p. 322.

217. *Ibid.*, p. 323, note.

218. *Ibid.*, p. 424. Note also that, in the copies of the thesis that do not contain this last chapter, the necessity of religious practice was presented as "the last link in the determinism" (pp. 404–405). In the commercial edition, religious practice is presented as a "new link" (p. 406); it is at the end of the chapter that we find the "last link," the one that joins together "the two ends of the chain" (p. 462).

219. *Ibid.*, p. 425.

220. *Ibid.*, p. 452.

221. *Ibid.*, p. 452.

222. *Ibid.*, p. 435.

223. *Ibid.*, p. 436.

224. We also understand why Blondel hesitated about the proper place for

this chapter. In place of putting it at the end of the fifth part, he might have put it at the end of the fourth.

**225.** The additions Blondel introduced into the definitive text of the conclusion are of three kinds. Some have as their only purpose to explain what had already been said in the text of the thesis, for example, those found on pp. 467–470, 474–476, 492. Others recapitulate Blondel's reply to Emile Boutroux on the day of the thesis defense; they are to be found on pp. 489–490, and to a great extent they repeat verbatim a passage in "Une soutenance de thèse" (*Et. blond.*, I:82–83). Finally, several additions incorporate into the conclusion material from the last chapter; they can be found on pp. 480–483 and 486–488. We are only interested in this final category.

**226.** *L'Action* (thesis edition), pp. 426–427.

**227.** *L'Action* (commercial edition), pp. 486–487.

**228.** *Ibid.*, p. 487.

**229.** See above: "In order not to see it where it is not, it must be seen solely where it is." Cf. *L'Action* (commercial edition), p. 487. The modifications of the first text are minimal.

**230.** *L'Action*, p. 41.

**231.** *Ibid.*, p. 41.

**232.** "It is not a question of considering this *something* as exterior, as interior, or as reducible to the representation we have of it. It is a question of analyzing the content of willed action." (*L'Action*, p. 43, note 1).

**233.** In *L'Etre et les êtres*, instead of justifying the ontological affirmation by showing that it is the ultimate condition of action, Blondel will have directly in view the spontaneous affirmation of being, so as to draw out its implications. It is a reflexive and prospective ontology, but no longer phenomenology. Coming out after the work on Being, the second edition of *L'Action* (vol. II, 1937) will no longer have to develop it.

**234.** de Montcheuil, *Pages religieuses*, p. 30.

**235.** *Ibid.*, p. 30.

**236.** *Ibid.*, p. 53.

**237.** *Ibid.*, p. 42.

**238.** *Ibid.*, pp. 45–46.

**239.** *Ibid.*, p. 28.

**240.** *Ibid.*, p. 46.

**241.** *Ibid.*, p. 46.

**242.** *Ibid.*, pp. 47, 57.

**243.** *Ibid.*, pp. 54–55.

**244.** *Ibid.*, p. 54.

**245.** *Ibid.*, p. 46.

**246.** *Ibid.*, pp. 54–56.

247. It is in this passage that *to affirm* has as its synonym "to have legitimate certitudes," an expression which is soon retranslated as "to be able to attribute a value of being" (p. 55). We also read that all the judgments made about the world by those who have rejected the supernatural are "profoundly false" (p. 56). The context indicates that this term is to be understood in the ontological sense and not in the epistemological sense; but the reader who has been misled by the expression "legitimate certitude" will once more be fooled here.

248. *Pages religieuses*, pp. 54–55.

249. There were two drafts of this study: the one, already old; the other, quite different and much more nuanced, destined for publication. The friends of Père de Montcheuil already had a copy of the latter draft when *Pages religieuses* made its printed appearance in 1942. They were surprised not to find the same text. Père de Montcheuil, cut off by circumstances (the blockade and travel restrictions) from his manuscripts in Jersey and at Lyons, much taken up with resistance to the Nazis, and, in addition, quite detached from the literary expression of his thought, may have inadvertently sent his first draft to the printer.

250. See *La philosophie de l'action*, p. 152; *Blondel et la religion*, p. 102, note 2 (first, second, and fourth citations).

251. *La philosophie de l'action*, p. 152.

252. *Pages religieuses*, p. 57.

253. *Blondel et la religion*, p. 102.

254. *Pages religieuses*, pp. 50–51.

255. *Blondel et la religion*, p. 101.

256. *Pages religieuses*, p. 51.

257. *Blondel et la religion*, p. 102, note 2.

258. *Pages religieuses*, p. 44.

259. *Ibid.*, p. 28.

260. *Ibid.*, pp. 51–52, etc.

261. *Ibid.*, p. 24.

262. *Ibid.*, p. 42.

263. *Blondel et la religion*, p. 102, note 2.

264. *Ibid.*, pp. 77–79 and p. 79, note 3.

265. Here is what Blondel wrote to Père Auguste Valensin, November 3, 1948: "Your book of extracts from *L'Action*, has borne fruit for which I have not sufficiently thanked you. Then you entrusted the second volume to Père de Montcheuil, whose Introduction I have just had read to me: I did not recall that it was so penetrating and, in summary, so favorable! And in the posthumous volume of *Mélanges théologiques*, he offers a remarkable study, which greatly surpasses the occasional review of a publication. And if you have read these pages, you will have noted the depth of his adher-

ence in my regard. This testimony is all the more important and opportune since many misapprehensions still persist." (No reserve is expressed here on either of the two studies.)

266. *La philosophie de l'action*, p. 183.

267. *Blondel et la religion*, p. 28, note.

268. "Blondel et la méthode reflexive," *Etudes Philosophiques* (1952), 390.

269. *Ibid.*, pp. 390–393; *Blondel et la religion*, p. 28, note.

270. Chapter entitled "L'option et ses conséquences" (*Blondel et la religion*, pp. 95–105).

271. *Blondel et la religion*, pp. 102–103, note.

272. *Ibid.*, pp. 102–103, note.

273. *Ibid.*, p. 95 cf. p. 102, note 2, and p. 104.

274. *L'Action*, pp. 452–453.

275. *Ibid.*, p. 453.

276. *Pages religieuses*, p. 36.

277. *Ibid.*, p. 36.

278. *Blondel et la religion*, p. 102, note 2.

279. Père de Montcheuil was personally little inclined to confuse natural and supernatural values, or to believe the first impossible when the second are not recognized. In an article on *Dieu et la vie morale*, published several months before the Introduction to *Pages religieuses* of Blondel, he even tried to show that "there could be a moral life truly independent of the recognition of God" (*Mélanges théologiques*, pp. 145ff).

280. Lettre, p. 87 (77–78).

281. *Blondel et la religion*, p. 97.

282. *Lettre*, p. 87.

283. *Blondel et la religion*, p. 98.

284. *Ibid.*, pp. 98–99.

285. *Ibid.*, p. 100.

286. *Ibid.*, p. 99.

287. *L'Action*, p. 370.

288. *Ibid.*, p. 370.

289. *Ibid.*, p. 371.

290. *Ibid.*, p. 372.

291. *Blondel et la religion*, pp. 101–102.

# NOTES TO CHAPTER FOUR

1. This sheet, torn out of the notebook, is preserved at the Blondel Archives in Aix-en-Provence. The text has been published by A. Hayen in *Etudes Philosophiques* (1952), 353–354.

2. See *L'itinéraire*, pp. 64–65.

3. *Ibid.*, p. 65.

4. Letter from Blondel to Boutroux, September 16, 1886.

5. Made at Saint-Joscph-du-Tholonet, near Aix-en-Provence.

6. The manuscript is preserved in the Blondel Archives. It is in a large notebook and bears the title: *"L'Action:* Etude sur la métaphysique de la science et de la morale, et sur la nature de la pratique religieuse." Blondel himself wrote at the top of the first page: "Premier brouillon" (first rough draft).

7. "Premier brouillon," p. 13.

8. *Ibid.*, pp. 3–5.

9. *Ibid.*, pp. 106–113.

10. *Ibid.*, p. 114.

11. *Ibid.*, p. 13.

12. *Notes-semailles*, no. 1132.

13. His method, as he sometimes defines it, is identical with that practiced by so many apologists: "One must take one by one the truths of the catechism, and show philosophers that nothing more beautiful or better can be conceived; that this passes imagination and man" (*Notes-semailles*, no. 1134).

14. "Premier brouillon," p. 9.

15. Letter from Blondel to Delbos, July 23, 1894.

16. Letter from Blondel to Delbos, May 6, 1889.

17. Letter to Maurice Léna, March 23, 1890.

18. *La science de l'action*, dictated to Charles Despins, pp. 39–40 of the MS.

19. Entitled simply *L'Action.* Above the title, to the left, Blondel wrote: "Projet de Thèse."

20. Dated July 25, 1892.

21. Letter from Boutroux to Blondel, July 28, 1892.

22. In this part only the development on "Les succédanés et les apprêts de l'action parfaite" was not rewritten but simply corrected.

23. Letter from Blondel to Paul Archambault, February 15, 1917: cited in *L'oeuvre phil.*, p. 51, note. The complete text can be read with profit.

24. Extract from a note sent by Blondel, November 29, 1924, to a Canadian Franciscan, Père Bruno. A copy of this note is preserved in the Blondel Archives.

25. *L'itinéraire*, p. 41.

26. This private letter is to be distinguished from the official letter that would be published in the *APC* in November, 1895, and reprinted in *Les premiers écrits*, II:3–4.

27. "L'anti-Cartésianisme de Malebranche," *RMM* 23 (1916), 24, note 3.

28. *Lettre*, p. 51.

29. Note sent to the Canadian Franciscan, Père Bruno, November 29, 1924.

30. *Lettre*, p. 5.

31. *Ibid.*, pp. 16–26.

32. *Ibid.*, pp. 21–22.

33. *Ibid.*, p. 48. Re-editing several fragments of the *Lettre* in 1932 for *Le problème de la phil. cath.*, Blondel corrected this passage without mentioning the fact. We read on page 39: "Only philosophy is capable of putting aside prejudicial objections, of exposing to full light the exigencies and insufficiencies of nature and, consequently, of clearly defining *a contrario* the notion of the supernatural." This formulation is clearly better than the first.

34. *Lettre*, p. 50.

35. *Ibid.*, p. 47.

36. Letter to Abbé Denis, reproduced in *Les premiers écrits*, II:3.

37. *Ibid.*, p. 3; *Lettre*, pp. 47–48.

38. *Lettre*, p. 48.

39. Cartier, *Existence et vérité*, p. 213.

40. *Lettre*, pp. 54, 91–92.

41. According to a letter from Blondel to Laberthonnière, February 26, 1921.

42. *Le problème de la phil. cath.*, p. 5.

43. *Ibid.*, p. 6.

44. E. Bréhier, "Y a-t-il une philosophie chrétienne?", *RMM* 38 (1931), 160.

45. *Ibid.*, p. 161.

46. M. Blondel, "Y a-t-il une philosophie chrétienne?", *RMM* 38 (1931), 599.

47. *Ibid.*, p. 604.

48. *Le problème de la phil. cath.*, pp. 44–45.
49. *Lettre*, p. 53.
50. *Le problème*, p. 44.
51. "L'illusion idéaliste" in *Les premiers écrits*, II:99.
52. In *RMM* 38 (1931), 604.
53. "Une soutenance de thèse," in *Et. blond.*, I:83.
54. In *RMM* 38 (1931), 604.
55. Henry Bars, *Maritain en notre temps* (Paris: Grasset, 1959), p. 220.
56. *Ibid.*, p. 330.
57. *Lettre*, p. 47.
58. *Ibid.*, p. 54.
59. In *RMM* 38 (1931), 605.
60. H. de Lubac, "Sur la philosophie chrétienne," *NRT* (March, 1936), 245.
61. J. Maritain, *Science et sagesse* (Paris: Labergerie, 1935), pp. 146–147. This statement is cited with approval by H. Bars, *Maritain en notre temps*, p. 217. According to Bars, Blondelian philosophy claims "to owe nothing to revelation," whereas it is "saturated with historic Christianity," and the constant use of Christian and even theological themes easily gives the reader the illusion that it "furnishes precisely what it claims it gets along without" (p. 217). "Christian philosophy according to Blondel refuses to be fecundated by revelation; but it is much more rigorously led, much less free than any philosophy of a Christian . . ." (p. 220).
62. *Lettre*, p. 53.
63. *Ibid.*, p. 94.
64. *Le problème de la phil. cath.*, p. 39, note.
65. *Ibid.*, p. 39, note.
66. *L'itinéraire*, p. 42. The eighth centenary of the birth of St. Bernard was celebrated at Dijon in June, 1891. It was at this time that Blondel came to know his work.
67. Letter to Paul Archambault, February 17, 1917; cited in Archambault's *L'oeuvre phil.*, p. 51, note.
68. Blondel reread and recommended *Le combat spirituel* by Laurent Scupoli, the Theatine (1530–1610).
69. He made a retreat at Saint-Joseph-du-Tholonet, near Aix-en-Provence, in 1899, and another in 1909 at the "campagne Gavoty" (Marseille).
70. The Ignatian theme of indifference is developed on p. 378 of *L'Action*. Note especially this sentence, which is an implicit citation from the *Exercises*: "Should we not judge in all things, for ourselves, as though it were a question of someone else . . . as though dead?" (See *Spiritual Exercises*, no. 339–340).
71. *L'Action*, pp. 383–384.

72. "After having done everything as though expecting nothing from God, we must expect all from God, as though one had done nothing of oneself" (*L'Action*, p. 385). This sentence, which we have already seen, is a rendering of a maxim of St. Ignatius, one treated at length by Fessard in *La dialectique des Exercices Spirituels*, pp. 305–363.

73. Two other texts in *L'Action* (and the list is by no means exhaustive) recall the *Exercises* of St. Ignatius, implicitly or explicitly: the "agere contra" of p. 192; and on p. 340 we read: "In the acts of the will, when we think about the presence of this unique necessary, it is for us to exhibit a greater respect than if we were exercising the understanding by reflection" (cf. *Exercises*, no. 3).

74. Père Fessard readily admits that the study of *L'Action* helped him understand the dialectic of the *Exercises* of St. Ignatius. This is to be expected in that Blondel's thought was itself nourished on the *Exercises*.

75. See the letter to Maurice Léna, March 23, 1890.

76. *Lettre*, p. 77.

77. *Ibid.*, pp. 77, 80–82.

78. Cf. *Le problème de la phil. cath.*, pp. 53–54, note. Here Blondel indicates who Père Beaudouin was, what his relations with him were, and what he owes him, especially on the question of the theological notion of the supernatural.

79. Speaking of university people in this period, Gilson wrote: "Out of so many Catholic philosophers—Lachelier, Delbos, Maurice Blondel, and others—not a single one had ever studied theology or had any great scruples on this score" (*Le philosophe et la théologie* [Paris, 1960], p. 72). As far as Blondel is concerned, this statement seems to be exaggerated.

80. *Lettre*, p. 54.

81. *Ibid.*, p. 54.

82. *Ibid.*, p. 53.

83. *Ibid.*, p. 55.

84. *Ibid.*, p. 58.

85. *Ibid.*, pp. 59–66.

86. *Ibid.*, pp. 59–66.

87. *Ibid.*, p. 64.

88. *Ibid.*, pp. 66, 76.

89. "Une des sources de la pensée moderne; l'évolution du Spinozisme," *APC* 128 (1894), 260–275, 324–341. Here Blondel uses the pseudonym Bernard Aimant.

90. *Ibid.*, p. 261.

91. *Ibid.*, 339.

92. *Ibid.*, p. 262.

93. *Ibid.*, p. 341.

94. *Lettre*, p. 92.

95. Letter to the *RMM* (1894), reprinted in *Et. blond.*, I:101.

96. *Lettre*, pp. 91–92.

97. Letter to the *RMM* (*Et. blond.*, I:99).

98. *L'Action*, p. 473.

99. *Ibid.*, p. 475.

100. *Les premiers écrits*, II:98.

101. *Ibid.*, p. 141.

102. *Ibid.*, p. 125.

103. "Blondel et la méthode réflexive," article reproduced in *La tentation*, p. 185.

104. *Ibid.*, p. 185.

105. *Blondel et la religion*, p. 3. The same distinction, as we have seen, is presented by Duméry in different terms: reflexive plane and concrete plane, phenomenological plane and ontological plane, order of intelligible conditions and order of effective realizations. (See, for example, *La tentation*, pp. 185–186).

106. *La tentation*, p. 187.

107. *Blondel et la religion*, p. 38, note 1.

108. *Ibid.*, p. 38, note 1.

109. *Ibid.*, p. 38, note 1; *Critique et religion*, p. 107, note 1; *La tentation*, p. 141, note.

110. *L'Action*, p. 425.

111. *Ibid.*, p. 425.

112. *Critique et religion*, p. 105.

113. *L'Action*, p. 406.

114. *Ibid.*, p. 406.

115. *Blondel et la religion*, p. 79, note 3.

116. *Lettre*, p. 41; cited in *Blondel et la religion*, p. 38, note.

117. *Blondel et la religion*, p. 38, note.

118. *Ibid.*, p. 68, note 1.

119. *La tentation*, p. 187.

120. *Ibid.*, p. 187.

121. *Ibid.*, p. 187.

122. *Ibid.*, pp. 168–70.

123. *Critique et religion*, p. 101.

124. *Ibid.*, p. 109.

125. *Ibid.*, p. 125.

126. *Blondel et la religion*, p. 54, note 2.

127. "Maurice Blondel et la philosophie de la religion," *Recherche de Science Religieuse* (1960), 316–317, 321–324.

128. *L'Action*, p. 391.

129. *Ibid.*, pp. 400–401.

130. *Critique et religion*, pp. 107–112.

131. *Ibid.*, p. 107; *Blondel et la religion, passim.*

132. *L'Action*, pp. 390–392.

133. *Ibid.*, p. 391.

134. *Ibid.*, p. 397.

135. *Ibid.*, p. 395.

136. This has not been sufficiently recognized by a number of Catholic theologians who have expressed their reservations. It has even happened that one or another has not so much as entertained a suspicion of the sense of the enterprise with the result that they have leveled criticisms that miss the point.

137. *Lettre*, p. 67. Duméry refers to this text in *La tentation*, p. 140, note.

138. *La tentation*, p. 140.

139. *Lettre*, pp. 67–68.

140. In *APC* 151 and 152 (1906), 337–360, 225–250.

141. *APC*, 151 (1906), 341.

142. *Ibid.*, p. 342.

143. *Ibid.*, p. 342. Blondel will indicate later on that prospection also includes a reflection *sui generis*. He will then name reflection, properly so called, "retrospection" or "analytic reflection." See under *Prospection* and *Réflexion* in Lalande's *Vocabulaire de la philosophie.*

144. "La philosophie de l'action" in *La tentation*, p. 169.

145. *APC* 152 (1906), 225–227, 240–242, 246, etc. The phrase "prospection pratique" appears on p. 242.

146. The text of these preparatory notes has been published in *Et. blond.*, II:21–46.

147. *Ibid.*, p. 44.

148. *Ibid.*, pp. 20–22.

149. *Ibid.*, p. 22.

150. *L'Action*, p. 475.

151. *L'Action* (1937), II:411.

152. *L'Action* (1893), p. 127.

153. *Ibid.*, pp. 281, 296.

154. *La tentation*, p. 185.

155. See the article "Aspiration et réflexion," *Les Etudes Philosophiques*, 1954, no. 4. Duméry says here that without the work of Jacques Paliard "important chapters would be lacking to Blondelism; it would even lack a

certain noetic structure which it presupposes and implies everywhere, and which the 'reflexive' Jacques Paliard, has managed to explicitate better than the 'prospective' Maurice Blondel" (p. 420). For "with Blondel, synthesis always had the primacy over analysis" (p. 420). (How can this be reconciled with the habitual statements of the same interpreter?) Paliard has "extended and completed Blondel" in making the distinction between concrete action and the ideal conditions of action fructify, a distinction "that Blondel did not always maintain with equal firmness" (p. 424).

156. *L'Action* (1937), II:8.

157. *Ibid.*, p. 11.

157. *Ibid.*, p. 12.

159. "Le point de départ de la recherche philosophique," *APC* 152 (1906), 239; cf. p. 240: "Philosophy is never limited to the reflection that analyzes."

160. *Ibid.*, p. 227.

161. *Blondel et la religion*, p. 28, note 1; *Critique et religion*, p. 132.

162. Expression of Jean Trouillard, "La structure de la recherche métaphysique selon Maurice Blondel," *Les Etudes Philosophiques*, 1952, no. 4, p. 368.

163. See Duméry, *La philosophie de l'action*, Conclusion; *La tentation*, pp. 193–203.

164. *L'Action* (1937), II:409.

165. *Blondel et la religion*, p. 38, note.

166. *Lettre*, p. 64; and cf. pp. 65, 67.

167. This last proposition is unilateral. For, according to Blondel, "we necessarily think that our thought, *immanent* in itself, bears within it an element of *transcendence*, a real heteronomy postulated by its ideal autonomy" (*Les premiers écrits*, II:113; italics added). There is an *"immanent affirmation of the transcendent"* which "in no way prejudices the transcendent reality of immanent affirmations" (*Lettre*, p. 40; italics added).

168. "L'illusion idéaliste," *Les premiers écrits*, II:109.

169. *Ibid.*, p. 113.

170. *Lettre*, p. 39.

171. "L'illusion idéaliste," *Les premiers écrits*, II:112.

172. *Ibid.*, p. 114.

173. *Ibid.*, p. 116. That the word *being* is here synonymous with *absolute* is indicated on the preceding page: "It seemed that it was either necessary that thought . . . attain by itself alone being and the absolute . . . ." This is again indicated on p. 121, where Blondel once more rejects this form of the "intellectualist illusion": "Thought is the highest and, seen more closely, the only form under which the absolute can be grasped." This proposition, which the author puts in quotation marks without any reference, had already been cited by him, with the reference, in the article on

the evolution of Spinozism *APC* 128 [1894], 337). It is taken from Hegel's *Logic* (tr. Véra, I:216).

174. *Les premiers écrits*, II:117.

175. *Ibid.*, p. 119.

176. "Question of fact" or "judgment of existence" identified with "ontological problems" (cf. *Blondel et la religion*, pp. 54–55, note). "Question of fact" or of "reality" identified with "question of being" (*Critique et religion*, pp. 105–106).

177. *La tentation*, p. 170.

178. *Lettre*, p. 66.

179. *La tentation*, pp. 170, 187; *Blondel et la religion*, p. 27.

180. *Critique et religion*, p. 131.

181. *La tentation*, p. 187, note.

182. *Lettre*, p. 41.

183. *Ibid.*, p. 67. The distinction between theory and practice is better indicated in this formula than in the one brought to our attention. For, if the method of immanence forbids us to pronounce "at first" on the subjective or objective sense of our representations, it constrains us *finally* to recognize their objective sense, that is, their ontological scope. It is true that it makes us aware at the same time that this necessary affirmation of being puts us in possession of being only by means of a positive option in the presence of the unique necessary. It is in this way that we recover the effective solution given by practice.

184. *La tentation*, p. 185.

185. *L'Action* (1937), II:131.

186. *L'Action* (1893), pp. 489–490.

187. Cartier, *Existence et vérité*, p. 229.

188. See *Et. blond.*, I:82–83.

189. *L'Action*, p. 464.

190. *Ibid.*, p. 127.

191. *Ibid.*, pp. 40–41.

192. *Ibid.*, p. 41.

193. *Ibid.*, p. 43.

194. *Ibid.*, p. 43.

195. Cartier, *Existence et vérité*, p. 233.

196. *Ibid.*, pp. 223–224.

197. *Ibid.*, p. 231.

198. *Ibid.*, p. 231.

199. *La Pensée*, II:98–109.

200. *L'Action* (1936), I, Excursus 12 and 16 (pp. 261 and 271 in the 1949 edition).

201. *Ibid.*, Excursus 16 (p. 271 in the 1949 edition).
202. *L'Action* (1937), II:410–411.
203. *Existence et vérité*, p. 251.
204. *Ibid.*, p. 229.
205. *L'Action* (1937), II:14. Cartier also uses the word fidelity.
206. Cartier, *Existence et vérité*, p. 228.
207. *Ibid.*, p. 233.
208. *Ibid.*, p. 233.
209. *Ibid.*, p. 233.
210. *Ibid.*, p. 233.
211. *Ibid.*, pp. 173–180.
212. "L'illusion idéaliste" in *Les premiers écrits*, II:115.
213. Cartier, *Existence et vérité*, p. 178.
214. *Ibid.*, pp. 179–180.
215. *L'Action* (1937), II:411.
216. Eric Weil, *Logique de la philosophie*, p. 345.
217. *Ibid.*, p. 50.
218. *Lettre*, pp. 83–84.
219. *L'Action* (1893), p. 389.
220. *Lettre*, pp. 86–87.
221. In a letter to *RMM*, printed in *Et. blond.*, I:103.
222. *Lettre*, p. 41.
223. *Ibid.*, p. 41.
224. *Ibid.*, p. 42.
225. *Ibid.*, p. 70.
226. From Vatican Council I, cited here by Blondel himself.
227. *Lettre*, p. 71.
228. *Ibid.*, pp. 70–71.
229. *Ibid.*, p. 71.
230. *Ibid.*, p. 71. In his letter of 1894 to the *RMM*, Blondel had described philosophy, as he conceived it, as an application of reason, not simply to itself, but to human action. "In being applied to action, reason discovers more than in being applied to reason, without ceasing to be rational" (*Et. blond.*, I:102). This definition agrees with the one given in the *Lettre* (1896) in that both place the essence of philosophy in the method of immanence, which guarantees its rational autonomy. But the definition of 1894, because it introduces action, is more specifically Blondelian; and it also indicates the mediating element between philosophy and theology, while the 1896 formulation only indicates what distinguishes them.
231. *Lettre*, p. 77.

232. *Ibid.,* p. 78.
233. *Ibid.,* p. 71.
234. *Ibid.,* p. 49.
235. *Ibid.,* p. 50.
236. *Ibid.,* pp. 50–51.
237. *Blondel et la religion,* p. 106.
238. *Lettre,* p. 75.
239. *Ibid.,* p. 75.
240. *Ibid.,* p. 77.
241. *Ibid.,* p. 74.
242. *Ibid.,* p. 79.
243. *Ibid.,* p. 73.
244. *Ibid.,* p. 49.
245. *Ibid.,* p. 73.
246. *Ibid.,* p. 72.
247. *Ibid.,* p. 53.
248. *Ibid.,* p. 80.
249. *Ibid.,* pp. 87–88.
250. *Ibid.,* p. 90.
251. Except for some writings that Blondel did not publish under his own name and which are more theological in scope.
252. *Lettre,* p. 53.
253. *Monologion,* Prologue; *Epistola de incarnatione Verbi,* ed. Schmitt (Florilegium Patristicum, fasc. 28; Bonn, 1931), p. 16.
254. *Monologion,* chapter I.
255. *Monologion,* chapter LXXIX.
256. On the thought of St. Anselm, see the pages devoted to him by Paul Vignaux, *Philosophie au Moyen Age* (Paris: A. Colin, 1958); by the same author, "Structure et sens du *Monologion,*" *Rev. des Sc. Ph. et Th.,* 1947. Also my own interpretation of the proof for God in the *Proslogion,* in *Karl Barth,* III:143–170, and in *Spicilegium Beccense,* I (Paris: Vrin, 1959), pp. 191–207, and in *The Knowledge of God* (New York: Herder, 1968), pp. 63–95.
257. While the unbeliever Blondel has in mind is a real person, the one Anselm is thinking about seems to be hypothetical: the *insipiens* of Sacred Scripture.
258. This, specifically, is the procedure of the celebrated proof for God given in the *Proslogion.* Following others, we have shown this in the three studies mentioned in note 256.
259. *Monologion,* chapter LXXIX.
260. Vignaux, "Structure et sens du *Monologion,*" *Rev. des Sc. Ph. et Th.* (1947), pp. 211–212.

261. *La Pensée*, II:274–276; *La philosophie et l'esprit chrétien*, I:1–31.

262. St. Anselm, *Cur Deus Homo*, Preface.

263. *Lettre*, pp. 87–88.

264. Vignaux, "Structure et sens du *Monologion*," *Rev. des Sc. Ph. et Th.* (1947), p. 197.

265. *Ibid.*, p. 198.

266. *Epistola de incarnatione Verbi*, ed. Schmitt, p. 9.

267. In *Karl Barth*, III:146–167, but especially pp. 151–153.

268. *Proslogion*, chapter IV.

269. M. Nédoncelle, *Existe-t-il une philosophie chrétienne?* (Collection, Je sais, je crois; Paris: A. Fayard, 1956), p. 35. Instead of saying "independent of theology," we would prefer "independent of faith."

270. *Ibid.*, p. 36.

271. *Ibid.*, 36–37.

272. On the subject of this comparison, originally outlined in our early article on Blondel's fundamental intention (*Recherche de Science Religieuse* 36 [1949], 390–391), Jacques Paliard had the kindness to write to me: "Your sketch of a solution by a comparison with Anselm [which I did not dare to make explicitly] delights me" (Letter of Jan. 9, 1950). This approval is the more precious in that Paliard, a disciple and friend of Blondel, has himself grasped admirably the specific character of Anselmian thought, as can be seen from his article, "Prière et dialectique: Méditation sur le *Proslogion* de saint Anselme," *Dieu Vivant* 6 (1946).

273. *Contra Gentiles* I:2.

274. *Contra Gentiles* I:9; cf. II:2, 4.

275. *Lettre*, p. 42.

276. *Lettre*, p. 90.

277. Well before I turned to the subject, Paul Vignaux had compared what Blondel thought he could say, as a philosopher, about the Trinity (in *La Pensée*) with what various theologians in the Middle Ages said about it (Richard de Saint Victor, Duns Scotus). "Philosophy and not theology, Blondel insists on this energetically when he speaks of Trinity. . . . I see that M. Blondel reasons with an evident concern for rigor; but speculative theology offeres us reasoning on the Trinity that aims to be rigorous; so I ask myself regarding the mode of thought: Is it philosophical or theological?" And the author adds that the mode of theological thought "appears, today, not to belong entirely to the past" ("Quelques tendances de la philosophie de Maurice Blondel," *Recherches Philosophiques* [1936–37], 371–372).

278. *Lettre*, p. 74.

279. *Ibid.*, p. 75.

280. Blondel's letter to the *RMM* (*Et. blond.*, I:101).

281. *Blondel et la religion,* p. 68.

282. *Ibid.,* p. 69.

283. *Ibid.,* p. 70.

284. *Ibid.,* p. 70.

285. Historical criticism also plays an important role, but there is no need to go into the matter here.

286. *Blondel et la religion,* p. 69.

287. *Ibid.,* p. 72.

288. *Lettre,* pp. 75–76.

289. M. Heidegger, *Essais et conférences,* tr. A. Préau (Paris: Gallimard, 1958), p. 142.

290. *Critique et religion,* p. 278.

291. *Ibid.,* p. 279.

292. *La Foi n'est pas un cri,* followed by *Foi et institution* (Paris: Ed. du Seuil, 1959), p. 324.

293. *Ibid.,* p. 324.

294. *Ibid.,* p. 202, note.

295. See under the word *Philosophie* in Lalande's *Vocabulaire de la Philosophie.*

296. This is the reason why we have formerly shown some discomfort over Lachelier's formula (*Recherches de Science Religieuse* 36 [1949], 384). It immediately follows this statement: "As for the relationship between philosophy and religion, it is in Schelling (not in Voltaire) that we must look for it." Duméry offers the following remark: "He [Lachelier] opposes Schelling to Voltaire, not to instigate a naturalization of dogma, but to stress the superiority of a reflection that takes positive religion as its object over every attempt to construct a natural religion. Lachelier perfectly respects the mystery . . . ." (*Critique et religion,* p. 9, note 3.) We know that Lachelier respected the mystery; he respected it insofar as he was a fideist in its regard. Nor have we challenged Schelling's superiority over Voltaire in the area of philosophy of religion. It has seemed to us, though, that Schelling naturalized Christianity. This was also Blondel's view. He specifically wanted to produce a work analogous to Schelling's, but one that would respect the supernatural.

297. "L'intention fondamentale de Maurice Blondel et la théologie," *Recherches de Science Religieuse* 36 (1949), 386–387.

298. *Blondel et la religion,* p. 73, note 3.

299. *Ibid.,* pp. 72–73.

300. "L'intention fondamentale," p. 386.

301. As a matter of fact, Blondel does not always use the term "pure philosophy" in the same sense. He used it to describe philosophy that pretends to take hold of being and the absolute by itself (*Letter,* p. 57), or

the philosophy that abstains from all reference to the positive data of Christianity (*Le problème de la philosophie catholique*, p. 167.). But he also wrote in the same book (p. 6) that his own personal work is "pure philosophy" in order to indicate that it is not an irrational apologetics, as Bréhier called it. Because of the ambiguity created by these different uses, we now prefer to avoid the term.

302. *Critique et religion*, p. 100.

303. *Ibid.*, p. 101.

304. "L'intention fondamentale," *Recherches de Science Religieuse* 36 (1949), p. 387.

305. *Ibid.*, pp. 389–390.

306. *Blondel et la religion*, p. 73, note 3.

307. *Ibid.*, p. 73, note 3.

308. *Ibid.*, p. 71.

309. *Ibid.*, p. 73, note 3. Duméry's reference is to H. de Lubac, "Sur la philosophie chrétienne. Réflexions à la suite d'un débat," *NRT* 63 (1936), 247.

310. "Sur la philosophie chrétienne," *NRT* 63 (1936), 245.

311. *Ibid.*, p. 247.

312. *Ibid.*, pp. 245–247.

313. *L'Action* (1936), I:311, note.

314. *Blondel et la religion*, p. 73, note 3. Duméry's reference is to "Le motif de la création dans *L'Etre et les êtres*," *NRT* 65 (1938), 222–225.

315. *Blondel et la religion*, p. 71.

316. *NRT* 65 (1938), 222–223.

317. *Ibid.*, 220.

318. *Ibid.*, 220.

319. *Blondel et la religion*, p. 74, note.

320. *NRT* 65 (1938), 221.

321. "L'intention fondamentale," *Recherches de Science Religieuse* 36 (1949), p. 400.

322. *Blondel et la religion*, p. 74, note.

323. *Ibid.*, p. 74, note.

324. M. Gueroult, *Malebranche* (Paris, 1955), I:17.

325. *Ibid.*, I:17.

326. M. Blondel, "L'anti-cartésianisme de Malebranche," *RMM* 23 (1916), 1–26. Blondel points out the difficulties raised by Malebranche's thought from the point of view of orthodoxy and of philosophy because of the continuity it establishes between the two orders, natural and supernatural (p. 24). But he also says: "We can thank Malebranche for having main-

tained and extended the domain of speculative philosophy against the artificial limitations of a philosophy without religious horizons" (p. 25).

327. Gueroult, *Malebranche*, III:374.

328. H. Gouhier, "Philosophie chrétienne et théologie. A propos de la seconde polémique de Malebranche," *Revue Philosophique* (1938), p. 65.

329. Emanuel Hirsch, *Geschichte der neuern evangelischen Theologie* (Gütersloh, 1954), V:268: "Wenn einer, so gehört er in eine Geschichte der Theologie."

330. Etienne Gilson, *La philosophe et la théologie* (Paris, 1959), p. 106. This remark seems justified, even though one may have reservations about the idea of Christian philosophy that Gilson proposes.

331. Peter Henrici, *Hegel und Blondel. Eine Untersuchung über Form und Sinn der Dialektik in der "Phaenomenologie des Geistes" und in der ersten "Action"* (Pullach bei München: Verlag Berchmanskolleg, 1958). This book was reviewed in *Archives de Philosophie* (April–June, 1960), 309–312.

332. *Hegel und Blondel*, pp. 181–185.

333. *Ibid.*, pp. 181–182, 197.

334. "L'intention fondamentale," *Recherches de Science Religieuse* 36 (1949), 386.

335. *Hegel und Blondel*, p. 181. He cites from the German translation, which is correct.

336. *Ibid.*, p. 155.

337. *Ibid.*, p. 155.

338. *Ibid.*, p. 155.

339. *Ibid.*, p. 158.

340. *Ibid.*, pp. 181–182.

341. *Ibid.*, pp. 187.

342. *Ibid.*, p. 188. Hegel himself cited with praise St. Anselm's principle (*Encyclopedia*, Sec. 77, note)

343. *Ibid.*, p. 187.

344. The remarks we have just made on Henrici's interpretation now have little more than retrospective interest. They move in the very direction of the modifications he would spontaneously make in his work were he to write it again today. But this work, even in its present form, is a valuable working tool.

345. *Critique et religion*, p. III. In itself this formula is quite correct. But Duméry states that it expresses only one of the two directions he discerns in the Blondelian enterprise. The second would be "a will to penetrate to the heart of religion and to bring the critical instrument to bear within the area of religious expressiveness" (p. III). He adds that, although this intention was only realized in part, it is for this and for the method created with

a view to realizing it that Blondel should be praised above all (p. 112). We have already shown that there is no reason for thus presenting the critical intention as an orientation different from the project of developing a Christian philosophy.

346. *Regards sur Platon . . ., Blondel* (Paris: 1955), p. 311. "It was in this book, as a philosophical commentary on the Gospel, that I found my final reasons for being a Jesuit—at the same time that certain of my companions drew from it their reasons for remaining Christians."

347. *Hegel und Blondel*, p. 185.

348. *La Pensée*, II:370.

349. *L'Action*, p. 442. We underline the last proposition because Blondel often repeated it in his "Cahiers intimes" and in the notes he used for preparing his book.

# BIBLIOGRAPHY

We offer here a list of the principal works and articles of Maurice Blondel, divided according to the major steps in the development of his work. The items generally are listed chronologically, but for the period prior to 1920 a distinction has been made between the apologetic writings and the writings that are strictly philosophical. A more complete list will be found in *Bibliographie blondélienne*, published by Père André Hayen in the collection *Museum Lessianum* (Desclée de Brouwer, 1953), which includes an almost exhaustive list of publications by Blondel and on Blondel from 1888 to 1951. See also the valuable bibliography, shorter but copiously annotated, published by Henry Duméry at the end of his work *La philosophie de l'action* (Paris: Aubier, 1948).

## I. PHILOSOPHY OF ACTION

*L'Action: Essai d'une critique de la vie et d'une science de la pratique.* Paris: Alcan, 1893. Copies of the thesis contain xxv–433 pages. The commercial edition has xxv–495 pages. The text was reworked, beginning with page 401, and augmented by a final chapter of 42 pages. This edition was reprinted in photo-offset in 1950 by Presses Universitaires de France.

*De vinculo substantiali et de substantia composita apud Leibnitium.* Lutetiae Parisiorum: Alcan, 1893. Latin thesis, 79 pages, out of print.

Letter to *Revue de métaphysique et de morale* (January, 1894), pp. 5–8 of the Supplément. Reproduced in *Etudes blondelienes.* I Paris: P.U.F., 1951. Pp. 100–104.

"Une des sources de la pensée moderne: L'évolution de Spinozisme" (article published under the pseud. Bernard Aimant), *Annales de philosophie chrétienne* 128 (June and July, 1894), 260–275, 324–341.

"Lettre sur les exigences de la pensée contemporaine en matière d'apologétique et sur la méthode de la philosophie dans l'étude du probléme religieux," *Annales de philosophie chrétienne* (January–July [except April], 1896), Vol. 131, pp. 337–347, 467–482, 599–616; Vol. 132, pp. 131–147, 255–267, 337–350. This also has appeared as a reprint of 86 pages, reproduced in *Les Premiers écrits de Maurice Blondel II.* Paris: P.U.F., 1956. Pp. 5–95. (All references are to this last edition, abbreviated as *Lettre*.

"Le Christianisme de Descartes," *Revue de métaphysique et de morale* 4 (July, 1896), 531–567.

"L'Illusion idéaliste," *Revue de métaphysique et de morale* 6 (November, 1898), 727–746. Reprinted in *Les Premiers écrits de Maurice Blondel II.* Pp. 97–122. (References are to the recent edition.)

"Principe élémentaire d'une logique de la vie morale," *Bibliothèque du Congrès International de Philosophie* for 1900. Vol. II. Paris: Colin, 1903. Pp. 51–85. Reprinted in *Les Premiers écrits de Maurice Blondel II.* Pp. 123–147.

"Le point de départ de la recherche philosophique," *Annales de philosophie chrétienne* 151 (January, 1906), 337–360; 152 (June, 1906), 225–250.

"Une soutenance de thèse," *Annales de philosophie chrétienne* 154 (May, 1907), 113–143. Reprinted in *Etudes blondéliennes I.* Paris: P.U.F., 1951, Pp. 79–98. This text, published by Abbé J. Wehrlé, is almost entirely Blondel's work. He drew up the essential outline the night following the defense. It was reworked and completed at the time of publication.

"L'Anticartésianisme de Malebranche," *Revue de métaphysique et de morale* 231 (January, 1916), 1–26.

## II. APOLOGETIC WRITINGS

"A propos de la certitude religieuse." Reply to Abbé Pêchegut, in *Revue du clergé français* 29 (February 15, 1902), 643–659.

"Histoire et dogme: Les lacunes philosophiques de l'exégèse moderne," *La Quinzaine* 56 (January 16, February 1, February 16, 1904), 145–167, 349–373, 433–458. Reprinted in *Les Premiers écrits de Maurice Blondel II.* 149ff.

"De la valeur historique du dogme." Letter to the editor of *Bulletin de littérature ecclésiastique* (de Toulouse) 7 (1905), 61–77. Also in *Les premiers écrits de Maurice Blondel II.* 229–245.

Series of articles, published under the signature of Abbé Mallet, on the apologetic work of Cardinal Dechamps, in *Annales de philosophie chrétienne* 151 (October, 1903), 68–91; 152 (February and March, 1906), 449–472,

625–645; 153 (March, 1907), 561–591. Reproduced with modifications in *Le Probléme de la philosophie catholique* (1932), 58–123.

"La Notion et le rôle du miracle" (under the pseudonym Bernard de Sailly), *Annales de philosophie chrétienne* 154 (July, 1907), 337–362.

*Qu'est-ce que la foi?* (under the signature of Abbé Mallet). Paris: Bloud, 1908.

*La Semaine sociale de Bordeaux et le Monophorisme* (under the pseudonym testis). Paris: Bloud, 1910. A collection of articles that appeared in *Annales de philosophie chrétienne* in 1909 and 1910.

Letter on the report of M. Le Roy: "Le Problème du miracle," *Bulletin de la Société Française de Philosophie* 12 (1912), 152–162, 165–166.

*Comment réaliser l'apologétique intégrale: Thèses de rechange ou points d'accord?* (under the pseudonym Bernard de Sailly). Paris: Bloud, 1913. A collection of articles published in *Annales de philosophie chrétienne* between October, 1912, and May, 1913.

## III. TRANSITION

*Le Procès de l'intelligence* (in collaboration with P. Archambault). Paris: Bloud et Gay, 1922. Pp. 217–306. A reprinting of three articles that appeared in *La nouvelle journée* the year before.

*Léon Ollé-Laprune: L'achèvement et l'avenir de son oeuvre.* Paris: Bloud et Gay, 1923.

*"Le Jansénisme et l'anti-jansénisme de Pascal,"* Revue de métaphysique et de morale* 30 (1923), 131–163.

"Le Problème de la mystique," in *Qu'est-ce que la mystique?* Cahiers de la Nouvelle Journée 3 (Paris: Bloud et Gay, 1925), 1–63.

*L'itinéraire philosophique de Maurice Blondel. Propos recueillis par Frédéric Lefèvre.* Paris: Spes, 1928. The text (questions and replies) was edited by Blondel himself, except the pages on the theories of Père Jousse. New edition, with *Avertissement* by Henri Bouillard and different page numbers. Paris: Aubier, 1966. (References are to the first edition.)

*Une Énigme historique: Le "Vinculum Substantialie" d'après Leibniz et l'ébauche d'un réalisme supérieur.* Paris: Beauchesne, 1930.

"La Fécondité toujours renouvelée de la pensée augustinienne," Cahiers de la nouvelle Journée 17 (1930), 3–20.

"Le quinzieme centenaire de la mort de saint Augustin (28 août 430). L'unité originale et la vie permanente de sa doctrine philosophique," *Revue de métaphysique et de morale* 37 (1930), 423–469.

"Y a-t-il une philosophie chrétienne?" *Revue de métaphysique et de morale* 38 (1931), 599–606. Reply to Emile Bréhier.

"La Notion de philosophie chrétienne," *Bulletin de la Société française de Philosophie* (1931), 82–86. Letter on the report of M. Gilson.

*Le Problème de la philosophie catholique*, Cahiers de la nouvelle journée 20 (Paris: Bloud et Gay, 1932).

## IV. THE TRILOGY AND THE CHRISTIAN SPIRIT

*La Pensée. I. La genèse de la pensée et les paliers de son ascension spontanée.* Paris: Alcan, 1934. Reprinted Paris: P.U.F., 1948.

*La Pensée. II. Les responsabilités de la pensée et la possibilité de son achèvement.* Paris: Alcan, 1934. Reprinted Paris: P.U.F., 1954.

*L'Etre et les êtres. Essai d'ontologie concrète et intégrale.* Paris: Alcan, 1935.

*L'Action. I. Le problème des causes secondes et le pur Agir.* Paris: Alcan, 1936. Reprinted Paris: P.U.F., 1949.

*L'Action. II. L'action humaine et les conditions de son aboutissement.* Paris: Alcan, 1937.

*La philosophie et l'esprit chrétien. I. Autonomie essentielle et connexion indéclinable.* Paris: Presses Universitaires de France, 1944.

*La philosophie et l'esprit chrétien. II. Conditions de la symbiose seule normale et salutaire.* Paris: P.U.F., 1946.

*Exigences philosophiques du Christianisme.* Paris: P.U.F., 1950.

## V. POSTHUMOUS PUBLICATIONS

*Le premiers écrits de Maurice Blondel: L'Action (1893): Essai d'une critique de la vie et d'une science de la pratique.* Paris: P.U.F., 1950. Exact reproduction of the 1893 edition.

*Les premiers écrits de Maurice Blondel: Lettre sur les exigences de la pensée contemporaine en matière d'apologétique* (1896). *Histoire et dogme.* Paris: P.U.F., 1956.

*Etudes blondéliennes, I* (Paris: P.U.F., 1951), 7–77. Texts prepared by Maurice Blondel for a new edition of the 1893 *L'Action.*

*Etudes blondéliennes, II* (Paris: P.U.F., 1952), 7–46. Inedita of Maurice Blondel: Notes and project for the second edition of *L'Action.*

*Etudes blondéliennes, III* (Paris: P.U.F., 1954), 5–132. An unpublished text of *Dialogues sur la pensée* by Maurice Blondel.

*Maurice Blondel et Auguste Valensin: Correspondance (1899–1912).* 3 vols. Paris: Aubier, 1957, 1965.

*Au coeur de la crise moderniste. Le dossier inédit d'une controverse.* Paris: Aubier, 1960. Letters of Maurice Blondel, Henri Bremond, Friedrich von Hügel, Alfred Loisy, etc., presented by René Marlé.

*Lettres philosophiques de Maurice Blondel.* Paris: Aubier, 1961. (Most of the letters from which we have cited extracts in the present book can be found *in extenso* in this collection.)

*Correspondance philosophique (Maurice Blondel and Lucien Laberthonniere)*, published by Claude Tresmontant. Paris: Editions du Seuil, 1961.

*Carnets intimes* (1883–94). Paris: Editions du Cerf, 1961.

*Carnets intimes II* (1894–1949). Paris: Editions du Cerf, 1966.

*Dialogue avec les philosophes* (Descartes, Spinoza, Malebranche, Pascal, Saint Augustin), collection of articles, presented by Henri Gouhier. Paris: Aubier, 1966.

# INDEX OF NAMES